Jens Mittag

Characterization, Avoidance and Repair of Packet Collisions in Inter-Vehicle Communication Networks

Characterization, Avoidance and Repair of Packet Collisions in Inter-Vehicle Communication Networks

by
Jens Mittag

KIT Scientific Publishing

Dissertation, Karlsruher Institut für Technologie (KIT)
Fakultät für Informatik, 2012

Impressum

Karlsruher Institut für Technologie (KIT)
KIT Scientific Publishing
Straße am Forum 2
D-76131 Karlsruhe
www.ksp.kit.edu

KIT – Universität des Landes Baden-Württemberg und
nationales Forschungszentrum in der Helmholtz-Gemeinschaft

KIT Scientific Publishing 2012
Print on Demand

ISBN 978-3-86644-880-3

Characterization, Avoidance and Repair of Packet Collisions in Inter-Vehicle Communication Networks

zur Erlangung des akademischen Grades eines

Doktors der Ingenieurwissenschaften

der Fakultät für Informatik
des Karlsruher Instituts für Technologie (KIT)

genehmigte

Dissertation

von

Jens Mittag

aus Freudenstadt

Tag der mündlichen Prüfung: 25. Mai 2012

Erster Gutachter: Prof. Dr. rer.nat. Hannes Hartenstein
                                   Karlsruher Institut für Technologie (KIT)

Zweiter Gutachter: Prof. Dr. Erik G. Ström
                                   Chalmers University of Technology, Schweden

Zusammenfassung

Basierend auf einer drahtlosen Kommunikation zwischen Fahrzeugen wurde in der Vergangenheit die Idee sogenannter intelligenter und kooperativer Transportsysteme entwickelt, welche die aktuellen und zukünftigen Anforderungen an Sicherheit und Effizienz sicherstellen sollen. Um dieses Ziel in die Realität umsetzen zu können muss die verwendete Kommunikationstechnologie jedoch mehrere Herausforderungen meistern: eine hohe Mobilität der Teilnehmer, stark schwankende Eigenschaften des Funkkanals, und die strikten Latenzanforderungen der zu implementierenden Anwendungen. Aufgrund der Paraderolle für zukünftige, allgegenwärtige Netze die zu der Vision von "a thousand radios per person" beitragen, ist es notwendig ein solches kooperatives Transportsystem so zu entwerfen dass eine robuste Leistung auch dann erzielt wird wenn mehrere hundert Fahrzeuge aktiv teilnehmen oder die Übertragungseigenschaften des Kanals auffallend stark schwanken. Das Ziel dieser Arbeit besteht deshalb darin, die Kommunikationstechnologie IEEE 802.11p, die in einer ersten Generation von Fahrzeugnetzen verwendet werden soll, bezüglich ihrer Robustheit, Zuverlässigkeit und Leistungsfähigkeit zu untersuchen und zu bewerten. Voraussetzung hierzu ist ein solides Verständnis der Eigenschaften des Funkkanals sowie dessen Auswirkungen auf die Signalverarbeitungsschritte des Physical Layers und die Effektivität der Koordinierung auf Medienzugriffsebene.

Die Arbeit beginnt mit einer Einführung in die fachübergreifenden Themen der digitalen Signalverarbeitung und der Modellierung des drahtlosen Übertragungskanal. Anschließend werden die dazugehörigen Sichten auf das Kommunikationssystem sowie die daraus resultierenden Modellierungsansätze untersucht, welche sich von den Ansätzen eines Netzwerkingenieurs deutlich unterscheiden, und die jeweiligen Vor- und Nachteile bewertet. Um die dabei identifizierten Modellungenauigkeiten existierenden Netzwerksimulatoren zu eliminieren, wird im folgenden ein neuer Simulator entwickelt und vorgestellt. Dieser vereint alle drei Modellierungssichten in einem Werkzeug und ermöglicht eine akkurate Modellierung des Kanals, des Physical Layer, und der darauf aufbauenden Netzwerkprotokolle. Der vorgestellte Simulator wird gegen kommerzielle IEEE 802.11 Sende- und Empfangseinheiten innerhalb kontrollierten Kanalbedingungen validiert, sowie um Kanalmodelle erweitert, welche die real gemessenen Eigenschaften des Zeit- sowie Frequenzselektiven Übertragungskanals nachbilden. Da die Einführung einer sehr akkuraten Modellierung einen signifikanten Rechenaufwand nach sich zieht, wird abschließend der Einsatz von GPU-basierten Simulationsarchitekturen untersucht und der erzielbare Laufzeitgewinn ermittelt.

Mit Hilfe des vorgestellten Simulators wird im zweiten Teil der Arbeit die Effektivität des Medienzugriffs in IEEE 802.11p basierten Fahrzeugnetzen untersucht und bewertet. Die vorgestellten Ergebnisse quantifizieren das Maß der Koordinierung (bzw. das Maß der nicht vorhandenen Koordinierung, im folgenden Inkoordination genannt) welches aus schwankenden Kanaleigenschaften resultiert, decken die Gründe einer Inkoordination auf, und charakterisieren den negativen Einfluß von Inkoordination aus der Sicht eines einzelnen Empfängers. Basierend auf den Ergebnissen wird anschließend folgendes Fazit gezogen: 1. Eine perfekte Koordination ist nicht zu erreichen; 2. Ein Schwanken der Kanaleigenschaften führt nur zu einem leicht erhöhten Grad an Inkoordination; 3. eine Überlastung der Kanalkapazität ist der primäre Grund für Leistungseinbußen.

Im Folgenden werden das identifizierte Skalierungsproblem sowie existierende Kontrollverfahren, welche durch die Anpassung der Senderate und Sendeleistung versuchen die Last auf dem Kanal zu begrenzen, analysiert. Im Gegensatz zur simulationsbasierten Charakterisierung der Leistungsfähigkeit von IEEE 802.11p wird das verteilte Kontrollproblem aus Sicht der Kontrolltheorie untersucht sowie Designkriterien identifiziert die eingehalten werden müssen um eine robuste und effektive Lösung zu erhalten. Obwohl diese Kriterien intuitiv erscheinen, zeigt die nachfolgende Bewertung existierender Lösungsansätze dass diese Kriterien bisher keine ausreichende Akzeptanz gefunden haben und nur von wenigen Vorschlägen vollständig erfüllt werden.

Zuletzt untersucht die Arbeit einen alternativen Ansatz um der auftretenden Inkoordination und den daraus resultierenden Paketkollisionen zu begegnen: Successive Interference Cancellation (SIC). Entsprechend der Erkenntnisse aus der Informationstheorie erlaubt SIC das erfolgreiche Dekodieren zweier sich überlappender Signale, sofern diese gewisse Bedingungen bzgl. ihrer relativen Signalstärke einhalten. Gemäß den Ergebnissen, welche im Rahmen weiterer Simulationen gesammelt worden sind, werden diese Bedingungen in einem IEEE 802.11p basierten Fahrzeugnetzen jedoch nicht ausreichend oft erfüllt, weswegen der Mehrwert von SIC in diesem Szenario als minimal betrachtet wird.

Abstract

Inter-vehicle communication networks have been identified as a promising solution to establish cooperative vehicular systems that overcome the current and future needs for increasing traffic safety and efficiency. To achieve their objectives, cooperative vehicular systems will be based on wireless communications between vehicles, and will have to deal with a highly dynamic mobility of the nodes, challenging radio propagation conditions, and stringent application requirements. As a prime example of upcoming ubiquitous networks that contribute to the vision of "a thousand radios per person", inter-vehicle communication networks need to be designed to scale to high densities of radios while being robust and adaptive to varying radio propagation conditions but not making use of any centralized coordination entity. The goal of this thesis is an analysis and performance evaluation of the IEEE 802.11p communications technology based on which such inter-vehicle communication networks will be deployed. Since the performance is going to be affected by fast fading channel characteristics, employed signal processing algorithms, and medium access control, a solid understanding of all those three aspects is required.

To establish the required inter-disciplinary expertise, a tutorial style introduction to signal processing and wireless channel modeling is given in the beginning of this thesis. In a subsequent step, the different perspective and modeling approaches that exist in the corresponding but co-existing research communities are surveyed. Since the modeling approaches and the resulting simulators are incompatible to each other, a holistic approach is proposed that integrates all perspectives into one single evaluation framework. The developed simulator is validated against commercial transceivers in a controlled and emulated radio environment, and extended to include state of the art channel models that describe the time- and frequency-selective properties of the wireless channel adequately well. In order to reduce the computational efforts that are introduced by this new simulator, several GPU-based software architectures are evaluated with respect to their benefit on the simulator's runtime performance.

With the help of this new simulator, the coordination performance of inter-vehicle communication networks based on IEEE 802.11p is evaluated. The presented evaluation quantifies the level of incoordination that exists in such networks, indicates the reason of incoordination, and characterizes the negative impact of incoordination on the successful reception of transmitted packets. The obtained results indicate that (i) incoordination is inevitable due to the hidden terminal problem, (ii) fading does not influence the coordination performance significantly, and (iii) congestion of the network is the primary reason for a deterioration of the reception performance.

The identified scalability issue is discussed from the perspective of distributed congestion control mechanisms that adapt the transmission power and/or the packet generation rate of all vehicles. In contrast to the characterization of the coordination performance, the control problem is analyzed from the perspective of control theory with the objective to establish a set of design criteria which have to be met in order to obtain an effective solution. The microscopic considerations of this analysis show that cooperative detection of and cooperative as well as synchronized reaction to congested situations is essential. Unfortunately, the following survey of recent congestion control proposals shows that these insights are not widely recognized by the networking community.

In a last step, the inevitable incoordination that occurs in a decentralized network is addressed using the principle of successive interference cancellation (SIC) at receiving nodes. According to information theory, SIC allows to successfully decode two overlapping packet transmissions (one after the other) if they satisfy certain conditions with respect to their relative signal strength. According to the results obtained through a simulation-based assessment, these conditions are not fulfilled often enough in inter-vehicle communication networks, hence, the benefit of SIC is marginal in this context.

Contents

List of Tables

List of Figures

1
Introduction

For several decades, researchers and engineers from all over the world have been attracted and fascinated by the idea of vehicles being "inter-connected" through wireless communications. Their research was initially motivated by the idea of an increased safety level on the roads. Through a periodic exchange of status (or awareness) messages vehicles are envisioned to establish a mutual awareness, which can be used to avoid dangerous situations or to coordinate multiple vehicles during complex driving maneuvers such as a lane change or an overtake process. More recently, the initial motivation behind inter-vehicle communications was extended to a larger scale and researchers started to improve the overall efficiency of the transportation system in terms of reduced travel times, reduced energy consumptions and gas emissions. While the retrospective view at history shows that there have been variations with respect to the motivation behind inter-vehicle communications, one key issue remained unchanged: an inter-vehicle communication network will only be successful if many vehicles are participating and contributing to the network, but the capacity of the wireless communication channel is limited. It is therefore crucial to efficiently and reliably coordinate concurrent access to the wireless channel by multiple vehicles such that transmissions by neighboring vehicles do not collide with each other. At the same time, not only a small but also a large number of communicating vehicles has to be supported.

Since coordination is the key factor to success, not only for the transportation system itself but also for the communication system, it is of high importance to deploy a communication system that provides robust and efficient coordination. To achieve this goal, any potential coordination mechanism has to fulfill certain constraints and master several challenges. First of all, a potential mechanism should not depend on a central coordination entity, i.e. it should incorporate a distributed operation mode. Second, due to the well-known hidden terminal problem, it has to deal with the fact that every vehicle has only a local view on the topology of the network. Third, the mechanism has to support scenarios that are comprised of only a few vehicles as well as scenarios that include a large number of vehicles, i.e. it has to be scalable. In addition, frequent topology changes due to the high vehicular mobility, as well as the wide range of radio propagation and shadowing conditions that exist in different environments (e.g. urban, rural or highway) have to be taken care of. Finally, fast-fading channel conditions due to multi-path signal propagation and significant Doppler effects have to be considered, which can prohibit successful communication even over short distances.

According to recent standardization activities in Europe and the U.S., the first generation of inter-vehicle communication networks will be based on the IEEE 802.11p standard for wireless access in vehicular environments (WAVE) [IEE10]. The medium access control (MAC) mechanism that will coordinate concurrent access in such networks is therefore Carrier Sense Multiple Access (CSMA). With CSMA, each node in the network performs a clear channel assessment prior to an own packet transmission and delays the transmission in case a busy channel is determined. Although such coordination belongs to the class of distributed control mechanisms, and is self-adapting to frequent topology changes without any delay, it has been shown that the performance of such a communications system does not degrade gracefully if the number of communicating vehicles is increased beyond a so called saturation level [TCSH06, TMSH09].

The coordination is additionally challenged by a fading of the radio propagation characteristics, which leads to situations in which even nodes located next to the transmitter are not able to successfully decode or even to sense its transmissions. Such situations can have a significant impact on the distributed coordination performance. According to recent channel measurement campaigns [PKC$^+$07, CHS$^+$07, RKVO08, KP08, CHC$^+$08, TTLB08], the inter-vehicle communication channel exhibits a severe time- and frequency-selective fading even within the short transmission period of a single packet. Since the OFDM-based IEEE 802.11p was derived from the IEEE 802.11a standard specification that did not consider such channel effects, IEEE 802.11p may not be protected sufficiently well against a time- and frequency-selective fading. Whether this is really the case, and whether this impairment has also a significant impact on the performance of distributed network protocols can not be answered easily: previous performance evaluations of IEEE 802.11p based communication networks did not consider a time- and frequency-selective fading. This is attributed to the fact that employed network simulators are not able to model a time- and frequency-selective fading, which in turn is attributed to the fact that they do not consider individual bits and corresponding signals of a packet. The latter is however required to evaluate the impact of a time- and frequency-selective channel.

Apparently, aspects that belong to different research communities relate and potentially impact each other significantly: radio propagation effects, digital signal processing capabilities, and wireless networking protocols. However, all these aspects are usually evaluated independently of each other, and the corresponding research communities co-exist without a strong interaction. For instance, a network engineer typically does not know about the details of the physical layer, and hence, existing evaluation methods targeted at wireless communication networks are based on simplifying assumptions and lack an accurate representation of the physical layer and the wireless channel. The significance of this lack in accuracy is twofold: first, and this is specific to this thesis, it prevents a proper evaluation of the coordination performance of an IEEE 802.11p based inter-vehicle communications network; second, and this is fundamentally even more important, it prevents an evaluation of emerging concepts, technologies, and ideas that may increase the capacity and performance of future communication systems and ubiquitous networks. The idea of cognitive radios that adjust their transmission and reception parameters such that the locally available radio spectrum is used in the most efficient way is only one example in which a combined consideration of channel, physical layer, and networking aspects will be beneficial. Advances in the field of information theory – e.g. interference cancellation based solutions that allow to receive multiple packets "simultaneously", or techniques such as network coding and multiple-input multiple-output antennas – represent additional examples that motivate the need to break up with a strict co-existance of the involved research communities and to bridge the gaps that exist between them.

To summarize the above elaborations, the following fundamental problems with respect to IEEE 802.11p based inter-vehicle communication networks and their evaluation exist:

1. IEEE 802.11p is a technology that has not been designed for the radio propagation environment it is going to be used in.

2. The inter-vehicle communication channel has been reported as being time- and frequency-selective, which challenges a robust and reliable communication based on IEEE 802.11p.

3. Existing methods to evaluate the performance of IEEE 802.11p based inter-vehicle communication networks lack the capability to model time- and frequency selective channels.

Due to the above problems, the following research questions arise:

1. How can the characteristics and details of the wireless channel and the physical layer efficiently be integrated into an evaluation method that is targeted at networks of up to several hundreds of nodes?

2. How significant is the impact of a time- and frequency-selective channel on the performance of an inter-vehicle communication network based on IEEE 802.11p, in particular on the coordination of concurrent access by multiple nodes?

3. How can potential incoordination be avoided or reduced, under the requirement of zero changes to the IEEE 802.11p physical layer and medium access control specification?

4. Is the avoidance of incoordination the only solution to encounter the problem, or is it possible to effectively repair resulting packet collisions, in the sense that all packets are successfully decoded despite being involved in a collision?

In order to give proper answers to the above research questions, a solid understanding of all involved aspects is required, i.e. an inter-disciplinary expertise in channel modeling, wireless digital signal processing, network engineering, and the relationship between all aspects is inevitable.

Main contributions of this thesis

This thesis makes contributions to the field of wireless communications in general and to the field of inter-vehicle communications in particular:

Consolidation of the perspectives taken by experts coming from different research communities: in order to properly analyze the effects of a time- and frequency-selective channel with respect to physical layer and MAC layer coordination performance, a solid understanding of all three aspects and their relationship to each other is established. In comparison to existing work that is usually targeted at only one of the three corresponding research communities and which usually simplifies or disregards the two other perspectives, a holistic approach is followed in this thesis. Thereby, a first differentiation between model characteristics (or details) which are most likely relevant and details which are most likely irrelevant is established.

Development of a new network simulation architecture which integrates the separate perspectives into one evaluation framework: based on the consolidation of the different perspectives, a new network evaluation method is proposed which adopts the complex time sample as the smallest unit under consideration. The resulting level of detail bridges the gap between complex wireless channel models that describe the characteristics of a time- and frequency-selective multi-path channel, the signal processing algorithms that are employed at the physical layer, and the aspects typically considered in the context of a network of nodes. The proposed network simulator enables an accurate assessment of the performance of inter-vehicle communication networks based on IEEE 802.11p, and further allows the study of new research questions that could not be studied before. For instance, the proposed method allows to quantify the impact of cross-layer optimizations based on either advanced signal processing techniques such as successive interference cancellation, or on the usage of multiple antenna techniques such as multiple-input multiple-output (MIMO). Emerging concepts such as cognitive (or software-defined) radios that will probably help to address the issue of insufficient spectrum bandwidth will benefit from such an evaluation framework as well. Since the adoption of the complex time sample increases the computation effort required to simulate a network significantly, the benefit of GPU-based simulation is evaluated. The results of this evaluation show that a large amount of the additional overhead can be compensated through a GPU-based processing.

Characterization of IEEE 802.11p based access coordination in time- and frequency selective channels: the proposed simulation framework is used to evaluate the coordination performance of CSMA over a wide range of scenario and channel conditions. Initially, deterministic channel effects in terms of a path loss only configuration are used to determine how CSMA schedules transmissions in a scenario in which the assumptions made by the protocol are valid: every vehicle within a certain range to the transmitter is able to sense and successfully decode one of its packet transmissions. Afterwards, fading effects are added and stepwise increased in order to determine how CSMA reacts to conditions which are not inline with the assumptions made by the protocol. The observed differences with respect to the non-fading case are evaluated and discussed. Independent of the channel conditions, the effect of different packet generation rates, different transmission power settings, and different vehicle densities is analyzed.

Identification of protocol requirements which have to be met by congestion control solutions that aim to keep the level of incoordination within a certain limit: since the coordination performance of a IEEE 802.11p based inter-vehicle communication network decreases significantly once the load that is generated by neighboring vehicles increases, previously proposed methods that aim to limit the load in the network are surveyed and analyzed with respect to their effectiveness. While it is no secret that the load in the network can be reduced through an adaptation of the packet generation rate or the transmission power, there is still no consensus on how an effective and robust congestion control solutation has to look like. To address this issue, the underlying distributed control problem is analyzed and fundamental requirements with respect to the architecture and design of an effective controller are identified: cooperative detection of and cooperative reaction to congested channel situations.

Standardization of distributed congestion control for intelligent transportation systems: the identified design requirements which have to be met in order to effectively restrict the load offered to the wireless channel have been contributed to the European Telecommunications Standard Institute (ETSI). Within a specialists task force, a technical specification on the *Configuration and validation of decentralized congestion control methods for Intelligent Transportation Systems (ITS)* [TS111] was developed which ensures that all of the above identified requirements can be fulfilled.

Evaluation of solutions that address a lack of coordination by means of successive interference cancellation: a second approach that deals with the negative impact of incoordination, namely colliding packet transmissions at a receiver, is analyzed with respect to its effectiveness. In comparison to congestion control methods which approach the problem by an adjustment of each node's transmission behavior, successive interference cancellation aims to solve the problem on a receiver side. From information theory it is known that two overlapping packet transmissions can be decoded and successfully received (one after the other) if they satisfy certain conditions with respect to their relative signal strength. In a simulation-based evaluation, the benefit of successive interference cancellation in inter-vehicle communication networks is evaluated, again over a wide range of scenario configurations and radio propagation conditions.

Parts of the contributions presented in this thesis have been previously published in

- M. Torrent Moreno, J. Mittag, P. Santi, H. Hartenstein; *Vehicle-to-Vehicle Communication: Fair Transmit Power Control for Safety-Critical Information*, In: IEEE Transactions on Vehicular Technology, Volume 58, Issue 7, pp. 3684–3707, September 2009

- J. Mittag, F. Schmidt-Eisenlohr, M. Killat, M. Torrent Moreno, H. Hartenstein; *MAC Layer and Scalability Aspects of Vehicular Communication Networks*, In: H. Hartenstein (Editor), K. Laberteaux (Editor), VANET – Vehicular Applications and Inter-Networking Technologies, Chp. 7, Wiley, pp. 219–272, 2010

- S. Papanastasiou, J. Mittag, E. Ström, H. Hartenstein; *Bridging the Gap between Physical Layer Emulation and Network Simulation*, In: Proceedings of the IEEE Wireless Communications and Networking Conference, Sydney, Australia, April 2010

- P. Andelfinger, J. Mittag, H. Hartenstein; *GPU-based Architectures and their Benefit for Accurate and Efficient Wireless Network Simulations*, In: Proceedings of the 19th Annual Meeting of the IEEE International Symposium on Modeling, Analysis and Simulation of Computer and Telecommunication Systems, Singapore, July 2011

- J. Mittag, S. Papanastasiou, H. Hartenstein, E. Ström; *Enabling Accurate Cross-Layer PHY/MAC/NET Simulation Studies of Vehicular Communication Networks*, In: Proceedings of the IEEE, Volume 99, No. 7, pp. 1311–1326, July 2011

- M. Sepulcre, J. Mittag, P. Santi, H. Hartenstein, J. Gozalvez; *Congestion and Awareness Control in Cooperative Vehicular Systems*, In: Proceedings of the IEEE, Volume 99, No. 7, pp. 1260–1279, July 2011

Overview of this thesis

This thesis is structured as follows: Chapter 2 starts with an overview of inter-vehicle communication networks, the motivation behind the idea of "inter-connected" vehicles, and a brief presentation of the corresponding research history. Afterwards, the fundamental challenges of inter-vehicle communication networks are discussed and the differences to traditional wireless networks are presented in detail. Then, the IEEE 802.11p standard specification including its distributed medium access control mechanism is introduced with a focus on aspects relevant to the ad-hoc type of communication that will be used in inter-vehicle communication networks.

As emphasized above, a proper assessment of IEEE 802.11p based inter-vehicle communication networks requires a solid understanding of all effects that can influence the outcome of the evaluation. Chapter 3 therefore provides a tutorial style introduction to wireless digital signal processing and channel modeling. First, the process of transmitting a data packet, i.e. the modulation of a sequence of bits as a sequence of complex signals, is explained. Then, the reverse process of a receiver is discussed, with a focus on the general tasks such as signal detection, channel estimation, channel tracking and demodulation. Afterwards, the structure of an inter-vehicle communication channel is illustrated in order to describe all relevant phenomena that can be observed in such a channel: shadowing, multi-path propagation and Doppler effects. Based on these basics, relevant metrics and channel modeling approaches that characterize the impulse response of an inter-vehicle communication channel are introduced, followed by a survey of results obtained within recent channel measurement campaigns. The relevance and impact of these results with respect to the physical layer of IEEE 802.11p is discussed in the following.

Chapter 4 starts with a survey and comparison of simulation and modeling approaches used by the networking and signal processing research communities. Based on the identified differences and discrepancies in the taken perspectives, a combination, or merge, of both perspectives is proposed and motivated through examplary research questions which would benefit from the existance of such a combined simulation approach. After this motivation, the design and implementation of a network simulator that actually integrates the perspectives of a physical layer or wireless channel simulator is presented. The proposed simulator is validated against a small-scale wireless channel emulation testbed that simulates the radio propagation effects between two commercial wireless transceivers. The physical layer implemented in this simulator is further evaluated in a one sender one receiver setup with reference to time- and frequency-selective channels. Since the computational effort is significantly increased by the integration of the additional aspects, the benefit of GPU-based signal processing and simulation is also discussed in this chapter.

With the help of the network simulator developed in Chapter 4, the coordination performance of IEEE 802.11p is assessed in Chapter 5. First, related work that also focuses on a performance evaluation of IEEE 802.11 is surveyed and compared to the work presented in this thesis. Afterwards, the own evaluation methodology, i.e. the employed performance metrics and the corresponding simulation setups, is specified. The obtained simulation results are then presented and intensively discussed.

Chapter 6 continues with an analysis of congestion control from the perspective of distributed control theory. Existing proposals are classified with respect to being based either on the principle of an open- or closed-loop controller, and on being either proactive or reactive. With the help of an exemplary scenario, the sensitivity of the underlying distributed control problem is presented in detailed. It is further shown how easily a controller can be ineffective if not every single aspect is not treated properly. The result is a set of design requirements, which have to be implemented by any control solution that aims not to be fundamentally wrong.

As an alternative to a transmitter side reaction to resolve congested channel situations, Chapter 7 evaluates the benefit of successive interference cancellation at receiving stations. In analogy to previous chapters, existing related work is surveyed in the beginning of this chapters. Furthermore, the carried out simulations are based on the same configuration and channel conditions used for the characterization of IEEE 802.11p's coordination performance.

Finally, Chapter 8 reports the conclusions that can be drawn from this thesis' results and provides directions for further research. Appendix A provides a detailed description of the state machine used in the implementation of the proposed network simulator. Appendix B elaborates on the parametrization of the signal detector implemented at the physical layer of the proposed network simulator.

2
Overview on V2V communication networks

On the New York World's Fair already back in 1939, Normal Bel Geddes introduced his vision of future transportation systems to the public, and illustrated how such systems may look like 20 years into the future. In his Futurama exhibit that was being sponsored by the General Motors Corporation, Bel Geddes sketched an automated highway system that is focused on safety, comfort, speed and economy [Ged40]. In his design of a network of motorways that inter-connect cities from all over the country, automobile collisions and accidents were envisioned to be impossible and congested traffic situations were expected to be a problem of the past.

Albeit the fact that many of his ideas were adopted in the following 20 years and are implemented today, road accidents, fatalities, and traffic congestion are still an everyday problem faced by citizens that merely desire to get from one place to the other. One major reason for this state is the lack of technical advances back at that time, which lead to a focus on infrastructure based solutions that require an upgrade of the existing road network by means of magnetized stainless-steel spikes that are driven one meter apart in the center of each lane. The spikes were envisioned to be used by each vehicle to measure its speed, locate its current position, as well as to receive information about the current driving direction, recommended speeds, or similar aspects. Since the deployment of such a system requires an upgrade of the whole traffic network, the vision of an automated highway system was eventually abandoned and replaced by the idea of intelligent autonomous vehicles, an idea which is studied using the term *Intelligent Transportation Systems* (ITS) today.

Intelligent transportation systems employ wireless communication technologies to enable information exchange between equipped vehicles in order to extend the set of locally available information. In combination with a positioning system such as GPS, and information provided by street maps, or geographic information systems in general, vehicles are envisioned to act cooperatively, derive sound decisions with respect to potentially dangerous driving maneuvers, and to adjust their routes if specific areas of the road network are congested. Whereas traffic efficiency related applications will probably be implemented using infrastructure based communication technologies, e.g. UMTS or LTE, a direct exchange of information between vehicles is envisioned for most safety-related use cases. Through a periodic broadcast of status messages that contain information about the current position, driving direction, velocity, etc., a mutual awareness among neighboring vehicles is established, which can then be used to detect and avoid dangerous traffic situations. In comparison to the approach followed in the late 60's, the introduction of wireless communication technology allows a smooth transition from non-intelligent to intelligent transportation systems.

The following Section 2.1 provides a very brief summary on the evolution of intelligent transportation systems, or more specifically of inter-vehicle communication networks. Section 2.2 then discusses the challenges of inter-vehicle communication networks by highlighting the aspects that differentiate them from traditional wireless networks. Afterwards, the IEEE 802.11p standard specification including its distributed medium access control mechanism is introduced in Section 2.3 with a focus on the most relevant aspects that are required in the remainder of this thesis. Finally, Section 2.4 summarizes this chapter and provides concluding remarks. In the interest of this thesis, a complete introduction to the wide range of aspects under which inter-vehicle communication networks have been studied in the past is avoided. Those desiring deeper background are refered to [HL10].

2.1 History

One of the first research projects that considered the exchange of information using wireless communication technologies was carried out from 1973 to 1979 in Japan, with the objective to develop a Comprehensive Automobile Traffic Control System (CACS) that reduces road traffic congestion and exhaust fumes, avoids traffic accidents, and enhances the public and social role of automobiles. Although the project was able to setup a pilot operation with 330 test vehicles and 98 roadside units in the end, CACS was never implemented on a large scale.

In the following decades, different research activies were initiated in Europe, Japan and the U.S: e.g., the PROMETHEUS (Programme for European Traffic with Highest Efficiency and Unprecedented Safety) framework was initiated and supported by 19 European countries and the Commission of the European Communities to foster research and development activities in 1986 [Wal92]. Similarly, the California Partners for Advanced Transport and Highways (PATH) demonstrated a prototype for cooperative autonomous driving at the San Diego demo in 1997, and initiatives such as the Intelligent Vehicle Initiative (IVI) in the U.S. [HS05] or the CarTalk and FleetNet projects in Europe [FHM05] continued to investigate the feasibility of active safety and cooperative driver assistance systems using wireless technologies.

The success of the IEEE 802.11 WLAN technology, the availability of a satellite-based global position system (GPS), and the allocation of a 75 MHz bandwidth in the 5.9 GHz frequency band by the US Federal Communication Consortium in 1999 stimulated a shift in the focus of subsequent research projects. These studies put more emphasis on the evaluation of architecture and protocol related issues, on a systematic exploration of possible application scenarios and use cases, as well as on the analysis whether the IEEE 802.11a standard specification is suited to support these applications and able to serve as a foundation for inter-vehicle communication systems. In parallel, standardization activities were intensified and consortia were established to develop a harmonized communication architecture that enables inter-operability between all major car manufacturers. All these efforts lead to the final approval of the IEEE 802.11p standard specification in 2010, which is considered to be used by the first generation of inter-vehicle communication networks in the U.S. an Europe, as well as to the availability of a standardized base communication architecture which all major car manufacturers agree on and which is being used in current and future field operational tests.

2.2 Challenges and requirements

While the envisioned scenario of vehicles that exchange information using wireless communication technology to increase safety on the roads is intuitively convincing to many people, the technical implementation of just that is not as straight forward as one might think. Indeed, inter-vehicle communication networks are challenged by several issues and requirements, which exist either due to the inherent characteristics of the considered scenario, or due to the fact that a communication technology has been selected which has not been designed for the usage in such an environment in the first place.

Within the research community and standardization bodies, there is a common agreement that the following requirements have to be met by an inter-vehicle communication network that aims to increase the safety level on the road:

- The network has to support two types of safety messages: *periodic awareness messages* which are broadcasted by any vehicle to inform neighboring vehicles about the own presence and status, as well as *event-driven alert messages* which are sent out in case of an emergency situation that requires an immediate notification of possibly affected neighbors. Whereas periodic messages are envisioned to be only one-hop broadcasted and termed either Cooperative Awareness Message (CAM) or simply "beacon", event-driven messages may be disseminated over more than one hop.

- Although periodic beacon messages are the building block for a communication based active safety system, the importance of their content is typically lower compared to the content of an event-driven message. Consequently, the communication system should be able to differentiate between both types and

11

assign higher priorities to emergency messages whenever they need to be disseminated.

– Due to the wide range of scenarios in which inter-vehicle communication networks will be deployed, the underlying communication system has to cope with a wide range of environmental conditions while providing optimal performance, hence it needs to be *adaptive* and *robust*.

– The network has to support scenarios in which only a small number or up to several hundreds of vehicles have to communicate, hence its has to be *elastic* and *scalable*.

Apart from the requirements described above, several challenges have to be faced, in particular by the physical layer and the medium access control layer:

– Due to the lack of a central coordination entity, communication will be performed in a distributed manner. This implies that resource and bandwidth allocations have to be determined in a self-organized fashion. However, since every vehicle acts out of its own perspective, message (or packet) transmissions by multiple vehicles will be difficult to synchronize, multiple access interference (or packet collisions) will not be an exception, and suboptimal medium access coordination among vehicles has to be expected.

– Frequent topology changes as a result of high vehicular mobilities prohibit a simple 1:1 adoption of principles that have shown to work efficiently in static networks. For instance, an offline (or a priori) optimization of the MAC layer, an approach that is often used in static networks, is not able to adapt to the topology changes that exist in vehicular environments.

– The IEEE 802.11a standard specification, from which IEEE 802.11p has been derived, was not optimized for a usage in vehicular environments in which the radio channel is fading significantly with respect to time and frequency domain. As a result, successful packet reception will be challenged even in the absence of interference.

– The laws of physics, in particular the fact that signal strength decays over distance, and the lack of a central coordination entity lead to the well known problem of hidden terminals. This issue is further intensified by fading channel characteristics, that introduce hidden terminal situations even within small geographic areas. Medium access control mechanisms have to consider that aspect.

– Only a bandwidth of 10 MHz has been reserved for safety-related communication, and a data rate of 6 Mbps is envisioned to be used within this bandwidth. However, this capacity will easily be exceeded if scenarios with high vehicular densities are considered. To address this issue, medium access control has to introduce "controlled" packet collisions.

While each requirement or challenge alone could easily be solved, the combination poses a big challenge for the design of an optimal solution. Already prior to the design of an optimal solution, the combination also makes it difficult to understand all negative and possibly positive impacts contributed by each single requirement or challenge, and aggravates a sound decision on how to design the to be used communication system. This is emphasized by the fact that there is still no consensus within the research community whether IEEE 802.11p already employs an "optimal" medium access control to meet the above requirements and challenges.

2.3 The IEEE 802.11p standard

This section provides a brief overview of the IEEE 802.11p standard for wireless access in vehicular environments (WAVE) [IEE10]. The p amandment extends the existing IEEE 802.11-2007 standard family [IEE07] by a communication mode termed *communication outside the context of a basic service set*. This mode is of special interest for safety-related communication, since it does not require association and authentication on medium access layer prior to a data transmission. Within the context of this thesis, a complete introduction to the IEEE 802.11p standard with all of its functionalities is omitted in this section, and only the decentralized medium access control mechanism for broadcast-oriented communication outside the context of a basic service set is addressed. Since Chapter 3 will elaborate on the fundamentals of digital signal processing, wireless channel effects, and the physical layer specification of the standard, these aspects are skipped in this section. Also, further details on the history and additional functionalities of the standard such as unicast or infrastructure-based communication are neglected. Those desiring deeper background are refered to [Gas02, MSEK+10] or the standard itself.

The coordination mechanism that is used by IEEE 802.11p for distributed medium access belongs to the category of *random access control protocols* and is called the *Distributed Coordination Function* (DCF). DCF employs the principle of "listen before talk" or Carrier Sense Multiple Access with Collision Avoidance (CSMA/CA). With CSMA/CA, each station has to check whether another station is already transmitting a frame before it is allowed to transmit an own frame. Hence, if a station wants to transmit a frame and the channel is free, it may start its transmission immediately. If however the channel is detected busy, the station has to defer its access until the channel becomes available again.

The channel is considered busy if the measured energy at the antenna exceeds a so called carrier sense threshold. The carrier sense threshold is arbitrary and does not reflect whether a signal can actually be decoded at that level. By using either a low or high carrier sense threshold, it is possible to implement a rather aggressive or conservative transceiver. In addition to such a *physical carrier sensing*, the channel is also marked busy if the preamble and signal header of a packet have been detected successfully and the frame duration has been obtained. Based on such a *virtual carrier sensing*, a station blocks own transmissions attempts until the last symbol of the frame that is currently "in the air" has been transmitted.

When virtual and physical carrier sensing indicate an idle medium again, the station does not just transmit its frame, but waits further for a so called *distributed inter frame space* (DIFS) during which the channel has to remain idle as well. Only if the channel remained idle during this period, the station will finally contend for the channel. Figure 2.1 illustrates this fundamental concept.

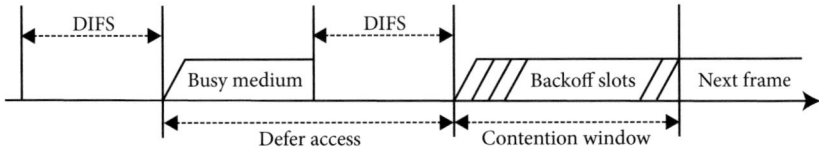

Figure 2.1: Illustration of the distributed coordination function for medium access in IEEE 802.11.

As mentioned above, a station enters the contention phase if it wants to transmit a data packet but the channel is detected as being busy. Since this could happen also to other stations, it would be a bad idea to start the transmission immediately after a DIFS – all contending stations would start to transmit at the same point in time. To avoid such a situation, every station waits for an additional, randomly selected time interval during which the channel has to remain idle. Each station draws a uniform random number that corresponds to a backoff slot in the *contention window* that starts directly after a DIFS, cf. Figure 2.1. The random number indicates how many backoff slots have to elapse before the own transmission may be started. The process of "counting down" time slots is called *backoff*. If the channel is determined busy again during the backoff process, the backoff is paused and resumed after the next observed DIFS. The size of the contention window and the number of backoff slots is a tradeoff: whereas an increased number of backoff slots reduces the probability of two stations selecting the same backoff slot, it will reduce the time that can be used for actual data transmissions. The contention window is therefore set to a size of 15 backoff slots with a time duration of 13 μs each.

As an extension of the distributed coordination function, IEEE 802.11p incooperates the Quality-of-Service (QoS) mechanisms defined in the IEEE 802.11e standard specification. The objective is to differentiate several packet types in the network and to prioritize packets that are most significant. The *Enhanced Distributed*

Access category index	Designation	AIFSN	Contention window size
0	Best effort	6	7
1	Background	9	15
2	Video	3	3
3	Voice	2	3

Table 2.1: Default EDCA parameter set for broadcast-oriented communication outside the context of a BSS.

Channel Access (EDCA) distinguishes four different access categories (AC), to which different arbitrary inter frame space numbers (AIFSN) and contention window sizes are assigned, cf. Table 2.1. AIFSNs replace the fixed DIFS in DCF and determine the number of time slots during which the channel has to be sensed idle in order to enter the channel contention phase. Through the usage of small AIFSNs and small contention window sizes for high priority access categories, packets that belong to this category have a high chance to gain access to the channel earlier than packets that belong to a category that uses longer inter frame spaces and larger contention window sizes. Note that the designations of the access categories indices (ACI) given in Table 2.1 do not relate to safety-related communication scenarios. Nevertheless, it is foreseen to use ACI 1 for non-prior background traffic (e.g. awareness messages), and to use ACIs of 2 and 3 for critical emergency messages.

2.4 Conclusions

This chapter provided a brief introduction to inter-vehicle communication networks with respect to their objectives and their long history of research projects. Further, existing challenges and requirements that have to be addressed (or fulfilled) by the communication system have been referenced and discussed, with the remark that a system that is being influenced by so many aspects is difficult to understand and difficult to design. As the foreseen IEEE 802.11p standard will be used in a first generation of inter-vehicle communication networks, although it has initially not been designed to master all challenges that are raised by radio channel characteristics at 5.9 GHz in vehicular environments, vehicular network engineers need to extend their horizon beyond their traditional expertise and have to consider the unreliabilities present on the physical layer and the wireless channel.

The following chapters elaborate on the challenges and requirements in more detail. Chapter 3 establishes a thorough understanding of the physical layer and the wireless vehicular radio propagation channel, with the objective to illustrate the shortcomings and weaknesses of IEEE 802.11p. Chapter 4 then surveys existing evaluation methods that are typically used to assess the performance of wireless communication networks, discusses their applicability in vehicular environments, and presents a new method in order to overcome the significant shortcomings that are present in existing evaluation methods. This new method is used in Chapter 5 to evaluate the performance of IEEE 802.11p based vehicular networks and to establish an in-depth understanding of the CSMA-based medium access control employed by that standard. The obtained insights are used to identify the fundamental weaknesses of CSMA in vehicular environments, and serve as the basis to discuss additional mechanisms in Chapter 6 which aim to avoid situations in which these weaknesses occur, and to evaluate the effectiveness of a cross-layer optimization approach in Chapter 7 that aims to repair these weaknesses through the application of successive interference cancellation.

3

From packets to signals: digital signal processing and channel modeling for the wireless network engineer

The following sections provide a tutorial-like introduction to the relevant aspects that have to be considered and well understood when studying the performance of wireless networks in general, and the performance of medium access control protocols in inter-vehicle communication networks in particular. Primarily, those aspects comprise physical layer internals and high-frequency channel characteristics, which on the one hand can have a significant impact on the performance of the to be used transceivers and the resulting network, but on the other hand are not sufficiently understood by traditional wired (and wireless) network engineers.

Section 3.1 therefore begins with an illustration of the fundamentals of digital signal processing, explaining how the data bits of a packet are modulated to signals and how signals are transmitted using sine waves (or sinusoids). An understanding of these fundamentals is required to recognize the inadequacy and inaccuracy of traditional network simulators when it comes to the simulation of the IEEE 802.11p physical layer in inter-vehicle communications. With these fundamentals in mind, Section 3.2 continues with an elaboration of the radio propagation effects that are typical for mobile-to-mobile channels and that will alter a transmitted signal. Section 3.2 further indicates how these effects challenge the successful reception of transmitted packets and how these impairments can be addressed by the physical layer. Afterwards, an outline of the Orthogonal Frequency Division Multiplex (OFDM) based physical layer specification of the IEEE 802.11 standard family is given in Section 3.3.

3.1 Introduction to digital signal processing

What is actually happening to all the bits of a data packet when the MAC layer is handing them over to the physical layer, with the request to broadcast them using digital wireless communication technologies? What sounds like an easy question for experts from the electrical engineering domain, will probably not be easy to answer for experts that originate from the computer science (or networking) domain. Most likely, a computer scientist will answer that bits are somehow modulated on a radio wave using different amplitudes, phases, codes and/or frequencies, but if you dig deeper, many of them will have to resign at this level of detail. Unfortunately for them, it is crucial to know and understand these details in order to consider and/or model all effects of the to be studied wireless communication systems accurately enough, and to recognize possible benefits that can be achieved through cross-layer optimization – cf. Section 4.1 for more details.

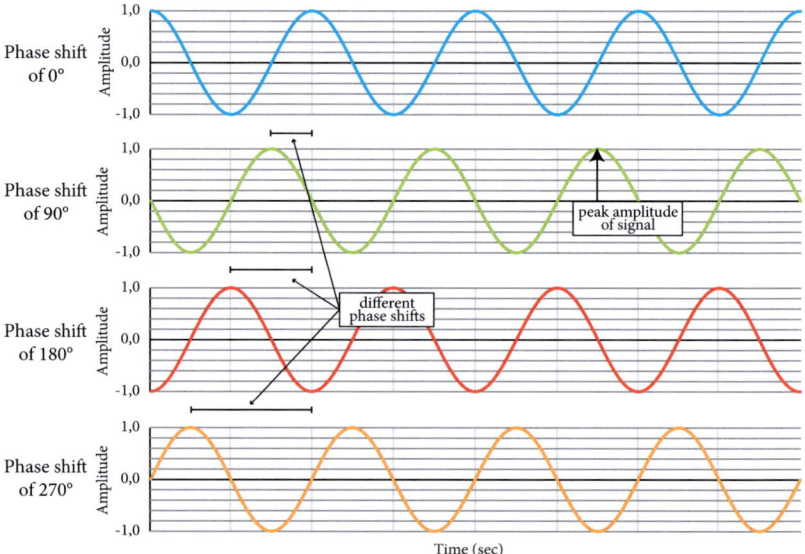

Figure 3.1: Illustration of four sine waves that differ only with respect to their phase offset, i.e. 0, 90, 180 and 270 degrees. The frequencies and peak amplitudes are identical.

To answer the question raised above, this section sketches the typical workflow of a transceiver. The sketch starts with the transformation of a sequence of bits (that constitute a data packet) into a sequence of complex signals, then describes how and for how long the generated signals are transmitted, and finishes with an explanation of the decoding process on a receiver side. Since the OFDM based specification of IEEE 802.11 does not make use of code based modulation, we omit this possibility in this thesis and consider only amplitude, phase and frequency as valid options to encode bits into signals.

3.1.1 Transformation of bits to signals

Let's start with an intuitive example: we assume that a transmitter is using the four sine waves shown in Figure 3.1 to encode the bits of a data packet and transmit them over the wireless channel. Each of the depicted sine waves can be described completely by its frequency, its peak amplitude and its phase offset. In the above example, the four sine waves have an identical peak amplitude of value of 1 (so far unitless), share the same fixed frequency, but differ with respect to the phase (namely 0, 90, 180 and 270 degrees) at which each sine wave starts. In mathematical terms, such sine waves are typically expressed by a periodic signal $x(t)$ with

$$x(t) = A \, cos(2\pi f_o t + \Phi) \tag{3.1}$$

where A is the peak amplitude, f_o the frequency, and Φ the phase of the signal in radians. Alternatively, if the frequency f_o is fixed (or known), the sine wave can also be characterized by a phasor V which is defined as

$$V = A \, e^{j\Phi} = A \, cos(\Phi) + jA \, sin(\Phi) \tag{3.2}$$

where A is again the peak amplitude and Φ the phase of the signal in radians. The above definition of a phasor allows us to describe each sine wave through a complex number that can be visualized in the complex plane, as illustrated in Figure 3.2. Hence, we can choose between a polar representation of a phasor V using its amplitude A and phase Φ, and a rectangular representation that is given through the x and y coordinates in the complex plane. In the illustrated example in Figure 3.2, the vector $\vec{z} = (x, y)$ in the complex plane describes a phasor with amplitude $A = |\vec{z}|$ and phase $\psi = tan(y/x) = 45°$. The vector $\vec{z}$ will be moving counterclockwise at a rate of $2\pi f_o$, e.g. it will turn by $360°$ once per second for a frequency of $f_o = 1 \, Hz$.

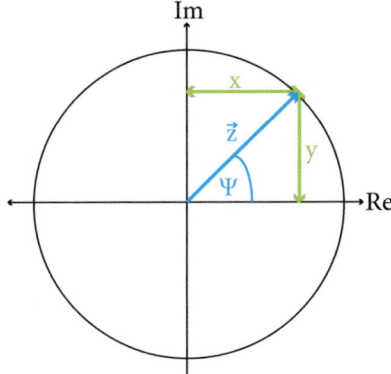

Figure 3.2: Expression of a sine wave with amplitude A, phase offset Φ and frequency f_o through a phasor with fixed frequency f_o: the length of $\vec{z}$ reflects the amplitude A, the angle ψ reflects the phase offset Φ, and the vector $\vec{z}$ is moving counterclockwise at a rate of $2\pi f_o$.

Now that we know that each periodic signal with a fixed frequency can be described by a vector in the complex plane, we can take a look at reasonable ways to encode a single (or a sequence of) bit(s) into a periodic signal and how to depict them in one single figure (using the complex plane notation of phasors). Using again

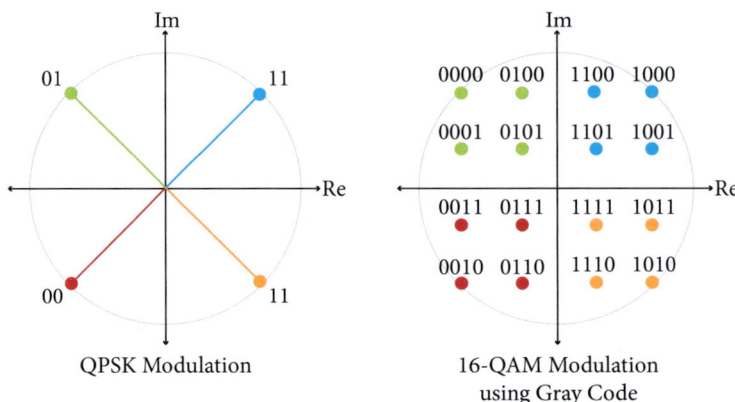

QPSK Modulation

16-QAM Modulation
using Gray Code

Figure 3.3: Several sine waves depicted as vectors in the complex plaxe, each one characterizing the periodic patterns of a phasor at fixed frequency: a) four different phasors that differ only with respect to their phase offset ($45°$, $135°$, $225°$ and $315°$); b) 16 different phasor that differ with respect to their phase offset and amplitude.

the example of four sine waves that differ only with respect to their phases, we can depict such sine waves as illustrated on the left in Figure 3.3: the red phasor ($225°$) represents the bit sequence 00, the green phasor ($135°$) represents the bit sequence 01, the orange phasor ($315°$) represents the bit sequence 10, and the blue phasor ($45°$) represents the bit sequence 11. Please note that the mapping between a specific bit sequence and phasor is arbitrary here and can be adjusted as long as transmitter and receiver employ the same mapping. Also, instead of using the term phasor or vector, one typically uses the term *constellation point* to refer to a specific phasor or vector, and *constellation diagram* to refer to the representation of a signal as a phasor in complex plane. In the following, we will use the terms phasor, vector and constellation point synonymously. Furthermore, we will use the term *bit modulation* to refer to the process of mapping a single bit or a bit sequence to a periodic signal.

When designing a communication system, one has to define a set of valid constellation points that may be used by a transmitter. In the above example, four constellation points that differ only with respect to their phases were used. Such a setup is typically called Quadrature Phase-Shift Keying (QPSK) and belongs to the class of bit modulation schemes that employ phase shift keying. Another often used phased shift keying method is called Binary Phase Shift Keying (BPSK) and distinguishes between two different phases only. While using two different phases allows to encode only one bit per signal (compared to two bits per signal in QPSK), i.e. it requires twice as many signals to encode the same bit sequence, BPSK comes with the advantage of being more robust since the two signals differ by $180°$ instead of only $90°$, and hence can be more easily distinguished by a receiver. Apart from phase shift keying, one can also employ the peak amplitude to differentiate signals. The example on the right side of Figure 3.3 for instance depicts the constellation points that are used by 16-Quadrature

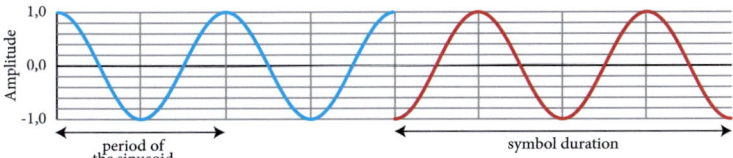

Figure 3.4: Sequential transmission of two digital signals: each signal has a sample period that is twice as large as the period of the signal itself.

Amplitude Modulation (16-QAM): each constellation point is uniquely identified by its phase and its peak amplitude. In the example the mapping between signals and bit sequences is further assigned such that neighboring constellation points differ in only one bit. Compared to QPSK, the spacing between the constellation points is significantly reduced in 16-QAM, and it can be reduced even further when using not only 16 constellation points but 64 constellation points in 64-QAM. Again, the increase of the number of constellation points allows us to increase the number of bits per symbol (4 bits in 16-QAM, and 6 bits in 64-QAM), but challenges a proper classification of the determined phase offsets and peak amplitudes on a receiver side.

In the above figures, the maximum peak amplitude of a phasor in the constellation diagram is always 1. The reason is quite simple: for digital signal processing, the absolute values that describe a phasor are not important, what matters is the relation of one phasor to another. Hence, one typically normalizes the constellation diagram such that the peak amplitude of the phasor with the greatest energy accounts to 1. Consequently, it is not a problem if the absolute values of the peak amplitudes used by a transmitter differ from the values observed by a receiver – as long as the relation between the amplitudes of the signals does not change.

3.1.2 Transmission of signals

After having clarified how bits are represented through signals in terms of sine waves (or phasors), the next question that needs to be answered is: how and for how long a radio should transmit a sine wave? In wireless communications digital signals are broadcasted using electromagnetic waves that exhibit the same periodic properties as the digital signal. That means, the radio frontend on the transmitter side will generate electromagnetic waves according to the given digital signals, and the radio frontend on the receiver side will transform the analog signals back to the digital domain. In order to make sure that the receiver determines the correct characteristics of a signal, the transmitter has to repeat each signal for a minimum period of time. This period is called *symbol time* (or symbol duration) and is typically several times longer than the period of the signal itself. Figure 3.4 illustrates an example where two different digital signals are transmitted sequentially for a symbol duration that is twice as long as the period of the signal.

In the example of Figure 3.4 we assumed that signals are transmitted one after the other at one single carrier frequency. Although it is a valid approach to use

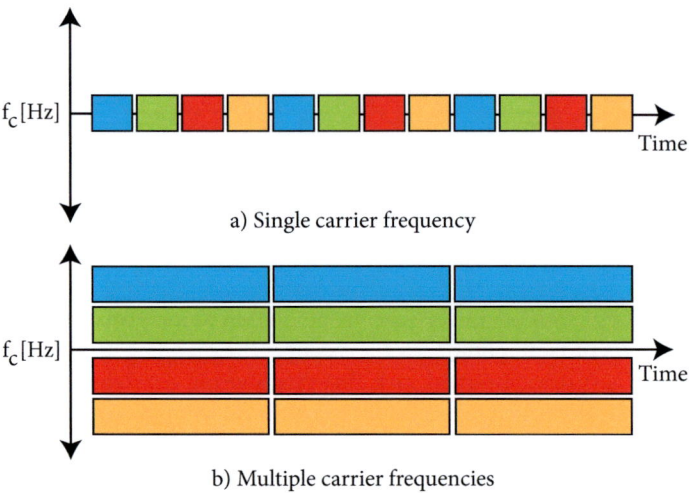

a) Single carrier frequency

b) Multiple carrier frequencies

Figure 3.5: Single versus Multiple carrier frequency transmission.

only a single carrier frequency for a transmission, todays communication systems do not employ it anymore. Instead, modern communication systems make use of multiple carrier frequencies and employ the concept of orthogonal frequency division multiplexing (OFDM) to transmit multiple signals simultaneously at different, non-interfering frequencies. As depicted in Figure 3.5(a), all symbols are transmitted on exactly the same frequency but for short periods in the single carrier case, whereas symbols are "spread" in time and frequency (for instance on 4 different carrier frequencies) when employing a multiple carrier frequency mechanism, cf. Figure 3.5(b). By the usage of several frequencies – typically called *subcarriers* – transmissions are more robust against frequency selective fading or interference that is present only at a specific frequency. While a permanent interference close to the center frequency would destroy all signals in the single carrier case, the impact of such interference would be limited in the multiple carrier case since not all carriers will be affected. In combination with additional forward error correction mechanisms, OFDM would in such a situation be able to recover all effective bits. In case of the single carrier system, additional forward error correction would be pointless. In the example in Figure 3.5(b), a simple mapping was used to map a signal to a specific subcarrier, i.e. every N-th signal was mapped to the subcarrier with index N. As we will see later in Section 3.3, IEEE 802.11p employs a more advanced mapping technique.

To be effective, OFDM requires that the used subcarrier frequencies are orthogonal to each other. Assuming that we have two subcarrier signals $s_1(t)$ and $s_2(t)$ of the form

$$s_i(t) = A_i cos(2\pi(f_c + i\Delta f)t + \varphi_i), 0 \leq t < T \qquad (3.3)$$

with A_i being the amplitude and φ_i the phase of the i-th signal, f_c being the center frequency, and Δf being the subcarrier spacing. Then, $s_1(t)$ and $s_2(t)$ are orthogonal to each other within the time interval $[0, T)$ if $f_c \gg T^{-1}$ and $\Delta f = T^{-1}$. That is

$$\int_0^T s_1(t)s_2(t)dt = 0 \tag{3.4}$$

If $\Delta f < T^{-1}$, $s_1(t)$ and $s_2(t)$ will not be orthogonal.

3.1.3 Detection and decoding of signals

After transmission, the signals propagate through the air and "arrive" at the receiver. Although we have not looked at all the details of radio propagation characteristics such as multi-path fading, Doppler effects or similar yet – these aspects are covered in Section 3.2 – we can already consider the fundamental tasks that a receiver has to perform in order to correctly decode the arriving signals: first, a receiver has to determine that there are relevant signals arriving at the own antenna at all and not just random thermal noise – i.e. it has to detect the signal; second, the receiver has to synchronize to the signals with respect to time in order to perform a proper mapping between signals and symbols – i.e. the receiver has to know when the first symbol starts; third, the receiver needs to estimate, track and equalize the signal alterations of the wireless channel, i.e. the receiver has to determine the phase shifts, the loss of the channel and possibly also frequency shifts; and finally, the receiver has to decode the signals, based on previously performed time synchronization and channel estimation.

Signal detection on a receiver side can be implemented in several ways. In a very simple solution a receiver "waits" until the energy that is observed at the antenna increases by a specific threshold and treats this event as an indicator for the beginning of a new data packet. However, such an approach can be vulnerable to unexpected interference that is not related to the wireless communication system at all. Therefore, many of todays wireless communication systems make use of so called *training symbols* which a transmitter will broadcast prior to the actual data symbols. Such training symbols adhere to a predefined pattern that is known by every transceiver, are repeated several times. Further, by using only a subset of the frequencies available in the used frequency band, e.g. by using only a subset of the available subcarriers of OFDM, a receiver can then also successfully detect the start of a valid transmission if the received signal strength is below thermal background noise.

Similarly to signal detection, a receiver can make use of training symbols to synchronize to the transmission in time and to estimate the impulse response of the channel. However, in order to estimate the channel over all frequencies, a second sequence of training symbols that covers all subcarriers is typically used. A "comparison" of the received and expected training symbols then yields the current phase shift as well as the gain in amplitude, and provides the necessary input in order to equalize the effects of the radio propagation channel at the receiver. Since the channel impulse response may change over time, modern OFDM-based communication systems employ so called *pilot subcarriers* that are used only for channel estimation. These subcarriers will not be used for actual data symbols, but instead contain well known training symbols in order to allow channel tracking by the receiver over time.

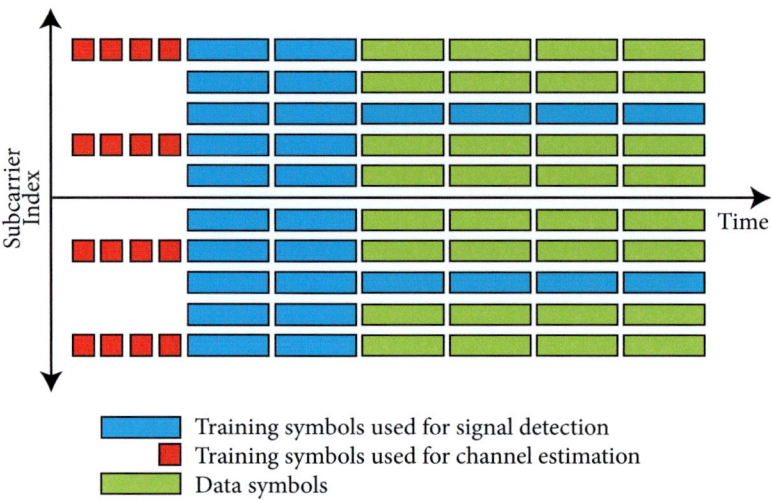

■ Training symbols used for signal detection
■ Training symbols used for channel estimation
□ Data symbols

Figure 3.6: Illustration of a typical subcarrier allocation: a repetition of several short training symbols in the beginning is used for signal detection, followed by two long training symbols used for initial channel estimation, and the actual data symbols. A subset of the subcarriers is further used to track channel variations over time.

Figure 3.6 illustrates the described subcarrier allocation over time: first only a few subcarriers are used to provide a robust foundation for signal detection; then, all subcarriers are used to transmit the training symbols for a complete initial channel estimation; afterwards, the actual data symbols and pilot symbols are transmitted.

Earlier, we briefly stated that a receiver finally decodes the received signals, which means that the signal is mapped back to the constellation point to which it has the closest distance. In order to be able to properly map the signal to the correct constellation point, and hence successfully decode the signal, the signal has to arrive sufficiently strong at the receiver. The importance of this aspect is illustrated in Figure 3.7 which shows a transmitted signal and an interfering noise component using their representatives in the complex plane. According to the superposition principle, their cumulation describes the received signal and is obtained through the addition of both vectors. As shown, the noise considered in this example results in a minor phase shift: while a BPSK or QPSK modulation will probably not suffer from such a small phase shift, higher order modulation schemes may be vulnerable. Similar arguments apply to the changes observed in the amplitude of the received signal.

The above discussion shows that noise (or interference) components are not necessarily destructive. Moreover, such components need to be sufficiently strong in order to challenge the decoding process at a receiver. These observations have to be kept in mind when the impacts of a multi-path radio propagation are evaluated later in this thesis.

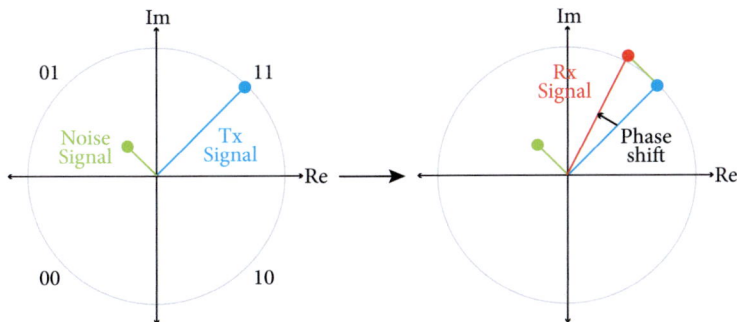

Figure 3.7: Impact of a single noise component on a transmitted signal, the resutling received signal and the implications on signal decoding.

3.2 Radio propagation

This section provides a brief introduction to radio propagation in vehicular environments and takes a look at what is happening to a signal once it is transmitted by the transceiver and radiated at the antenna. The introduction begins with a general description of multi-path propagation in Section 3.2.1, covering aspects such as multipath fading and characteristics such as Delay spread, Doppler shift, Doppler spread, coherence time and coherence bandwidth. Afterwards, Section 3.2.2 surveys existing vehicular channel measurement studies that have been carried out in the past, and Section 3.2.3 concludes with a discussion of the observed characteristics and the implications on physical layer. A more detailed survey on vehicular channel characterization, including antenna characteristics and vehicle-to-infrastructure channels, can be found in [MMK+11].

3.2.1 Vehicle-to-vehicle propagation channels

When a transceiver transmits a signal using an omnidirectional antenna the energy of the signal is typically radiated into all directions. Although directional antennas could be used to "guide" the radiated energy into a specific direction, the remainder of this subsection as well as the rest of this thesis assumes that omnidirectional antennas will be the default antenna type in vehicular communication networks. As a result, we assume that signals will propagate uniformly into all directions.

The propagation of signals that are transmitted by a vehicle is typically described by an infinite set of rays – in the following termed *paths* – that originate at the antenna with different angles of departure. The power of each path declines with an increase in distance to the origin. This phenomenon is called *pathloss* and is modeled as

$$P(d) = P_0 - 10n \, log_{10}(d/d_0) \tag{3.5}$$

where d is the distance, P_0 is the power level at the reference distance d_0 (typically 1 meter), and n the pathloss exponent. A subset of these paths arrives at the receiver,

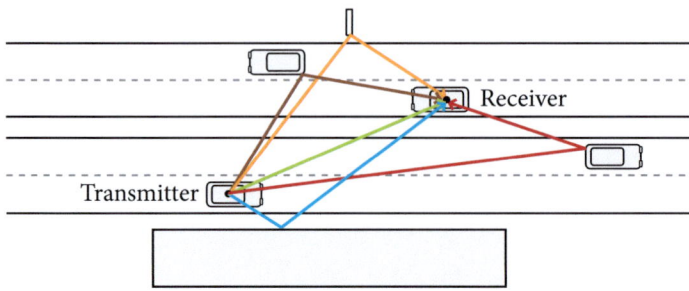

Figure 3.8: Illustration of a typical vehicle-to-vehicle propagation scenario with mobile and static scatterers that contribute to the multi-path impulse response between a transmitter and a receiver.

either directly in case of line of sight or indirectly through reflections and diffractions. Due to the distinct distance of each path, a different path loss, phase shift and propagation delay is exhibited by each path – similar to the timely dispersion of an accoustic signal and its echos. The sum of all paths defines the *impulse response* of the channel.

Figure 3.8 illustrates these basics using a simple scenario in which vehicles are moving on a straight road being surrounded by two obstacles next to the street (a sign post and a building). Due to comprehensibility, only five different paths have been drawn into this scenario, which all take different paths to reach the receiver. Usually, not only one but a collection of multiple paths is reflected at each of the objects (or scatterers) located in the surrounding of the transmitter or receiver, and each of the paths that belong to such a collection arrives at the receiver with a similar delay but with a different attenuation. Each collection can be described stochastically and is typically called a *tap*, a notion that is essential to understand the channel modeling approaches described later in Section 3.2.4. Note that not all scatterers bounce the signal equally well, and are therefore not equally important (or relevant) for the accurate description of the channel impulse response.

The relationship of all propagation paths with respect to their contributed signal strength and arrival time is described by the so called *power delay profile* (PDP). The power delay profile is deterministic for any scenario snapshot and does not change as long as the geometry of the environment does not change neither. An example (but arbitrary) power delay profile for the above scenario is shown in Figure 3.9: each of the five scatterers reflects a set of multiple paths (note the same colorcoding already used in Figure 3.8) and generates multiple "peaks" of different intensity at different points in time.

Based on many channel impulse response measurements within a similar environment, channel modeling experts often derive the *average power delay profile* (APDP) to describe the expected power at different delays. Typically, a 25 to 30 dB threshold is used during the generation of the APDP to remove weak paths and thermal noise that would else introduce errors in the derived characteristics. While such

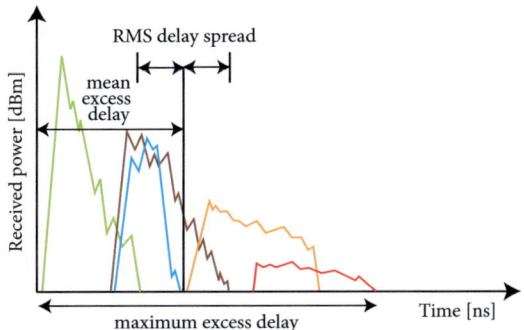

Figure 3.9: Illustration of a power delay profile and its derived metrics, i.e. mean excess delay, maximum excess delay and RMS delay spread.

a large threshold is chosen to satisfy the accuracy requirements of a channel modeling expert, it may be too large if a physical layer perspective is adopted. Indeed, from a physical layer point of view, only the paths that challenge a successful reception are of interest. Consequently, reported channel measurement results have to be evaluated carefully and with respect to the robustness of the employed modulation scheme.

The APDP is used to quantify statistics such as the *mean excess delay*, the *RMS delay spread*, and the *maximum excess delay*. The mean excess delay and the RMS delay spread are defined as the first moment and the second central moment of the APDP, i.e. they reflect the expected (or mean) value and the variance. The maximum excess delay is simply the delay between the first arriving path and the latest arriving path. The power delay profile and the average magnitude frequency response of the channel are further related through the Fourier transform [Rap09]. Hence, one can obtain an estimate of the frequency response characteristics from the time-domain description given by the power delay profile. For instance, the RMS delay spread and the *coherence bandwidth* of the channel, i.e. the range of frequencies over which the channel impulse response is strongly intercorrelated, are inversely proportional to each other. According to [Lee90], the coherence bandwidth b_c within which a correlation threshold of 0.9 is satisfied can be estimated by

$$b_c \approx \frac{1}{50\, \sigma_\tau} \tag{3.6}$$

where σ_τ is the RMS delay spread. Please note that the above formula is only an estimation and that the exact relationship depends on the individual shape of the PDP.

In analogy to the power delay profile of the channel, the so called *Doppler spectrum* describes how a transmitted signal is "spread" in frequency domain due to transmitter/receiver mobility and changes of the environment during signal propagation. Figure 3.10 illustrates two Doppler spectrums that describe the frequency characteristic of two different taps, one with a uniform distribution of the power spectral density, and one with a non-uniform distribution of the power spectral density. Based on the Doppler spectrum, one can derive the *mean Doppler shift*, the *RMS Doppler*

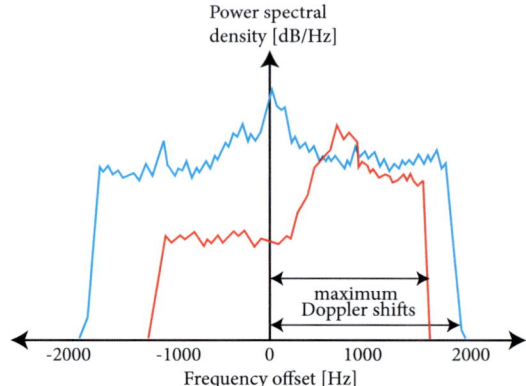

Figure 3.10: Illustration of two different Doppler spectrums. In comparison to the spectrum of the tap plotted in red, which is spread quite uniformly around the center frequency, the spectrum of the tap plotted in blue has a slight tendency towards higher frequencies.

spread, and the *maximum Doppler shift*. Further, the *coherence time* can be estimated through a Fourier transform of the Doppler spectrum. The coherence time is an indication of the time variance of the channel and quantifies the time duration over which the impulse response is invariant. According to [Rap09, TV05] a common rule of thumb for the computation of the coherence time T_c is given by

$$T_c = \frac{M}{D_S} \tag{3.7}$$

with D_S being the RMS Doppler spread and M being a constant factor between 0.25 and 1.

To summarize, the impulse response of a vehicular channel is described by the power delay profile and the Doppler spectrum. While the power delay profile is affected solely by the multi path nature of the channel, which leads to *frequency selective* fading, the Doppler spectrum is a result of the mobility of transmitter/receiver and leads to *time selective* fading. The two dimensions that are spanned by these independent effects lead to a classification into four different types of fading.

The first two classes are distinguished with respect to the multi path propagation effects and their relationship to the transmitted signal. For instance, a channel is termed to be a *flat fading* (or narrowband fading) channel if the coherence bandwidth is larger than the bandwidth of the transmitted signal. That means, the channel gain is constant over the full signal bandwidth and the spectrum of the transmitted signal will be preserved. If the coherence bandwidth is smaller than the bandwidth of the signal, the channel is said to undergo a *frequency selective fading*. The comparison of the RMS delay spread and the symbol period is an equivalent criterion, and indicates flat fading if the delay spread is smaller than the symbol period, or frequency selective fading if the delay spread is greater than the symbol period.

28

Fast fading and *slow fading* are the two remaining fading types and are a result of high or low Doppler spreads. A channel is said to be fast fading if the symbol period is greater than the coherence time or if the bandwidth of the signal is smaller than the Doppler spread. Contrary, a channel is said to be slow fading if the symbol duration of a transmitted signal is significantly smaller than the coherence time or if the Doppler spread of the channel is significantly smaller than the bandwidth of the transmitted signal. Hence, the distinction between fast and slow fading is simply based on a comparison of the rate of changes of the channel and the signal.

3.2.2 Measurement results

Within the past few years, several channel measurement studies have been carried out by experts all over the globe. This subsection provides a brief overview of these measurements by means of a comparison of the results obtained. While there have been measurement campaigns within a multitude of different environments – ranging from urban over rural to highway scenarios – this subsection puts its focus primarily on highway scenarios. Further, measurement campaigns that are not based on high resolution channel sounding, i.e. measurement campaigns that have been carried out using commody transceiver hardware that provides only statistics about the received signal strength indicator (RSSI) of successfully received packets, are also not considered here [YHE+06].

In 2007, Paier et al. carried out 4x4 multiple-input multiple-output (MIMO) channel measurements at 5.2 GHz in Lund, Sweden [PKC+07] with a focus on a determination of path loss characteristics, power delay profiles and Doppler spreads. According to their results, the path loss follows a traditional power law model, with a path loss exponent of 1.8. Further, a mean excess delay of 52 ns, a RMS delay spread of 247 ns and a maximum excess delay of 1300 ns has been observed. Their frequency domain analysis also indicates that, depending on the relative speed between vehicles, Doppler shifts up to 1 kHz and beyond have to be expected.

Cheng et al. analyzed path loss, RMS delay spread, maximum excess delay spread, coherence time and coherence bandwidth characteristics based on several measurement campaigns at 5.9 GHz in Pittsburgh, PA, USA. The path loss in suburban environments was fitted using a dual slope power law model with an exponent of 2.1 up to a critical distance of 100 m and an exponent of 3.8 beyond [CHS+07]. The observed large-scale fading was modeled using a zero-mean, Log-normal distributed random variable with standard deviation $\sigma = 2.6$ for distances up to 100 m and $\sigma = 4.4$ beyond. The authors also studied small-scale fading characteristics and concluded that fading follows a Rician distribution up to a distance of approx. 90 m, while following rather a Rayleigh like distribution beyond 90 m. In highway environments, Cheng et al. observed a slightly different path loss with an exponent of 1.9 up to a critical distance of 220m, and an exponent of 4.0 beyond [CHBS08]. Small-scale fading was fitted using again a Log-normal distributed random variable with a standard deviation of $\sigma = 2.5$ and $\sigma = 0.9$ respectively. The authors argue that the significantly longer critical distance of 220 m compared to the sub-urban environment is caused by the fact that there are less objects and obstacles (e.g. pedestrians) in a highway environment that could create reflections from points higher than the ground. In [CHC+08], Cheng et al. reported additional results from their time and frequency domain analysis, indicating a RMS delay spread of 200 ns, maximum excess delays of 1400 ns, and a 90 % coherence bandwidth of only 460 kHz.

In [TTLB08], Tan et al. reported the results of their channel measurement campaign which they carried out for urban, rural and highway environments in Detroit, Michigan, USA. The authors differentiate between line of sight (LOS) and non-line of sight (NLOS) conditions in the highway environment. They observed a mean excess delay of 175 ns and a RMS delay spread of 141 ns under LOS conditions, as well as a mean excess delay of 558 ns and a RMS delay spread of 398 ns under NLOS conditions. The maximum excess delayss account for 1576 ns under LOS conditions and 4773 ns under NLOS conditions. With respect to Doppler effects, Tan et al. report Doppler spreads of approx. 1 kHz on average and up to 2 kHz in more extreme situations. A more detailed presentation of their measurement results can also be found in [TB10].

A characterization of vehicular channels in highway environments has also been carried out by Sen et al. [SM08]. In their campaign, low and high density traffic situations have been distinguished, transmitting and receiving vehicles were driving with a velocity of approx. 26 m/s into the same direction, and signals were transmitted using a carrier frequency of 5.12 GHz. Their analysis of the low traffic density scenario revealed a mean excess delay of 127 ns, a maximum excess delay of 1773 ns, and a 90 % coherence bandwidth of 2 MHz. The characteristics under high density traffic conditions share quite similar values – 160 ns for the mean excess delay, 1276 ns for the maximum excess delay, and 1.2 MHz for the 90 % coherence bandwidth. Compared to the results reported in [CHC+08], the coherence bandwidth is significantly higher, which can be attributed to the low relative speed used in their evaluation setup.

The power delay profile in vehicular channels has also been measured and analyzed by Renaudin et al. in [RKVO08]. The used carrier frequency was 5.3 GHz and the measurements have been carried out in a highway environment in Helsinki, Finland. Their measurement data yields a mean excess delay of 165 ns and a maximum excess delay of 2083 ns.

In 2008, Kunisch et al. performed additional path loss, power delay profile and Doppler spread measurements for a carrier frequency of 5.9 GHz and published their results in [KP08]. The observed path loss on a highway in Germany is best fitted by a power law model using an exponent of 1.85, and a zero-mean, Log-normal distributed random variable with $\sigma = 3.2$ for the large-scale fading effects. Further, a RMS delay spread of 41 ns and Doppler shifts up to 1.3 kHz were measured.

Another path loss measurement has been carried out by Karedal et al in [KCP+11]. The authors performed channel sounding on a highway that cut itself directly through the city in Lund, Sweden, using the 5.2 GHz frequency band and vehicles that were driving in same and opposite directions. As in previous studies, the power law model with an exponent of 1.77 yielded the best fit. The large-scale fading was modeled using a zero-mean, Log-normal distributed random variable with $\sigma = 3.1$. Further, the authors observed a difference between the case in which vehicles are driving towards

	Path loss		Delay spread			Doppler spread		Coherence
	n	σ	Mean	RMS	Max.	RMS	Max.	bandwidth
Paier et al.	1.8	–	52 ns	247 ns	1300 ns	–	1 kHz	–
Cheng et al.	1.9^1	$2.5\,dB^1$	–	200 ns	1400 ns	–	–	460 kHz
	4.0^2	$0.9\,dB^2$						
Tan et al.	–	–	175 ns	$141\,ns^3$	$1576\,ns^3$	1 kHz	2 kHz	–
	–	–	558 ns	$398\,ns^4$	$4663\,ns^4$			
Sen et al.	–	–	$127\,ns^5$	–	$1773\,ns^5$	–	–	2 MHz
	–	–	$160\,ns^6$	–	$1276\,ns^6$			
Renaudin et al.	–	–	165 ns	–	2083 ns	–	–	–
Kunisch et al.	1.85	3.2 dB	41 ns	–	–	–	1.3 kHz	–
Karedal et al.	1.77	3.1 dB	–	–	–	–	–	–

[1] Up to a critical distance of 220 m
[2] Beyond a critical distance of 220 m
[3] Under line of sight conditions
[4] Under non-line of sight conditions
[5] In low density traffic situations
[6] In high density traffic situations

Table 3.1: Comparison of reported channel characteristics in highway environments. Since results depend significantly on the specific geometry a slight variation can be observed. But on average, a strong conformance among the results is visible.

each other, the case when vehicles are driving in the same direction, and the case when vehicles are driving away from each other. These findings have been modeled by a 3.3 dB offset that is either added to the path loss (driving away from each other) or substracted (driving towards each other). According to [KCP+11], these offsets can be attributed to the smaller combined gain of antennas and cars in the case of vehicles driving away from each other.

Table 3.1 summarizes the reported characteristics and the following conclusions can be made: first, measurements of the path loss indicate that signal energy loss is decreasing with an exponent close to 2. With respect to the time dispersion of a transmitted signal, all measurements indicate that the arrival times of the shortest and longest path will be in the order of a few hundred nanoseconds on average, and increase up to one or several thousand nanoseconds in rare and extreme situations. The significance of such "late arrivals" is not clear since the reported results do not answer properly whether the late arrivals are sufficiently strong (in comparison to the strongest path) to challenge the successful reception on physical layer. The signal will also be scattered with respect to frequency due to the Doppler effect and frequency shifts of up to 1-2 kHz. Despite the existence of only two measurements that quantified the coherence bandwidth, the vehicular propagation channel can be considered narrow band, in the sense that the channel impulse response correlates only over a small frequency band (only across a spectrum in the order of 460 kHz up to 2 MHz).

3.2.3 Implications on OFDM-based physical layer

The reported measurement results described in Section 3.2.2 show that multi path propagation and Doppler effects are significant in vehicular environments. As a re-

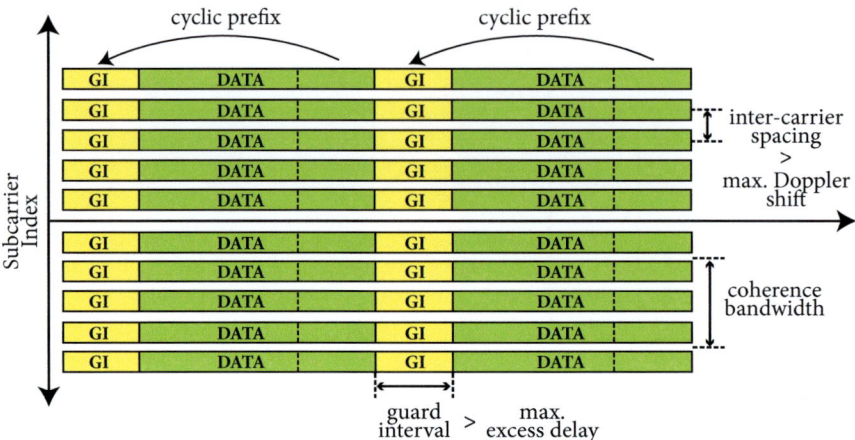

Figure 3.11: Influence of channel measurement metrics on communication system design: the power delay characteristics determine the length of the guard interval and the maximum spacing between pilot subcarriers, whereas the Doppler spectrum determines minimum inter-carrier spacing.

sult, small coherence bandwidths and coherence times have to be expected in vehicular communication networks. But how do these characteristics influence the communication system? And how can they be addressed during the design of the communication system?

The time dispersion of signals due to multi path has a significant impact on the timing of two consecutive (OFDM) data symbols. To ensure that "late arrivals" of the first data symbol do not interfere with "early arrivals" of the second data symbol, a transmitter has to insert short waiting periods called *guard intervals* between both of symbols. The guard interval has to be greater than the maximum expected excess delay of the channel in order to avoid *inter-symbol interference* (ISI) completely. Instead of being "silent" during these periods, a transmitter prepends a *cyclic prefix* to each data signal, which is simply a copy of its own tail, as illustrated in Figure 3.11. Time dispersion also influences the coherence bandwidth of the channel. For OFDM to work, it is required that the coherence bandwidth is greater than the bandwidth of a subcarrier. Further, in order to make sure that the channel coefficients can be tracked over time across the full OFDM signal bandwidth, pilot subcarriers have to be used at spacings no greater than the coherence bandwidth. Else the channel impulse response of the data subcarriers in between can not be estimated accurately enough.

The observed Doppler effects pose requirements on the communication system as well. For instance, the *inter-carrier spacing* between subcarriers should be chosen such that *inter-carrier interference* (ICI) is avoided, i.e. the inter-carrier spacing should be significantly larger than the maximum expected Doppler shifts. Furthermore, pilot subcarriers are needed to track the channel impulse variations over time in case the coherence time is shorter than the duration of all data symbols together.

Without pilot subcarriers, the estimation that is performed at the beginning of a frame (based on the short and long training symbols) gets more and more invalid over time. An alternative to pilot subcarriers is the usage of so called *midambles* that are inserted after every N-th data symbol to enable a full re-estimation of the channel over time.

With respect to the reported measurement results described in Section 3.2.2, the above requirements can be summarized as follows: First, successive data symbols should be separated by at least approx. 1200 ns to ensure that ISI is observed only in very rare cases. Second, the inter-carrier spacing should be significantly larger than 2 kHz to avoid ICI. And third, either pilot subcarriers at a separation smaller than 460 kHz, or midambles that are inserted in intervals smaller than the coherence time should be used.

3.2.4 Channel modeling approaches

During the design and development process of a communication system, the simulation of the wireless channel is an often used approach to test and evaluate the signal processing algorithms employed at the physical layer. Depending on the modeling approaches that are used during simulation, the results obtained might possess different levels of conclusiveness. In the following we survey three fundamentally different approaches to channel modeling: ray tracing, stochastic modeling, and geometry-based stochastic modeling. We further discuss their advantages and disadvantages, and assess whether they need to be considered for the evaluation of IEEE 802.11p based inter-vehicle communication networks.

The most accurate approach to channel modeling is based on the principle of *ray tracing*. Ray tracing requires a detailed description of the scenario and the environment in terms of a 3-dimensional model of all buildings, obstacles and vehicles that will influence the propagation characteristics of a transmitted signal. Based on the geometric description of the environment, ray tracing solves an approximation of Maxwell's wave equation for short wavelengths and calculates the phase shift, amplitude gain, and Doppler shift for every single path that exists between transmitter and receiver – visually speaking, ray tracing can be compared to the "shooting of thousands of rays into all directions". Ray tracing is therefore a deterministic approach and considers the specific geometry of the studied scenario. However, due to the great number of rays that have to be computed, ray tracing is known to be highly expensive with respect to computation times. Maurer et al. were among the first to employ such an approach for vehicle-to-vehicle communications [MSW01, MFW02, MFSW04].

The second approach is based on a stochastic modeling of the channel characteristics with the benefit of reduced computation times. Instead of a consideration of environment or site specifics, such models aim to be only statistically correct and accurate, e.g. by reflecting the average or worst-case characteristics that have been observed in measurement campaigns. In channel modeling literature, *stochastic channel models* are distinguished with respect to the propagation mechanism (or scale)

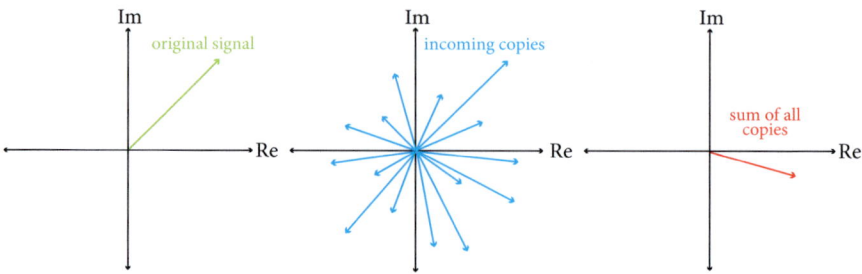

Figure 3.12: Illustration of the principle of a Rayleigh fading using the complex plane. The original (i.e. transmitted) signal arrives at the receiver in terms of multiple copies (i.e. paths), whereas the the phases uniformly and the amplitudes independent and identically distributed. The resulting received signal is then the sum of all copies.

that is addressed by the model. Path loss channel models are the most basic models and are common to researchers and engineers in the form of the *Free space*, *Two-ray Ground*, and the more generic *Power-law* or *Log distance* channel models. The second type of stochastic models are *shadowing channel models*, which address the large-scale fading of the channel. A *Log-Normal shadowing* – given by a zero-mean, normally-distributed random variate with standard deviation σ – is the most commonly used candidate for this type. The third and last type of stochastic channel models is given by models that aim to represent the fast fading characteristics of the channel. Whether the model includes frequency-selectivity or not, such models are either called *narrowband stochastic channel models* or *wideband stochastic channel models*. Narrowband stochastic channel models focus on the frequency dispersion of the channel and describe how the Doppler spectrum of the channel looks like. In time domain, the Doppler spectrum defines the autocorrelation function of the channel and determines the coherence time of the channel. The most common Doppler spectrum is the classical Jakes spectrum [Jak75], which assumes that scatterers are Gaussian distributed on a circle around the receiver, with the result that incoming propagation paths arrive uniformly from each direction. The Jakes spectrum is typically used to implement the autocorrelation function of a flat *Rayleigh fading* channel in which the phases of the (infinite number of) incoming paths are uniformly distributed, and the amplitudes are Gaussian distributed. In case of a significant line of sight component among the arriving paths, in other words the amplitudes are not Gaussian distributed anymore, the so called *Rician distribution* achieves a better match of the channel characteristics [Rap09].

Figure 3.12 illustrates the characteristics of a Rayleigh channel using the example of a single transmitted signal and its representation in the complex plane. Due to multi-path propagation multiple copies of the original signal arrive at the receiver. Each copy carries its own uniformly distributed phase shift and independent but identically distributed amplitude factor. The sum of all copies eventually determines the received signal. In case of a Rician fading channel, one of the signal copies is sufficiently stronger than the rest and therefore "dominates" the resulting received signal.

In contrast to flat fading channel models, *wideband stochastic channel models* are used if the channel exhibits frequency-selectivity. Such channels are usually modeled through a *Tapped Delay Line* (TDL) approach which describes the channel as a function of multiple narrowband stochastic channel models and their respective time delay. Each narrowband stochastic channel is called a tap and describes the average propagation characteristics of a group of paths that are reflected at identical or similar scattering objects, and which arrive at the receiver at approximately the same point in time. Although different grouping (or clustering) methods exist in literature (e.g. clustering based on the angle of arrival or the time delay of each path), their advantages and disadvantages is not discussed in this thesis. In the following, it is sufficient to know that a grouping is performed at all, and that the characteristics of the resulting groups (or taps) is described statistically – in analogy to narrowband channel modeling.

To clarify what this means in detail, let us consider the scenario illustrated in Figure 3.8 of Section 3.2.1 again. To model the channel impulse response in this setup using the TDL approach, one would usually come up with five taps, whereas each tap represents the collection of paths that is reflected at one of the five scatterers[1]. To reflect the different propagation delays of the taps, each tap is associated with the average (or mean) time delay of all corresponding paths. The frequency domain characteristics of each tap are then described by a matching Doppler spectrum, e.g. by the already mentioned Jakes spectrum, or other typically observed spectra such as the Round, Classic 3 dB, or Classic 6 dB spectrum.

In the context of mobile-to-mobile communications within the 5 GHz frequency band, several TDL channel models have been proposed, for instance by Acosta-Marum et al. [AI07], Matolak et al. [Mat08] and Renaudin et al. [RKVO09]. From these, only the six time- and frequency-selective channel models by Acosta-Marum et al. have been implemented for this thesis and will be used later to evaluate the performance of the IEEE 802.11p based physical layer. These six models simulate the characteristics of a vehicle-to-vehicle channel in either expressway, urban, or suburban environments by using up to 12 taps. The taps experience a propagation delay difference of up to 700 ns (with respect to the earliest tap), Doppler shifts of up to 1.5 kHz, and relative tap powers down to a value of -26 dB (in comparison to the strongest tap). As it was emphasized already in Section 3.2.2, it is not clear at this point whether all taps that arrive with a delay of up to 700 ns, or which are up to 26 dB weaker than the strongest (line of sight) path, have a significant impact on the performance of the IEEE 802.11p based physical layer. Particularly low data rates that employ only QPSK bit modulation, which is the default for safety-related communication, should be robust against any self-interference that is more than 10 dB weaker than the line of sight path. Chapter 4 will elaborate on this aspect.

A stochastic approach is to be preferred if low computation effort is desired. However, existing stochastic channel models are not able to reflect the fluctuations of the channel characteristics between transmitter and receiver over large time pe-

---

[1] Although one might come up with less than five taps in the end when using a different clustering method, a set of five taps is assumed in the following to ease comprehensibility.

riods, e.g. when transmitter and receiver are first approaching each other and then driving away from each other. In such a situation, the fixed time delay value associated to each tap as well as the characteristics of each tap do not match with what is really happening over time: the time delay of each tap will increase or decrease, and the characteristics of each tap may vary since the constellation of the scatterers changes. Such variations are simply "averaged out" in a stochastic channel model, which therefore belong to the class of models which are based on the wide-sense stationary uncorrelated scattering (WSSUS) assumption [Bel63].

Geometry-based stochastic channel models (GSCM) solve the issue described above through a combination of the ideas behind ray tracing and stochastic channel modeling. In general, such models place scatterers randomly within the surrounding of transmitter/receiver in order to generate a geometry that adheres to a desired statistical distribution. The geometry is then used to perform a simplified ray tracing: each scatterer is considered to be responsible for one single path that arrives at the receiver position. Each path represents an echo of the signal, and exhibits its own attenuation, stochastic amplitude gain, phase shift, and propagation delay. While the exact value of the distance dependent path loss and propagation delay are deterministic, the stochastic amplitude gain and the phase shift are randomly derived from a stochastic distribution.

Akki et al. [AH86] were the first to propose a geometry-based stochastic channel model. In their model, scatterers are placed on circles around transmitter/receiver to achieve a narrowband isotropic scattering in vehicle-to-vehicle environments with Rayleigh fading. Tsan-Ming et al. and Zajic et al. followed the same principle and developed three-dimensional models to determine the space-time-frequency [WK07], or additionally the space-Doppler power spectral density and the power space-delay spectral density of the channel [ZS08a, ZS08b, ZS09]. Zajic et al. could also show that their model matches empirical results from measurement campaigns quite accurately [ZSPN09]. In [CWL+09b, CWL09a] Cheng et al. proposed a geometry-based stochastic channel model that is further able to consider different vehicle densities in the surrounding of transmitter and receiver. Yet, all of the above models do not consider the non-stationarity of the vehicle-to-vehicle communication channel, since they consider only static scatterers that are placed randomly on regular shapes (e.g. circle or ellipse) around transmitter and receiver.

Recently, Karedal et al. proposed a geometry-based stochastic channel model for highway scenarios that addresses the non-stationarity of the channel [KTC+09]. Based on the results of their measurement campaigns [KP08], the authors developed a model in which discrete and diffuse scatterers are explicitly distinguished and placed on irregular shapes within a highway scenario. Whereas moving vehicles, buildings or sign posts are treated as discrete scatterers (either being mobile or static) that contribute significantly to the overall signal, diffuse scatterers cover objects such as trees, small objects along the road and other structures that do not contribute significantly to the channel gain on their own. Furthermore, discrete static and diffuse scatterers are placed randomly in valid regions of the scenario, and discrete mobile scatterers, i.e. vehicles, are placed according to their actual position on

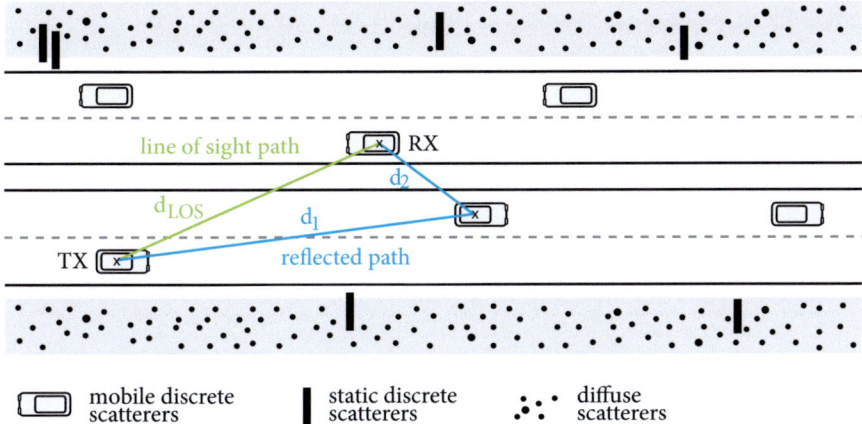

	mobile discrete scatterers		static discrete scatterers		diffuse scatterers

Figure 3.13: Geometry of the scenario that is considered by the geometry-based stochastic channel model developed by Karedal et al.: vehicles are driving on the highway and represent mobile discrete scattering objects; static discrete objects, e.g. sign posts, are located at the side of the highway, together with a large amount of diffuse scattering objects.

the road. Compared to previous GSCM channel models, the proposed model aims to reflect the geometry of a highway instead of using regular shapes such as circles and ellipses. Hence, the time-varying channel transfer function that is obtained through successive computations (with positions of vehicles slightly changed) fulfills the non-stationarity condition. An optimization of their model with respect to computation time is proposed in [CKZ+10].

Since the geometry based stochastic channel model by Karedal et al. will be used in Chapter 4 to evaluate whether the characteristics of a time- and frequency-selective channel have a significant impact on the performance of the physical layer, relevant details of their model are presented and discussed in the following. The model assumes a scenario as depicted in Figure 3.13: vehicles are driving on a two lane per direction highway and the highway is surrounded by so called static discrete (SD) and static diffuse (DI) scattering objects which scatter the transmitted signal. The vehicles that are in the surrounding of the transmitting and receiving vehicles are denoted as mobile discrete scatterers (MD). According to their model specification, five static discrete scattering objects per highway kilometer, and 1000 diffuse scattering objects per highway kilometer are assumed. And although the number of vehicles on the highway is specified to be five vehicles per kilometer, it is assumed that the exact number can be varied and that the location of each vehicle is derived and updated from its mobility pattern. Based on this layout, the channel impulse response for a sequence of input signals $S = [s(1), ..., s(n)]$ (and between two of the vehicles) is calculated as follows.

Parameter	Unit	LOS	MD	SD	DI
Reference loss, $G_{o,p}$	dB	-5	$-89 + 24n_p$		104
Pathloss exponent, n_p		1.8	$\mathcal{U}[0, 3.5]$		5.4
Random phase shift, ϕ_p			$\mathcal{U}[0, 2\pi)$		
Mean of σ_S^2		6.8	9.4	6.3	–

Table 3.2: Most relevant configuration parameters used by the geometry-based stochastic channel model of Karedal et al. [KP08] for the computation of the per path complex amplitude gain.

1. Calculate the per path (complex) amplitude gain $a_p(i)$ and the per path propagation delay $\tau_p(i)$ for each input signal $s(i)$ and

   (a) the line of sight (LOS) path

   (b) each path that exists due to one of the mobile discrete scatterers

   (c) each path that exists due to one of the static discrete scatterers

   (d) each path that exists due to one of the diffuse scatterers

2. Update the position of each mobile scatterer over time, i.e. when moving on to the next signal $s(i + 1)$

3. Apply each $a_p(i)$ to the input signal $s(i)$ and "delay" the result according to the corresponding propagation delay $\tau_p(i)$

4. Sum up all signal copies that arrive at the same point in time

According to [KP08], the complex amplitude gains (which result in a scaling and phase rotation of the signal vector) of the line of sight and the (mobile as well as static) discrete scatterer paths are calculated as follows:

$$a_p(i) = g_{S,p} \, e^{j\phi_p} \, G_{o,p}^{1/2} \left(\frac{1}{d_p}\right)^{n_p/2} \tag{3.8}$$

whereas $g_{S,p}$ represents a slowly varying stochastic amplitude gain, $e^{j\phi_p}$ represents a uniformly distributed phase shift, $G_{o,p}^{1/2}$ the reference loss at 1 meter, d_p the distance of path p, and n_p the path loss exponent. The stochastic amplitude gain $g_{S,p}$ is modeled as a correlated log-normal variable using an exponentially distributed variance σ_S^2. Of course, depending on the type of path – either a line of sight or a scattered path – a different parametrization is used in the formula above, cf. Table 3.2. For instance, a fixed path loss exponent of 1.8 is used for the line of sight path, compared to a random exponent in the range of $[0, 3.5]$ for each path that exists due to a discrete scatterer, or a fixed exponent of 5.4 for each path that exists due to a diffuse scatterer. Similarly, the reference loss $G_{o,p}$ at 1 meter and the mean value of variance σ_S^2 vary as well. Only the random phase shift is equal for all paths.

In case of a path that exists due to a scattering at one of the diffuse scattering objects, the complex amplitude gain is calculated as follows:

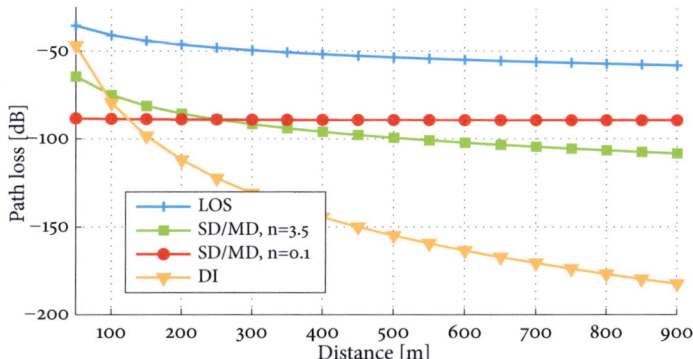

Figure 3.14: Illustration of the distance decaying path loss of each of the four different path types: line of sight (LOS), static and mobile discrete scatterer paths (SD/MD), and diffuse scatterer paths (DI).

$$a_p(i) = c_r \, G_{o,p}^{1/2} \left(\frac{1}{d_1 \cdot d_2} \right)^{n_p/2} \tag{3.9}$$

with c_r being zero-mean complex Gaussian distributed, $G_{o,p}^{1/2}$ being the reference loss at 1 meter, d_1 and d_2 being the distance from transmitter to scatterer and from scatterer to receiver, and n_p being the path loss exponent.

Apparently, the distance decaying part in the above equation has the most significant influence on the magnitude of each path. As can be seen in Figure 3.14, which plots the distance decaying path loss for each type of path and its respective parametrization, a line of sight path is significantly stronger than a scattered path, at least by more than 20 dB. Note that Equation 3.9 uses the product of the lengths d_1 and d_2 of the two subpaths in order to compute the path loss for a diffuse scatterer path. Since Figure 3.14 plots the path loss only over the total path length, d_1 and d_2 are set such that $d_1 = d_2 = 0.5(d_1 + d_2)$. This allocation of the total path length yields the smallest path loss value, and is therefore considered to be very optimistic. Of course, the stochastic amplitude gain might reduce this difference, but it will not diminish. As a result, it is questionable whether all paths, in particular the ones that result from diffuse scattering, will influence the performance of IEEE 802.11p at all, and if yes how significantly.

Independent of the answer to the question whether all paths have an impact on the physical layer performance, it can be concluded that the above way of modeling scatterers is close to how a Rayleigh fading channel is modeled: multiple copies arrive at the receiver (each on its own path) whereas each copy has its own angle of arrival and amplitude gain. However, in contrast to Rayleigh, the scatterer distribution in the scenario above is not uniform, and hence the angle of arrivals are not uniformly distributed neither. Also, since the amplitude gain is based on the distance decaying Power-law, the amplitudes of the paths are not derived from a uniform distribution.

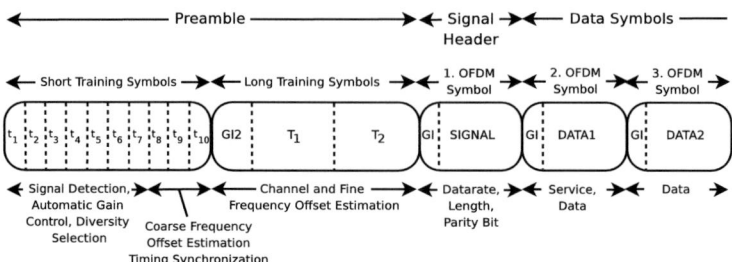

Figure 3.15: Frame format of the OFDM-based IEEE 802.11 PHY specification.

Further, the propagation delays of the corresponding paths are not equal and changing over time (since sender, receiver and mobile scatterers move).

3.3 The IEEE 802.11p physical layer specification

The IEEE 802.11p standard employs exactly the same physical layer specification that is already used in the IEEE 802.11a and g standard. As such, IEEE 802.11p uses 52 OFDM subcarriers in total, out of which 48 are used for data transmissions and four as pilots for channel tracking over time. Further, it offers a 5, 10 and 20 MHz channel spacing, as well as datarates up to 54 Mbps. The frame format is identical to IEEE 802.11a and contains the following sections, as illustrated in Figure 3.15: a preamble, a signal header, and a data unit section.

The preamble consists of a series of repeating time sample sequences, which are identical for every transmitted frame. These sequences are ten repetitions of short and two repetitions of long training symbols (cf. Section 3.1), which can be used by the receiver for signal detection, automatic gain control, diversity selection, timing synchronization as well as channel and frequency offset estimation. After the preamble, there exists the signal header, termed the SIGNAL in the standard, which contains information about the length of the data unit section, the modulation and coding scheme used and further, a parity bit to support basic error detection. The SIGNAL fits in one OFDM symbol and contains most of the frame's header information, apart from a 16-bit service field which is included in the first OFDM symbol of the data section. Finally, the data section is the last distinct part of the frame, can be several OFDM symbols in length and contains the payload to be transmitted.

To combat the large maximum excess delays of the channel, the first generation of V2V communication networks will use a profile standard that employs channels of 10 MHz bandwidth. The resulting 1.6 μs guard interval protects successive OFDM symbols from inter-symbol interferences (ISI), and the 156 kHz subcarrier spacing avoids inter-carrier interference (ICI). However, the reported coherence bandwidth of approx. 460 kHz (cf. Section 3.2.2) is too small to rely on four pilot subcarriers that are placed with a spacing of approx. 2 MHz (or 13 subcarriers). Further, relying solely on the initial training symbols that allow a channel estimation over the whole frequency band is also not recommened, since the envisioned datarate of 6 Mbps yields packet transmission times greater than the reported coherence times of the channel. Hence, the initial channel estimation becomes invalid at the end of a transmission.

The bits that constitute the data unit section are encoded into complex signals based on the principles explained in Section 3.1: first, the bits are shuffled by the scrambler to prevent the appearance of long sequences of o's or 1's; then, a convolutional encoder [VO79] adds redundancy to enable error correction and, finally, a block interleaver ensures that long runs of low reliability bits are avoided. Importantly, the block interleaver divides the bitstream into equally sized blocks, each of which can fit into a single OFDM symbol. Then, each block is modulated according to BPSK, QPSK, 16-QAM or 64-QAM, and pilot symbols are inserted in four of the 52 subcarriers to support channel tracking in the receiver. Finally, each block is modulated using OFDM. A similar process is applied to the signal header, with the special condition that no bit scrambling is done and a coding rate of $\frac{1}{2}$ and BPSK bit modulation is used regardless of the datarate that is used for the data section.

4
Combined physical layer and network simulation

As highlighted in the previous chapter, several radio propagation effects can have an impact on the performance of a wireless communication system. With respect to the IEEE 802.11p physical layer standard specification, those effects reside primarily at signal level and may cause decoding failures at individual receivers. Clearly, those effects influence the performance of higher layer protocols such as medium access control and data dissemination as well.

Since a direct evaluation of not yet deployed systems (or networks) is either impossible, expensive to set up and difficult to manage (simply consider field operational tests), or analytically not tractable, a simulation-based approach is employed in this thesis to assess the performance of inter-vehicle communication networks. Section 4.1 therefore analyzes to which extent existing wireless network and physical layer simulators – that are typically used independently by the networking and the electrical engineering community – employ appropriate models that include the effects mentioned above. The apparent gap that exists between the physical layer and networking perspective is discussed intensively, and possible benefits that could be exploited by means of combined physical layer and network simulation are motivated. Alternative evaluation (or experimentation) methods and existing work that proposes to combine both aspects as well is surveyed in Section 4.2. The following Section 4.3 then presents the implementation and integration of a physical layer simulator for the IEEE 802.11p standard specification into the popular NS-3 network simulator. The subsequent sections provide a validation of the implemented physical layer simulator, an evaluation of the physical layer performance in vehicle-to-vehicle radio propagation channels, as well as a runtime performance evaluation and optimization using GPU-based signal processing. The work presented in this section has been published in a condensed version in [MPHS11], upon which portions of this section are based.

4.1 Motivation

Based on the motivation given in [MPHS11], this section provides a brief outline of communication systems as viewed from a physical layer and networking perspective. Subsequent discussion highlights the differences in modelling such systems under each perspective as, intuitively, each view reflects different priorities and objects of study.

Networking perspective

Simulation studies performed from a networking perspective typically focus on aspects related to the performance and behavior of the whole network. For instance, studies that address existing medium access control issues often record the observed channel access times, the packet collision probability, fairness or scalability issues (e.g., [BUSB09, JC08, TSH05]). Similarly, studies that focus on network or transport layer aspects normally evaluate metrics related to routing, dissemination or point-to-point communication, such as the number of required retransmissions, dissemination delay or the number of routing hops (e.g., [HBSG06, MOL07]). At this level, the entity of interest for such studies is the packet (or frame), a fact which is reflected in the metrics used, many of which are measured in packets.

The adoption of the packet as the simplest unit of interest has lead to abstractions in the workings of the physical layer, where an unambiguous specification requires the use of lower level entities such as bits and signal time samples. Modern network simulators have largely adopted what can be termed as packet-level physical layer models, where the packet is considered an indivisible unit, i.e. there is no modelling of individual bits (or lower level components) in the collective whole.

The packet-level physical layer approach is reflected in the NS-2 [NS2] network simulator where, initially, the physical layer representation utilized a basic reception threshold model in order to simulate the carrier sense functionality and determine successful packet reception. In particular, a packet was only received successfully in simulations if its signal strength was above a pre-defined threshold and if it did not experience any collisions. This approach was found to be too disconnected from the workings of real transceivers by Chen et. al, who proposed an improved model which kept track of all incoming packets and used a signal-to-interference-noise ratio (SINR) to determine whether a packet could be received successfully [CJTD06]. Note that tuning the SINR thresholds in that model can reflect the level of sophistication and effectiveness of the receiver – with a particularly sophisticated receiver requiring a relatively low SINR to decode a packet. The model was further extended in [CSJ$^+$07] by the same authors to optionally enable packet capturing capabilities for the receiver. This facility accounts for advanced receiver technologies which allow synchronization (i.e. switching reception) to a new incoming packet even if the transceiver is already in the process of reception. Overall, the work of Chen et al. has been integrated in other popular network simulators, such as OMNeT++ [KSG$^+$08], NS-3 [ns3] and QualNet [RLLK08].

Apart from the SINR-based reception models there exist others based on statistical bit-error rate (BER) computations. Examples of this approach can be found in the NS-3, Jist/SWANS [jis] and GloMoSim [glo] simulators. BER-based models use the SINR to derive a corresponding average single BER and then use this for the calculation of the final packet error rate taking into account the number of bits in the packet. In such models a large packet experiences a higher error probability than a smaller one. Note that SINR-based models disregard the length of a packet in error computations; regardless of the packet size, if the SINR threshold is crossed, even for a very short time period, the packet is rejected. Similar to the thresholds used in the SINR-based approach, one can tune the receiver effectiveness in BER models by modifying the SINR to BER mapping, e.g., by using either analytical BER models [Pro01] or by employing lookup tables that have been populated through empirical measurements or detailed physical layer simulations.

Physical layer perspective

Broadly, physical layer oriented research studies, e.g. [HYW$^+$09], are primarily concerned with point-to-point link performance rather than the network wide implications of particular algorithms — this is unsurprising considering that the network level effects of a communications stack are viewed as dictated by higher layer protocol functions (e.g., MAC). At the physical level of inquiry, the metrics of interest are largely the power efficiency which is a measure of the minimum received power required to satisfy a target BER probability, and some measure of spectral efficiency; the two quantities are frequently viewed as opposing optimisation trends and discovering an optimal trade-off point (depending on the application) is a continuing research challenge. As can be expected, much of the relevant literature in the area of physical layer and channel modeling [MTKM09] considers the signal time samples as the basic unit of interest because they allow for precise enough description of the mechanisms covering the functionality assigned to the physical layer [IEE07, Int].

Simulation evaluation at this level, insofar as a broad characterization of it is possible, is conducted on dedicated simulators which are based on signal processing frameworks such as IT++ [ITP], Matlab [MAT], Simulink [SLI] or similar environments [Eat02]. Typically, simulations consider a transmitted signal (represented by sufficient time samples) that is altered by channel effects and experiences some level of interference and noise when it reaches the receiver. The time samples ultimately act as input data for the physical layer at the receiver, where the decoding process, that is the transformation to bits, takes place. Note, that during transmission and reception, signal processing techniques are employed to characterize and ameliorate the effects of the channel and interference. Broadly, a comparison of the original bits at the sender and the decoded bits at the receiver provides a measurable quantity of effectiveness of competing techniques in terms of BER.

The BER result, expressed in Packet-Error Rate (PER) terms, can be used in network layer oriented research, as described previously. However, the BER to PER transformation is not usually straightforward and, perhaps more critically, both the PER and BER measures reflect particular simulation parameters such as specific packet sizes and a particular channel model. Most network simulators work around this limitation by providing a look-up table where different packet sizes correspond to particular PERs or even consider a different table per channel model. As such, interactions of packets of differing sizes characterised by different signal propagation models can lead to a prohibited growth in the size of such tables and therefore significant compromises need to be made; normally coarse packet granularity is assumed (say only packets of 300, 500 and 1000 bytes are used in the simulations) and it is assumed that all packets propagate through the same channel. Depending on the level of detail required these limitations may be overly restricting.

Moreover, physical layer simulations do not model effects at higher layers. For instance, the error detecting (or even correcting) mechanisms of an encapsulated MAC frame, or of higher layer payloads, are not directly considered. Further, in several simulation studies the bits in the frame often do not exhibit any special structure, such as, say, the one dictated by the 802.11 standard, but are, instead, distributed randomly along the frame. Generally, the prospect of studying interactions with higher layer mechanisms is limited, as creating a simulator incorporating these layers is a non-trivial task and perhaps beyond the expertise of a non-interdisciplinary researcher. So, appreciating the impact of a proposed physical layer mechanism on the whole communications stack in the context of a network is frequently not immediately possible.

Problem statement

Treating the networking aspects and the physical layer as broadly abstract-able entities in simulations can lead to significant drawbacks when evaluating wireless communication systems in general and vehicular networks in particular.

Notably, network level simulation studies ignore the implications of significant effects observed at the physical layer and the wireless channel. Such effects are, for instance, the impact of high relative speeds between a transmitting and receiving vehicle on the communications channel or even the effect of scatterers between and around the communicating partners. Studying such effects and evaluating attempts to ameliorate them requires a particular level of detail commonly encountered only in physical layer oriented research. To appreciate the importance of the above, consider the fast-fading characteristics of the received power as well as the large root mean square delay and Doppler spreads reported by recent measurement campaigns in actual deployments, cf. Section 3.2.2. In this setting, inter-carrier and inter-symbol interference can exist within a single packet, which leads to reduced communication reliability, unless the effects are catered for by appropriate signal processing mechanisms at the receiver. Further, short coherence times and a small coherence bandwidth can affect system performance as well, cf. Section 3.2.3. Such considerations, however, are not reflected in modern network level simulators. Further, since the envisioned IEEE 802.11p standard for vehicular communications derives largely from IEEE 802.11, which was not original designed for highly mobile ad-hoc networks, these issues have to be reflected in simulations especially if high precision and detail are required (for instance, in safety-related use case evaluations).

Physical layer simulation studies, on the other hand, do not consider the effect of mechanisms present in upper layers nor make use of the added information they could provide. As an immediate consequence, there is no direct way to evaluate how feedback from higher layers (say the MAC or routing mechanisms) may aid in choosing appropriate signal processing techniques at the physical layer. For instance, consider that in a vehicular network information on the future mobility status of a communicating neighbour (as predicted by the routing agent which receives periodic updates of other vehicles' speed and direction) could help the physical layer switch to a more suitable mode of transmission — perhaps opting for a lower transmission rate if a neighbour is deemed to be moving away, so as to obtain increased communications range and reliability. Evaluating such a mechanism directly, i.e. not through statistical abstractions, is not possible unless both the node's transmission mechanisms and the network in its entirety are accounted for in sufficient detail.

Benefit of merging both perspectives

Consolidating the physical layer and networking perspectives into a common simulation framework provides two main benefits. First, it allows each perspective to consider a complete set of modeling aspects; network simulators can accommodate realistic physical layer phenomena, while physical layer studies may account for the impact of medium access mechanisms and network characteristics. Thereby simplifying assumptions which may impact simulation results need not be made. Second, the merge of both perspectives enables new types of research enquiries including cross-layer feedback and optimization studies, which have either been unrealizable, or difficult to perform directly. So, researchers may assess advanced physical layer techniques originating from information theory and evaluate their impact on network-wide performance.

To highlight the practical implications of the above, the work of Halperin et. al [HAW08] is considered in which the concept of interference cancellation at the physical layer is applied to a small wireless ad-hoc network testbed of ZigBee nodes in order to increase spatial reuse and reduce the negative effect of hidden terminals. By giving each node the ability to disambiguate and successfully receive concurrent overlapping transmissions from multiple sources, the authors were able to disable the carrier-sense mechanism of the medium access layer altogether and significantly increase, due to improved spatial reuse, the delivery rate for the median pair of links in the testbed. Evidently then, cross-layer optimization has been employed to reduce the complexity of the distributed medium access by using an advanced algorithm at the physical layer — the above work hints at the potential of studying such optimizations through simulations. Similar work, which further strengthens the case for a perspectives merge, has been undertaken by Tan et. al in [TLF⁺09] and Sundaresan et. al in [SSIC04]. Tan et. al studied the same concept as in [HAW08] for IEEE 802.11b networks, leading to the development of the Carrier Counting Multiple Access (CCMA) mechanism, in which up to a limited number of overlapping transmissions are allowed before transmission requests from upper layers are blocked. A novel MAC protocol, called stream-controlled medium acces (SCMA), was also presented by Sundaresan et. al. SCMA leverages the benefits of multiple input multiple output (MIMO) links in order to increase the performance and throughput of wireless ad-hoc networks. With MIMO, data to be transmitted can, e.g., be demultiplexed into several streams with each transmitted out of a different antenna with equal power, at the same frequency, modulation format, and time slot. A receiver can then, under certain conditions, distinguish the different streams when either no interference is present or as long as the total number of incoming streams (even if they originate from several different transmitters) is smaller than the number of receiving antennas. If this condition is not met, the receiver becomes overloaded and is unable to suppress the interference from other nodes. In order to exploit the potential of MIMO efficiently, the SCMA protocol determines the maximum number of usable streams for each packet transmission so as to enable successful suppression of interference at the receiver. Intuitively, the performance gain depends on the amount of correlation between the receiving antennas and reaches its peak if the streams at the antennas are not correlated at all. Since the authors used a traditional packet level network simulator to evaluate SCMA, they could only employ a simple model for the physical layer MIMO characteristics that assumes a minimum correlation level between the streams. With a network simulator that integrates both physical and network layer details, they could have assessed the performance more accurately.

Apart from enabling interference cancellation studies, fusing both perspectives can also enable the accurate study of simple and advanced network coding techniques, where the capacity of a network is increased by coding multiple packets into a single transmission, and the coding itself may be performed at the physical, link or network layers [Wu07].

4.2 Related work

Recently, several research efforts attempted to address the issues described in the previous section, at least partially and primarily using methods that do not employ a full simulation of the considered system. For instance, Judd et al. [JS04] developed a wireless network emulator which simulates the fine-grained effects of a mobile wireless communication channel by multiplexing the antenna in- and outputs of commodity communication systems with a software-controlled digital signal processor. Thereby, controlled and repeatable wireless experiments of e.g., up to 16 IEEE 802.11-based communication systems operating at 2.4 GHz are supported. Further, with respect to the evaluation of advanced signal processing techniques, the authors of [CH99, war, TZF⁺09] proposed several software defined radio platforms that provide the ability to implement (and emulate) the physical layer entirely in software by using dedicated hardware only for the radio frontend, e.g. using field programmable gate arrays (FPGAs) or commodity multi-core and many-core systems.

The above works propose emulation of either only the wireless communication channel or the physical layer but not both concurrently, and, further, are either expensive or difficult to use for studies of vehicular communication networks. The same observation is made by Kasch et al. in [KWA09], where the benefits and drawbacks of either hardware or software based simulation (or emulation) is discussed. While a hardware based approach is to be prefered due to a better runtime performance (i.e. smaller execution times), software based appoaches come with the advantage of an increased flexibility. After an evaluation of the pros and cons, Kasch et al. propose to pursue so called *high fidelity simulations* that are entirely software-based and optimized with respect to an increased runtime performance using distributed processing techniques.

The proposal of Kasch et al. was adopted by Massin et al. [MLBLMF10], who combined physical layer and networking aspects in an OMNET++-based cross-layer simulation framework. The proposed framework is stated to be reusable and extensible, and envisioned to simulate the complete protocol stack from application layer over network layer down to the physical layer. Further, to achieve its objective, individual bits of a packet are treated separately. Unfortunately, the proposed framework is not publically available, and the paper itself does not include any details on the implemented physical layer signal processing algorithms and the implemented channel models.

4.3 Implementation

The demands for a combined simulation of physical layer and networking aspects including the resulting benefits were motivated in the previous section. The following subsections now present how a physical layer simulator can be implemented and integrated into a discrete event-based network simulation framework. In the context of this thesis, the popular NS-3 network simulator is chosen as a starting point, and the open-source IT++ signal processing library is used to implement the physical layer simulator. The implementation is compliant to the OFDM-based IEEE 802.11 standard specification, but omits the legacy direct sequence spread spectrum (DSSS) modes as well as the infrared communication provisions of the standard. The proposed combination can therefore be used to simulate the IEEE 802.11 a, g and p amendments of the standard with data rates up to 54 Mbps.

An overview of the combined physical layer and networking simulator is given in Figure 4.1: medium access control forwards transmission requests down to the *Tx module* of the physical layer simulator according to its medium access policies (i.e. CSMA). The Tx module then transforms the contents of the data packet into a sequence of complex time samples[1], as described in Section 3.3 and as defined by the

---

[1]Traditionally, network simulators do not model the actual payload of each packet, but consider only the protocol headers added by each layer. To resolve this, a random payload (or bit sequence) is generated that serves as input to the frame construction process.

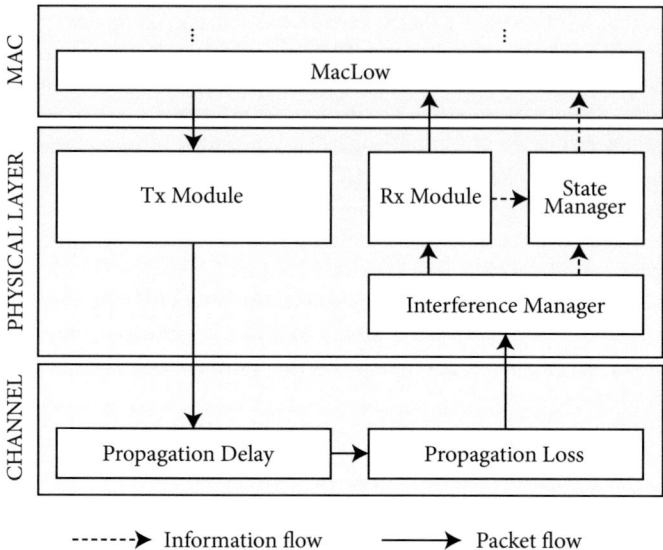

Figure 4.1: Overview of the joint networking and physical layer simulation architecture. In addition to the transmission and reception logic (cf. Tx and Rx modules), propagation delays and possible impacts of multiple transmitting nodes have to be considered as well (cf. interference manager and state manager).

standard. Afterwards, the packet (whose content is now represented by a sequence of complex time samples) is put on the channel, which multiplexes between all nodes that are transmitting and listening to that channel. To address space and time properly, a propagation delay and one (or multiple) propagation loss modules apply time delay and power loss characteristics. At each receiver the packet is delivered to the physical layer and first stored in the so called *Interference manager* which keeps track of all incoming packets (and signals), aligns them w.r.t. time and ensures that network aspects, i.e. multiple access interference, are implemented correctly. In a next step, the packet is handed over to the *Rx module* for reception, which starts the reception process depending on the current state of the physical layer, and finally delivers it up to the medium access control layer in case the decoding process completed without any errors.

Apart from being responsible for a proper treatment of multiple access interference, the interference manager will also report the energy level that is currently present at the receiver to the *State manager*. This feedback is necessary in order to support the clear channel assignment mechanism and to implement the carrier sense functionality of the medium access control layer in IEEE 802.11. The state manager distinguishes also between several processing (or reception) stages in order to emulate the reception behavior of a real transceiver properly, e.g. to support the different frame capture capabilities available in modern chipsets.

The following Section 4.3.1 further elaborates on the signal processing details, outlines the transmission and decoding algorithms used in the implementation. Section 4.3.2 then covers the network related aspects by means of an in-depth explanation of the underlying state machine and an illustration of how the continuous reception process of a real transceiver is modeled in a discrete event-based simulator. An overview of the implemented propagation loss models is given in Section 4.3.3, and several design decisions are discussed in Section 4.3.4.

4.3.1 Signal processing aspects

The main signal processing logic of the physical layer resides in the Tx and Rx modules. Whereas the frame construction process is straight forward and leaves no room for fundamental modifications, the reception process is not covered by the IEEE 802.11 standard specification and is also subject to optimisation in terms of decoding performance. Hence, after a short outline of the frame construction process in the beginning, the main focus will be on the logic of the reception module.

As a first step of frame construction, the bits of a packet are scrambled in order to prevent long sequences of zeros or ones. Then a convolutional encoder adds redundancy to enable error correction in the receiver and a block interleaver ensures that long runs of low reliability bits are avoided. The block interleaver further divides the bitstream into equally sized blocks, each of which can fit into a single OFDM symbol. Afterwards, the bits of each block are modulated onto complex signals using either phase-shift keying (BPSK or QPSK) or quadrature amplitude modulation (16-QAM or 64-QAM), pilot symbols are inserted in four of the 52 subcarriers to support channel tracking in the receiver, and OFDM modulation is applied to each block. The end product of the above transformations is a sequence of complex time samples — 80 samples per OFDM symbol. As interoperability among different vendors has to be guaranteed, minor deviations in this chain of processing steps are not allowed.

Since real transceivers will introduce carrier frequency offsets due to inaccuracies in the local oscillators (i.e. symbol clock), a uniformly distributed frequency offset is applied twice to the transmitted signals: once to model the offset on transmitter side, and once to reflect the inaccuracies on receiver side. According to the IEEE 802.11 standard specification for OFDM-based communication, the clock frequency tolerance shall be at most ±20 ppm for 20 MHz channel configurations, and ±10 ppm for 5 MHz channel configurations.

In contrast to the strictly defined transmission chain, the standard does not define the specific signal processing algorithms that have to be used in a receiver. Instead, the standard defines a minimum receiver sensitivity that has to be met by any receiver implementation. Of course, each receiver has to execute the inverse of the frame construction process, i.e. it has to perform OFDM and bit demodulation, error correction (using a Viterbi decoder), as well as to deinterleave and to descramble all data bits. However, it is not standardized how the beginning of a new frame is detected, how timing synchronization has to be performed, how (or even whether) a receiver has to use the feedback provided through pilot subcarriers, how it should

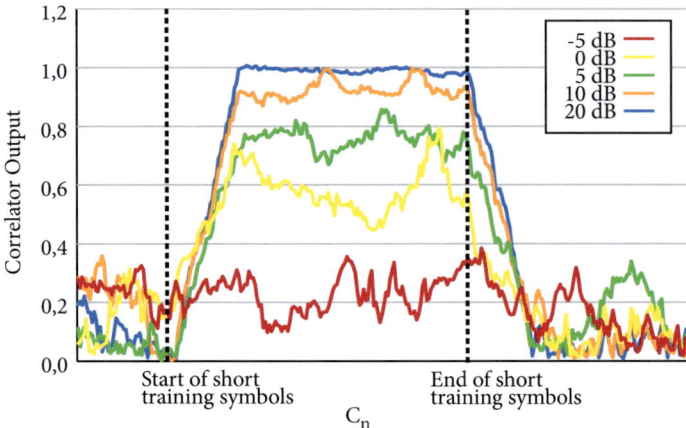

Figure 4.2: Time-variant and signal-to-noise ratio dependent output of the auto-correlator that is used by the signal detector.

equalize channel effects, and how to correct frequency offsets due to inaccurate oscillators in the transmitter and the receiver.

In the proposed physical layer implementation, the process of signal detection is based on two mechanisms: energy detection and preamble detection. The receiver assumes that a valid frame is present if the energy level increases by at least 4 dB, and if the auto-correlation of the received signal exceeds a specific correlation threshold. The auto-correlator computes the correlation among the short training symbols, i.e. each sample is correlated against its counterpart that arrives with a delay of 16 time samples, and returns a moving average using a window size of 32 time samples in order to suppress white noise [Liu03]. In mathematical terms, the correlator computes

$$C_n = \sum_{k=0}^{L-1} s_{n-k} s_{n-k-16}^* \tag{4.1}$$

with $L = 32$ being the window size of the moving average, s_i being the i-th received time sample and s_i^* being the complex conjugate of it. Depending on the SNR of the received signal, the time-varying output of the correlator will look similar to the values shown in Figure 4.2. As can be seen, the correlator has its difficulties to identify the repeating pattern of the short training symbols if the SNR is smaller than zero. However, as soon as the signal strength is equal to or greater than the noise level, C_n exceeds a correlation value of 0.4 and reaches the maximum value of $C_n = 1$ for SNRs of 10 dB and greater. Due to reasons that will be explained later in Section 4.3.4, a correlation threshold of 0.85 is used in the remainder of this thesis.

The receiver also performs a coarse time synchronization using the short and long training symbols. The point in time at which the correlator output drops below the correlation threshold is taken as an estimate for the end of the short training symbols. In a next step, a more accurate time synchronization is achieved through an (auto-)correlation of the long training symbols. In analogy to signal detection, Equation 4.1 is used to auto-correlate the received samples that belong to the long training symbols, however, using a delay of 64 time samples.

Based on the short and long training symbols and following the proposal presented in [SEM04], the receiver performs also an initial phase offset estimation and uses the estimate to correct the responsible frequency offset. First, the last 5 short training symbols are used to obtain a coarse estimate $\hat{\alpha}_{ST}$ of the per sample phase rotation (or drift). Assuming that s_m, where $m = 0, 1, ...79$, are the time samples representing the second half of the short training symbols, $-\pi < \angle(z) \leq \pi$ being the phase of the complex variable z, $\hat{\alpha}_{ST}$ can be computed as

$$\hat{\alpha}_{ST} = \frac{1}{16} \angle \left(\sum_{m=16}^{79} s_m s_{m-16}^* \right) \tag{4.2}$$

In a second step, the long training symbols are used to obtain a more accurate estimation of the frequency offset. Therefore, the 128 samples of the two long training symbols are first corrected using the coarse estimate $\hat{\alpha}_{ST}$, i.e. the time samples s_m of the long training symbols are multiplied by $e^{-jm\hat{\alpha}_{ST}}$ such that

$$s_m = s_m e^{-jm\hat{\alpha}_{ST}}, m = 0, 1, ..., 127 \tag{4.3}$$

and are then used to compute the (per sample) fine estimate $\hat{\alpha}_{LT}$, given by

$$\hat{\alpha}_{LT} = \frac{1}{64} \angle \left(\sum_{m=64}^{127} s_m s_{m-64}^* \right) \tag{4.4}$$

The total phase estimation $\hat{\alpha} = \hat{\alpha}_{ST} + \hat{\alpha}_{LT}$ is finally used to correct the carrier frequency offset present in the remaining part of the frame. Hence, all time samples after the long training symbols are multiplied by $e^{-jm\hat{\alpha}}$.

In addition to the initial frequency offset channel estimation and correction, the implemented receiver further uses the four pilot subcarriers to track channel variations over time. Therefore, the accumulated (or residual) phase rotation at the n-th OFDM symbol is estimated and corrected using the same technique as described above [SEM04]. For each OFDM symbol, the receiver further computes a channel estimate using the knowledge provided in pilot subcarriers. This estimate is frequency-dependent and has to be computed for each subcarrier. For the four pilot subcarriers with index $i \in \{-21, -7, 7, 21\}$, the estimate $\hat{h}_i$ can be derived directly by a division of the (known) reference samples and the received samples. For subcarriers in between, the pilot-based estimates are simply linearly interpolated. With this approach, variations in the channel response can be tracked over time and equalised.

4.3.2 Network aspects

The combination of physical layer and network layer simulation is not complete by the sole adoption of complex time samples in a network simulator. Indeed, apart from the signal processing details, the characteristics of a network with respect to

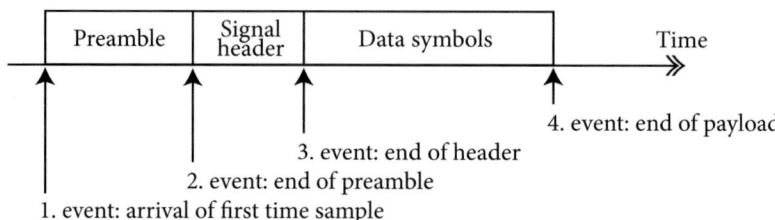

Figure 4.3: Subdivision of the continuous frame decoding process of a real transceiver into three logical stages in order to model the receiver as a discrete event-based process.

time and space have to be reflected and integrated into the signal processing logic as well since network nodes may impact each others transmission behavior. As a consequence, and in contrast to the frame construction process of IEEE 802.11p which can be considered time-discrete and independent from other events that occur in the network, the reception process can not be considered to be atomic and time-discrete: while a transmitting node will stay in transmission state until the last OFDM symbol has been transmitted, a receiving node will change its physical layer state several times until the whole packet is successfully received.

The set of events that reflect this sequence of state changes is illustrated in Figure 4.3: first, the arrival of the first time sample of a packet at the receiving node is reflected by a *StartReceive* event. The term "receiving" might be misleading here, since the node is not decoding the samples at this point in time. The time samples rather arrive at the antenna of this node and contribute to the cumulative signal strength of multiple arriving packets. At this point in time, the received time samples will be added to the interference manager and a decision is made whether the packet will be considered for reception or not. For instance, if the node is in transmission state itself, if the signal strength of this packet is below thermal noise, or if other reasons prohibit the start of the reception process, no further action is taken. Otherwise, the reception process is started and an *EndPreamble* event for this packet is scheduled. Upon expiration of the end preamble event, it is checked whether the preamble can be detected successfully using the methods described in Section 4.3.1. In case of a successful signal detection, time synchronization and channel estimation is performed, followed by the scheduling of an *EndHeader* event that marks the point in time at which the last sample of the signal header arrives at the receiving node. When the end header event is executed, the receiver decodes the bits that constitute the signal header, checks the parity bit and performs a plausibility check on the obtained data rate and packet length information. If all checks are successful, an *EndRx* event is scheduled at which all remaining data symbols are decoded and a final decision on the success of the reception process is drawn. Please note that each event takes the cumulative signal of all overlapping transmissions and a white gaussian noise component as input to the signal processing mechanisms. Also, signal processing is only performed at these events and not during the (time) periods in between.

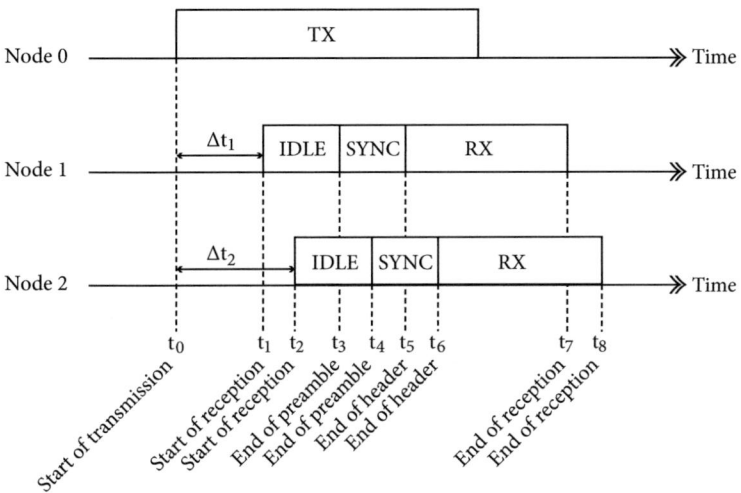

Figure 4.4: Examplary timeline of simulation events if one node is transmitting a packet, and two nodes are receiving it.

As described above, four different events span the successful reception process of a transceiver. To clarify the different states that will be adopted in the periods in between, a scenario with multiple nodes is used in the following. Figure 4.4 depicts the timeline of this scenario in which one node is transmitting a packet at time t_0, and in which two other nodes start a corresponding reception process at times t_1 and t_2. The starting times differ due to different distances to the transmitting node and the resulting propagation delays (compare $\triangle t_1$ and $\triangle t_2$). As annotated in this figure, the transmitter executes the frame construction process at t_0, computes all time samples that will represent the frame in complex time domain, switches to *TX* state and stays in this state for the full transmit duration. The two receiving nodes stay in *IDLE* state until the end of the preamble. Only then, the transceivers may establish a "receiving context" and switch to *SYNC* – cf. t_3 and t_4. Upon expiration of the end header event and a successful decoding of the signal header, the transceivers switch to *RX* state and stay in this state until the end of their individually calculated frame duration.

What is not shown explicitly in Figure 4.4 are the physical layer states during the periods in which neither a frame is "in the air" nor present as a candidate for reception. In the first case, the physical layer will be idle and ready for new receptions and transmission requests. In the latter case, i.e. frames are in the air but not considered for reception due to insufficient signal strength, the physical layer will also be ready for reception, but may block own transmission requests from upper layers if the cumulative signal strength at the antenna exceeds the carrier sense threshold of CSMA. Such a situation is reflected by the *CCA Busy* state, which implements the CCA.indicate primitive of the IEEE 802.11 standard specification – cf. clauses 17.3.6 and 17.3.10.5 of [IEE07]. The actual carrier sensing is performed on a per OFDM-

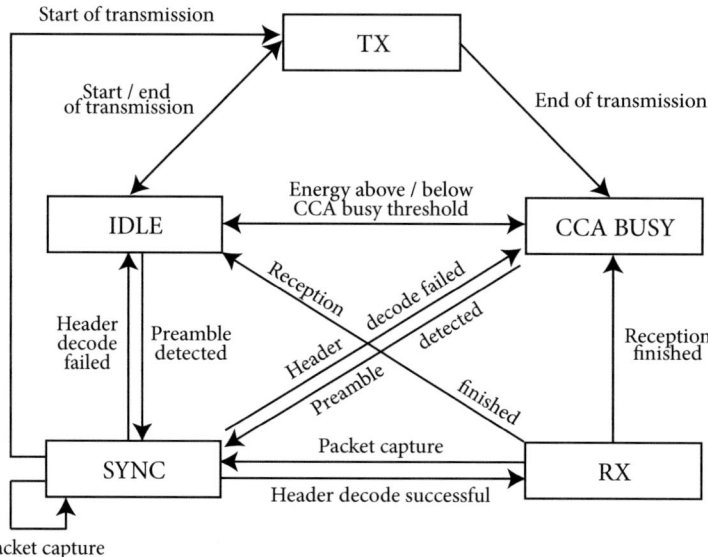

Figure 4.5: The physical layer state machine with its five different states and the allowed state transitions.

symbol basis, i.e. the signal strength is calculated over periods of 80 time samples. Please note that the receiver will also block higher layers, i.e. MAC, and indicate a busy medium if the state is changed to RX.

The total set of possible physical layer states contains five distinct states: transmit, idle, CCA busy, synchronized, and receiving, cf. Figure 4.5 for an illustration of the implemented state machine. As described previously, in the simple and optimistic case with a sufficiently strong incoming signal the state will switch from idle/CCA busy to synchronized, from synchronized to receiving, and from receiving back to idle/CCA busy. Under worse conditions, e.g. due to interference, the state transition sequence may differ: if the preamble can not be detected successfully, the physical layer will stay in idle/CCA busy state, and if header decoding fails, the state changes back to idle/CCA busy without going to receiving state. The sequence gets even less straight forward if packet capture on physical layer is enabled. With packet capture, the physical layer may start a reception process even if it is already synchronized to a signal and decoding either the signal header or the data symbols. Hence, transitions from synchronized to synchronized, and from receiving to synchronized are allowed and possible. As demonstrated by Lee et. al [LKL+07], such a re-synchronization is performed by off-the-shelf transceivers if the SINR of the new incoming signal satisfies an artificially chosen capture threshold.

More details on the implementation of the physical layer state machine — in particular of the corresponding event handlers for *StartReceive*, *EndPreamble*, *End-Header*, and *EndRx* — can be found in Annex A.

4.3.3 Radio propagation

Apart from the implementation of a more accurate physical layer and its integration into NS-3, several channel models that operate and exploit the improved granularity are part of the combined physical layer and network simulation approach.

As illustrated in Figure 4.1 and described in Section 4.3, the channel itself is only a multiplexer between all nodes that listen and transmit to the channel. In principle, the channel multiplexer employs a propagation delay and one (or multiple) propagation loss models which determine the channel transfer function based on the location and the relative velocities of the nodes. In the context of this thesis, two different types of channel multiplexers have been implemented: a channel multiplexer that uses only stochastic propagation loss models, and one that employs a geometry-based stochastic channel model.

The channel multiplexer that uses only stochastic channel models is the traditional approach used by most of todays network simulators. Each "link" between two nodes experiences the same stochastic channel properties, in the sense that a fixed path loss model, a fixed large-scale fading model, and a fixed small-scale fading model is applied. The parametrisation of these models can therefore be considered as uniform among all transmitter-receiver combinations. In addition to the common pathloss (e.g. Friis, Two-Ray Ground, LogDistance), large-scale fading (e.g. Log-Normal shadowing), and small-scale fading models (e.g. Nakagami-m, Rician, Rayleigh), the six vehicular channel models developed by Acosta-Marum et. al [AI07] have been implemented in order to simulate the time- and frequency-selective nature of vehicular environments. These channel models adopt the tapped-delay line model where each tap is characterized by a Rician or Rayleigh fading process and a Doppler power spectral density. Due to the sample-level granularity of the simulator, the implementation of the channel models in [AI07] is complete without further abstractions or approximations.

The usage of purely stochastic channel models for large- and small-scale fading has some obvious drawbacks, as outlined already in Section 3.2.4: such models do not reflect the geometry of the scenario and are only stochastically correct. For instance, they only capture the long-term average or the worst-case characteristics of the channel. Further, since they do not consider the geometry, a spatial correlation of the propagation conditions is not modeled at all, hence nodes located in similar locations may experience significantly different channel impulse responses, even if only marginal differences should be observed. In general, a wide-sense stationary uncorrelated scattering (WSSUS) assumption is made by such models, which is not valid for vehicular environments and a 5.9 GHz carrier frequency.

To solve the above issue, the second type of channel multiplexing employs the principle of geometry-based stochastic channel modeling and implements the model presented by Karedal et. al in [KTC+09]. Their model considers signal contributions that result from reflections at different kind of scatterers: mobile scatterers such as other vehicles driving on the street, static scatterers such as buildings or sign posts, and diffuse scatterers to reflect smaller objects along the road.

4.3.4 Discussion

The proposed implementation of a combined physical layer and network simulator is based on several assumptions. Indeed, from the perspective of a radio expert, the current implementation still involves several levels of abstraction. For instance, inaccuracies due to imperfect radio frontends are neglected, i.e. errors that are introduced during the quantization process of analog-to-digital conversion, imperfections in automatic gain control, and receiver nonlinearities are not considered. Furthermore, the presented implementation assumes a single omnidirectional antenna present in every transceiver. Nevertheless, such aspects can easily be introduced in the proposed physical layer and network simulator if needed.

Apart from the above aspects, it is important to discuss the parametrisation of the used signal processing algorithms. The autocorrelation threshold of the signal detector is only one but important parameter that can be optimized. While a low threshold leads to an increased preamble detection rate, it also leads to reception attempts that fail in the end due to insufficient SNR levels. Such attempts should be avoided, since they lead to unnecessary reception states and unneeded blocking periods at higher layers – which might have a negative impact on medium access control and network performance since inadequate feedback is provided. On the other hand, a threshold that is set too high leads to declined packets that could have been decoded without errors successfully. It is therefore important to find the optimal correlation threshold that achieves close to zero false positives but which does not miss too many potential packets. According to the results of a dedicated evaluation, a correlation threshold of 0.85 provides the best results with regard to this objective. An illustration of these findings is available in Section B.

4.4 Validation

The implemented physical layer and its signal processing algorithms have been validated against real hardware using off-the-shelf transceivers from Atheros, in particular transceivers based on the Atheros AR5112 chipset, and the wireless channel emulator testbed developed by Judd et. al at the Carnegie Mellon University (CMU) in Pittsburgh, USA [JS04]. The testbed allows to conduct controllable and repeatable experiments using wireless technologies. By means of an emulation of the wireless channel effects, i.e. path loss and frequency-flat fading such as Rayleigh or Rician, network and higher layer protocols can easily be tested or optimized without the need to care about external influencing factors that would usually alter the channel conditions and complicate a fair comparison of different protocol configurations. It further allows to miniaturise the propagation channel, emulates distances between nodes up to several hundred meters, and let nodes move at relatively high speeds, even though the nodes are located next to each other and not moving at all.

An overview of the wireless emulator testbed is given in Figure 4.6: a field programmable gate array (FPGA) based digital signal processing unit constitutes the core of the testbed and multiplexes the signals of all connected devices (e.g. laptops).

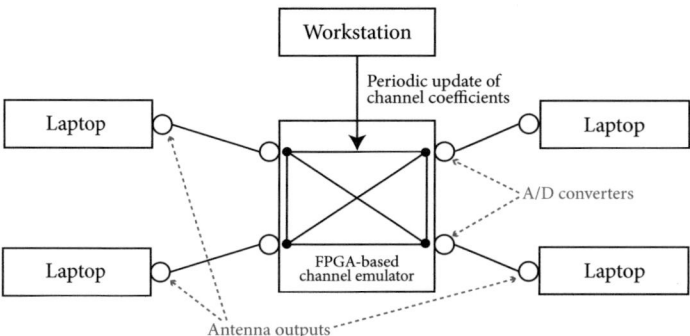

Figure 4.6: Architecture of the wireless emulator testbed at the Carnegie Mellon University.

Each device is connected to the FPGA through an antenna cable and an analog-to-digital conversion unit that transforms the analog signal transmitted by the device. The digitally sampled signal is then altered according to the channel configuration that is stored inside of the channel emulator, afterwards transformed back to the analog domain and provided as input to all other connected devices. The channel configuration itself is simply a table of channel coefficients, whereas each entry is applied to a single transmitter-receiver combination. Thus, it is possible to reflect different path loss conditions between the connected devices. By means of an external controller that is running on a workstation, the channel configuration can be adjusted in order to reflect either only the power law of distance-dependent path loss or to include also the characteristics of a Rician fading channel. To be able to compute the Rayleigh channel coefficients in real-time, the network emulator testbed implements the algorithm presented in [PNS00] and uses its output to update the fading table in the FPGA. The fading intensity (or speed) then determines the update rate that is used by the controller. Further, to protect the testbed from interference generated by other device operating at the same carrier frequency, the whole setup is operated inside an isolation chamber with shielded walls.

For the validation of the physical layer implementation, analog-to-digital and digital-to-analog radio frontends for the 2.4 GHz frequency band have been used. As a consequence, the transceivers in the simulator and the laptops were configured to use the OFDM-based transmission modes of the IEEE 802.11g standard specification with a channel bandwidth of 20 MHz. Although the simulator will later be used for vehicular scenarios with transceivers operating at 5.9 GHz, this will not be an issue, since the validated signal processing algorithms are independent of the actual carrier frequency.

With respect to the conducted experiments, a setup with one transmitting and one receiving device was used and repeated 10 times, on the simulator as well as on the testbed. During each repetition, 1200 packets were transmitted in total, but only the last 1000 packets were used to obtain the average frame reception ratio and the

Parameter	Value
Frame size	100, 500, 1000 bytes
Transmission rate	10 Hz
Transmission power	20 dBm
Data rate	6, 12, 24, 48 Mbps
Carrier frequency	2.4 GHz
Channel spacing	20 MHz
Non-fading conditions	Static pathloss, 90-130 dB
Freq.-flat Rayleigh-fading	Jake's Doppler spectrum
Relative vehicle speeds	10 m/sec

Table 4.1: Configuration parameters used for validation experiments.

corresponding 95 % confidence intervals w.r.t the configured SNR. The remaining relevant configuration parameters are listed in Table 4.1. Note that several packet sizes were used during validation and all of them yielded a successful result. Yet, only the results for a 500 byte configuration will be shown in the following.

Figure 4.7 shows the frame reception ratio with respect to SNR for different data rates. As can be seen, the reception curves show not only similar slopes, but also start to rise at very similar SNR values which, at lower data rates, are at most 1 dB apart. Only at the highest data rate did the simulator results diverge significantly from the testbed, which, based on a discussion with the team at CMU, can be attributed to the presence of too much phase noise in the analog to digital converter.

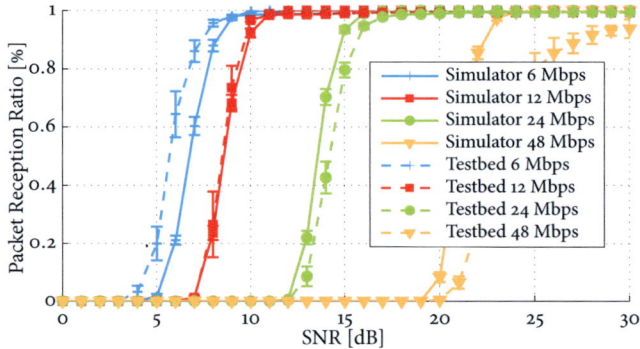

Figure 4.7: Frame reception ratio with respect to SNR for different data rates and a path loss only channel configuration: at lower data rates the difference between the implemented physical layer simulator and the testbed is at most 1 dB; at high data rates, the simulator yields significantly better reception results.

To compound the results of the previous comparison, the experiments and simulations of that scenario were repeated with a Rayleigh-fading effect added to the pathloss configuration. The frame reception ratios of the conducted simulations and testbed experiments with a Rayleigh fading channel are illustrated in Figure 4.8. The

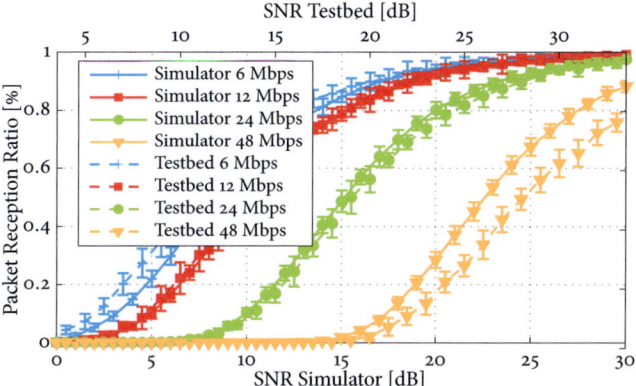

Figure 4.8: Frame reception ratio with respect to SNR for different data rates and a path loss plus Rayleigh fading channel configuration. Please note the two different x-axes that were used to align the curves obtained in both systems.

slopes of the observed reception curves are again very similar, but this time, the offset varies between 3-5 dB throughout all data rates and the performance of the Atheros AR5112 chipset is significantly worse than the one observed in the simulator (note the use of two different x-axes in this figure to ease a comparison of the corresponding curves). This discrepancy can be attributed to the channel estimation algorithms being used in the AR5112 chipset, which are probably different to the ones used in the simulator. More contemporary chipsets are further expected to provide better results. It should also be noted that the intention is not to reflect the performance of a particular chipset, but to ensure that the simulator provides a similar performance in comparison to real transceivers. Hence, based on the obtained results, the current implementation is assumed to reflect the performance of real transceivers sufficiently well.

4.5 Evaluation

To illustrate the benefits of an increased accuracy in the physical layer model, the following section provides a comparison between the frame reception ratios that are achieved with traditional packet-level simulation models and the signal-level physical layer model presented in Section 4.3. Further, a brief demonstration of the frame capture capabilities is presented. In contrast to the scenario setup that was used in the previous section, the conducted simulations in this section are based on an IEEE 802.11p configuration with a carrier frequency of 5.9 GHz, a 10 MHz channel bandwith and a background noise setting of -99 dBm. Again, following the same argumentation as before, only results for the 500 byte packet configuration are shown. To ease referencing of the two simulation models in the following, the term *PhySimWifiPhy* is used to refer to the model offering an increased accuracy, and

61

YansWifiPhy to refer to the traditional packet-level simulation model that is already available in NS-3.

In Figure 4.9 the observed frame reception ratios of both implementations is plotted w.r.t. the SNR that can be derived after the pathloss effect has been applied. Note that the YansWifiPhy model results are plotted against an x-axis with an offset of 5 dB compared to that of the PhySimWifiPhy results so as to highlight the similarities in the shape of the curves. It is clear though that the existing BER-based physical layer model in NS-3 generates more optimistic results compared to the new implementation, which, however, does not imply that one modeling approach is better than the other. Note that the slopes of the curves in this case show very similar characteristics — in fact they could coincide substantially if a linear offset was introduced for each data rate.

When simulating the scenario with a Rayleigh-fading channel, a similar conclusion can be drawn – at least initially. As illustrated in Figure 4.9(b), the observed frame reception curves for the data rates of 6, 12 and 24 Mbps follow very similar slopes as well and are separated by a linear offset of 4-5 dB. However, if a data rate

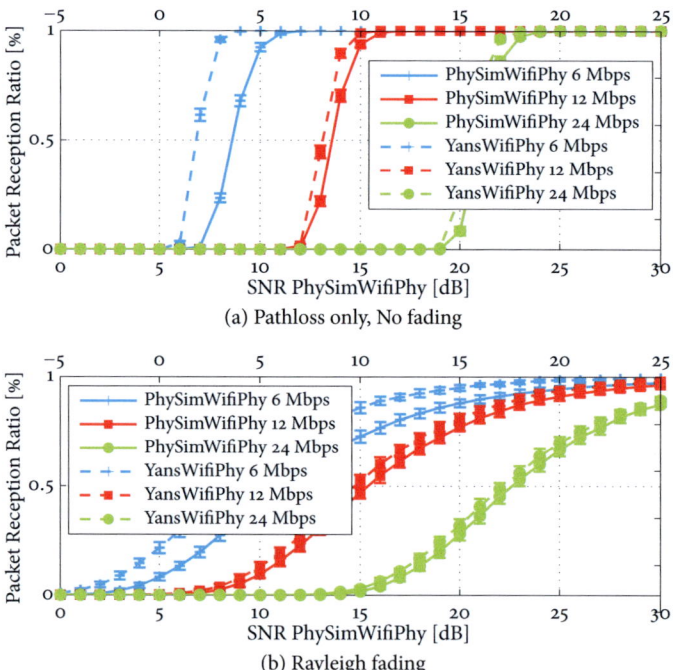

(a) Pathloss only, No fading

(b) Rayleigh fading

Figure 4.9: Comparison of the frame reception ratios using either the new and more accurate physical layer implementation (PhySimWifiPhy) or the traditional packet-level simulation approach (YansWifiPhy), and a path loss only channel (top) or Rayleigh fading channel (bottom) configuration. Please note the two different x-axes that were used to align the curves obtained with both simulators.

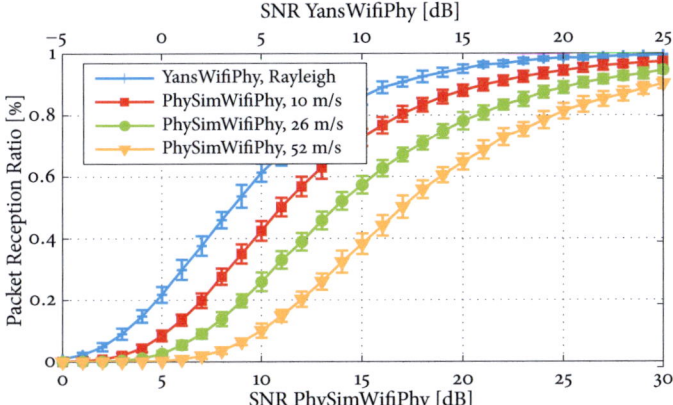

Figure 4.10: Comparison of the frame reception ratios using the new physical layer under a Rayleigh fading channel configuration with different speeds, and using the packet-level simulation with a block-fading Rayleigh channel. Please note again the two different x-axes that were used to align the curves obtained with both simulators.

of 6 Mbps and different fading speeds are considered — which are not modeled in a packet-level simulator — the slopes tend to divert from each other, cf. Figure 4.10. As a summary of the observations, it can be stated that packet-level simulators show inaccuracies when a Rayleigh-fading channel is modeled and cannot account for different relative speeds between a transmitter and a receiver. If only a path loss has to be reflected, a packet-level simulator is well suited to capture the performance appropriately — apart from the linear offsets which can easily be "corrected".

As previous measurement campaigns have shown [AI07, MTKM09] and as emphasised in Section 3.2, the vehicle-to-vehicle (V2V) channel is different from a frequency-flat Rayleigh fading channel. In particular, V2V channels have shown to be time- and frequency-selective, i.e. they exhibit fading over time and w.r.t. frequency. As a result, the frequency-responses of neighboring OFDM subcarriers are not necessarily strongly correlated and the four pilot subcarriers may not be sufficient to estimate the channel for all subcarriers correctly, cf. Section 3.2. To evaluate the significance of the frequency-selectivity on the reception performance, the six empirical models by Acosta-Marum et al. [AI07], which are based on vehicle-to-vehicle and roadside-to-vehicle measurements in expressway, urban canyoning and suburban environments, were used. In addition, the geometry-based stochastic channel model of Karedal et al. [KTC+09] is used to evaluate whether the large amount of diffuse scatterers located at the side of the road affects the physical layer layer performance.

Figure 4.11 starts with the illustration of the observed frame reception ratios with respect to the SNR when simulating the expressway oncoming and the urban canyon oncoming channel models by Acosta-Marum et al. Similar to the setup in which a Rayleigh fading channel was simulated, the implemented receiver is not able to estimate the V2V expressway oncoming channel sufficiently well, even at very high

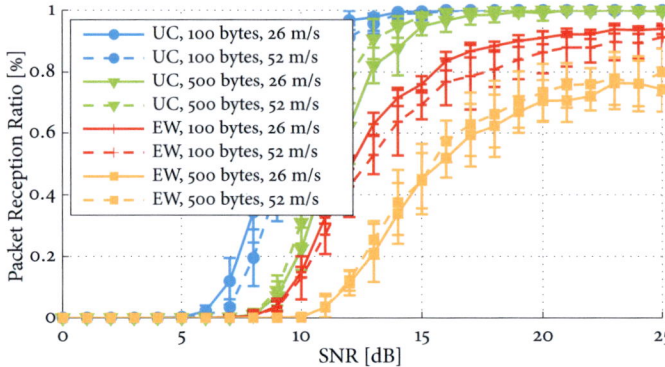

Figure 4.11: Illustration of the frame reception performance in vehicular environments, e.g. expressway (EW) oncoming and urban canyoning (UC) oncoming, with respect to different relative speeds, packet sizes and SNR.

SNRs. This is either a result of the significant Doppler effects or the lack of a sufficiently strong line of sight component in the randomly generated channel impulse response. On the contrary, the reception probabilities in the urban canyoning environment are significantly higher and even better than in the Rayleigh case. Indeed, the gradient of each curve is considerably steeper and very close to the curves obtained with a path loss only channel configuration.

If the geometry-based stochastic channel model by Karedal et al. is used to simulate the channel impulse response between two vehicles, frame reception ratios as the ones shown in Figure 4.12 are obtained. Since each path in this model experiences its own random path loss value, the ratios are plotted with respect to the distance between sender and receiver. In addition, the number of vehicles and the number of diffuse scatterers that are located at the side of the road is varied. However, as can be seen in this figure, it does not matter at all whether one or 1000 diffuse scatterers are simulated. Similarly, the impact of surrounding vehicles is also not significant. The shown results therefore confirm the considerations that were already expressed in Section 3.2.4: only because there are multiple paths that arrive with a significantly larger delay than the line of sight path, such paths do not necessarily harm a successful reception of the transmitted signal. The power at which those paths arrive at the receiver is important as well, and according to the parametrization of the model by Karedal et al., the difference between the line of sight and the remaining paths is most of the time greater than 20 dB. In the remainder of this thesis, a simulation of time- and frequency-selective channels is therefore omitted, since the resulting physical layer performance is not worse than the performance achieved in a frequency-flat Rayleigh fading channel.

In addition to the single sender, single receiver scenario used so far, a scenario with two transmitting and one receiving node is considered to demonstrate the frame capture capability implemented in the receiver. As illustrated in Figure 4.13(a), one of

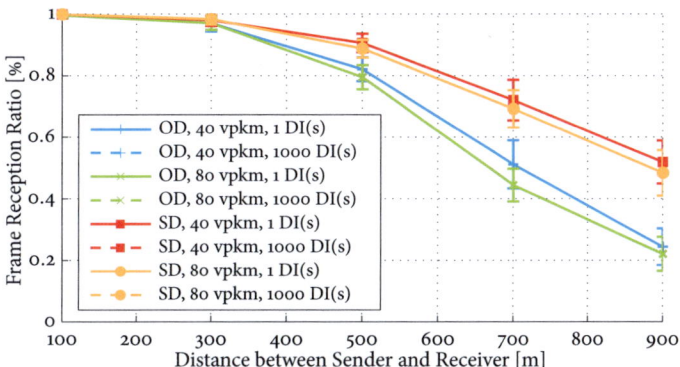

Figure 4.12: Observed frame reception ratios w.r.t. distance between sender and receiver when simulating the geometry-based stochastic channel model in scenarios with either 40 vehicles/km or 80 vehicles/km, either 1 or 1000 diffuse scatterers (DI) per highway kilometer, and two vehicles that are either driving in the same direction (SD) or oncoming direction (OD). The configured packet size accounts to 400 bytes.

the two transmitting nodes acts as the reference node from which the receiving node aims to decode as many packets as possible, and the second transmitter takes the role of an interferer. Both nodes start a packet transmission almost simultaneously, being separated in time only by a very small $\triangle t$ that is shorter than the packet transmission period, c.f. Figure 4.13(b). Together with an equal propagation delay between all nodes, this setup yields an overlap of the packets at the receiver, either completely if $\triangle t = 0$ or only partially if $\triangle t \neq 0$. The relationship w.r.t. the points in time at which the two nodes start their transmissions is depicted in Figure 4.13: if $\triangle t > 0$, the reference node starts its own transmission prior to the one from the interfering node, and if $\triangle < 0$, the reference node starts to transmit after the interfering node.

In order to simulate different conditions for the frame capture mechanism, the path loss between the reference and the receiving node is varied such that SNR values of 10 dB, 15 dB, and 20 dB are achieved. Similarly, the path loss between the interfering and the receiving node is varied, such that signal-to-interference ratios (SIR) in the range of 0 dB to 10 dB are achieved. While the first variation ensures that the packets sent by the reference node arrive with different power levels at the receiving node, the second variation leads to different levels of interference by the interfering node. For instance, a SIR of 0 dB creates a situation in which interfering packets arrive with the same power level as reference packets. A SIR of 10 dB setting however creates a situation in which interfering packets are 10 dB weaker than reference packets.

Note that it is not the objective to actually evaluate capture capability effects in the following, since such an evaluation has already been carried out by Lee et al. in [LKL+07] in an experimental using commodity IEEE 802.11a communication chipsets. Instead, the following results are included in this section to demonstrate the compliance of the present implementation with what has been observed empirically.

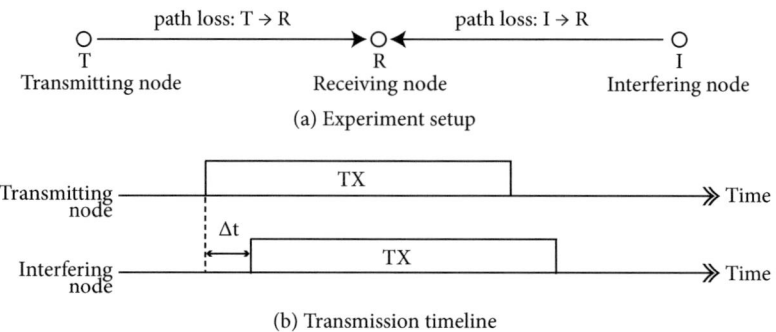

(a) Experiment setup

(b) Transmission timeline

Figure 4.13: Experiment setup used to demonstrate frame capture capabilities: (a) two nodes T and I transmit frames to a receiving node R, whereas different path loss values are applied between T to R and I to R; (b) the time difference between the transmissions of T and I is controlled by a small $\triangle t$ such that both frames overlap either completely or only partially at the receiving node R.

Figure 4.14 illustrates the frame reception ratios achieved by the receiving node when considering only the packets transmitted by the reference node, different SNR and SIR levels, values of $\triangle t$ in the range of $-160\mu s$ to $160\mu s$, and either capture being enabled or disabled. The packet size was set to 100 bytes, and the data rate to 6 Mbps in a 20 MHz channel, hence the duration of a single frame accounts to $160\mu s$ and is equal to the maximum absolute value of $\triangle t$. As can be seen in all subfigures, a successful packet reception is possible if the reference node starts to transmit prior to the interfering node ($\triangle t > 0$), and if the SIR of its packets is greater than 2-4 dB — independent of frame capture. If, however, the interfering node started its transmission prior to the reference node, i.e. if $\triangle < 0$, a successful reception is only possible if either frame capture is enabled, cf. Figure 4.14(c) and (d) as well as Figure 4.14(e) and (f), or if the interfering packet is not significantly stronger than the background noise level, as shown in Figure 4.14(a) and (b).

A closer look to Figure 4.14(c), (d), (e) and (f) shows that approx. 50 % of the reference packets are successfully decoded if frame capture is disabled, the SIR greater than 4 dB, and $\triangle t \in [-16 : 0)$. How can this happen? The explanation is simple: if the first time sample of the reference packet arrives at the receiver during the preamble period of the interfering packet, it can prevent a successful preamble detection of the interfering packet. As the physical layer will then still be idle at the end of the preamble that belongs to the reference packet, the receiver can successfully synchronize to it and achieve a successful reception.

Another interesting aspect that can be discovered in all subfigures of Figure 4.14 is the vulnerability of the reception process during the preamble period, i.e. if $\triangle t \in (-16 : 16)$. In particular when the preamble portion of the interfering packet overlaps with the preamble portion of the reference packet, the exact timing between both packets is highly significant. The reason is again quite simple: since the preamble portion of the interfering packet is identical to the preamble portion of the ref-

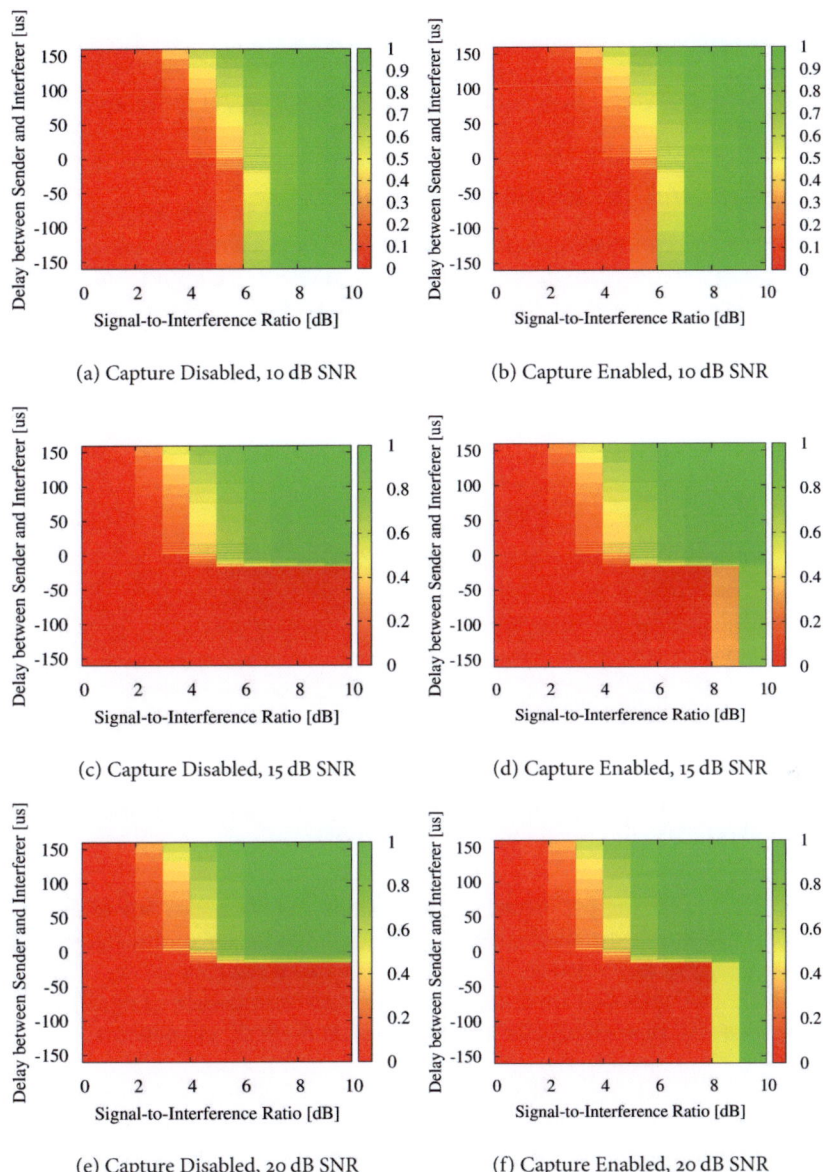

(a) Capture Disabled, 10 dB SNR

(b) Capture Enabled, 10 dB SNR

(c) Capture Disabled, 15 dB SNR

(d) Capture Enabled, 15 dB SNR

(e) Capture Disabled, 20 dB SNR

(f) Capture Enabled, 20 dB SNR

Figure 4.14: Demonstration of frame reception ratios (color coded) with and without frame capture enabled and with respect to the SNR of the frame sent by the reference node, the signal-to-interference ratio of the packet sent by this reference node, as well as the time difference $\triangle t$ of the packet transmission.

erence packet, it can be much more destructive than a random gaussian distributed background noise. As a consequence, the interfering packet can easily misguide the channel estimator, and subsequently cause decoding failures at the receiver.

4.6 Runtime performance evaluation

Enabling detailed simulations with the physical layer simulator increases simulation requirements both in terms of processing time and memory consumption. This section elucidates the added requirements and offers some analysis on the simulator's runtime performance.

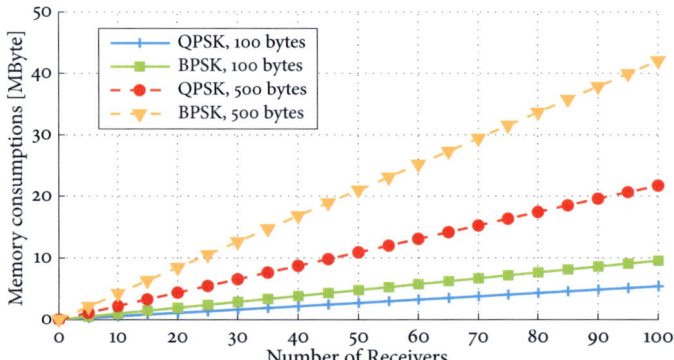

Figure 4.15: Illustration of the per packet memory consumptions with respect to the number of receivers that are present in the network.

When considering the memory requirements that are raised due to the adoption of complex time samples, a simple estimation of the per packet transmission memory footprint can be made. This memory footprint depends on the number of complex time samples that are necessary to represent the transmitted signal, and the number of nodes that are present in the network and which will potentially receive the packet. Consequently, the modulation scheme and the packet size used are the dominant factors, whereas higher order modulation schemes yield a lower memory requirement in comparison to lower order schemes. In mathematical terms, the number of time samples N that are necessary to represent an OFDM-based IEEE 802.11 compliant packet containing N_{bits} bits when using a modulation scheme that results in N_{DBPS} data bits per OFDM symbol is given by

$$N = 4 + 1 + 80 \left\lceil N_{bits}/N_{DBPS} \right\rceil \tag{4.5}$$

Under the assumption that each complex time sample is stored using two floating point values with double precision, i.e. 8 bytes per value, the memory footprint M (in bytes) per transmission is then given by

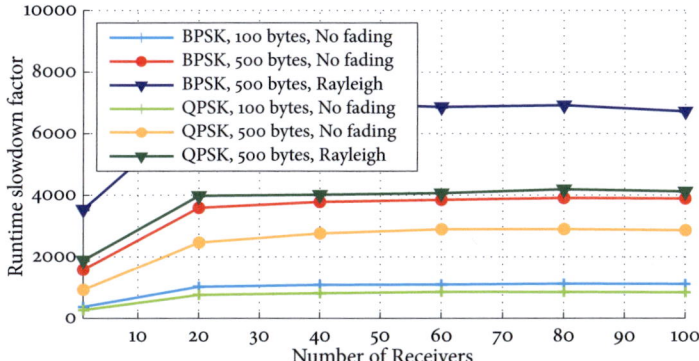

Figure 4.16: Illustration of the runtime slowdown caused by the increased accuracy. Depending on the packet size, the modulation scheme used, the complexity of the channel and the number of nodes simulated, the slowdown varies between factors of 260 and 6800.

$$M = 16\,R\,N \qquad (4.6)$$

whereas R is the number of potentially receiving nodes, and N the number of time samples according to Equation 4.5. In addition to the storage of the time samples that represent the packet bits, additional memory is needed to store the time samples that represent the Gaussian distributed background noise. Hence, the estimate given by Equation 4.6 has to be doubled. Figure 4.15 depicts the resulting per packet transmission memory footprint (including the background noise aspect) with respect to the number of potentially receiving nodes. Please keep in mind that the estimate given by Equation 4.6 accounts for a single transmission and all corresponding nodes that receive the packet with a signal strength greater than thermal noise, i.e. -104 dBm. If multiple nodes are transmitting simultaneously, the total memory footprint increases accordingly — all per packet footprints are added cumulatively, only the background noise footprint is added once. As a consequence, the overall memory footprint depends heavily on the transmission behavior of the nodes being simulated. Although configurations can be found which result in a very high memory footprint, the observed footprints of the most demanding scenarios simulated in subsequent chapters never exceeded a value of 7.5 GB.

Similar to the memory footprint, the runtime performance of the simulator is affected significantly as well. However, apart from the configured modulation scheme, the packet sizes used, and the network nodes present, the complexity of the channel has an additional impact on the overall runtime performance. For instance, a Rayleigh fading channel requires more computation efforts than a simple path loss model. Figure 4.16 illustrates the observed runtime slowdowns of the simulator in comparison to a traditional packet-level based simulation in NS-3. For the comparison, a scenario with one transmitting and one or multiple receiving nodes

69

was simulated, whereas the transmitter performed 1000 packet transmissions and the remaining nodes went through the whole reception process. To ensure that all transmissions lead to a packet reception process, the path loss was set to 20 dB for all transmitter-receiver combinations. All simulation runs were repeated ten times in order to obtain an average slowdown factor and a corresponding 95 % confidence interval. Please note that it is not necessary to simulate a scenario in which all nodes are transmitting as this is only a scalar multiplication of the runtime experienced in both, the packet-level and the signal-level simulator. Hence, it does not affect the relationship between both.

As illustrated in Figure 4.16, the usage of complex time samples leads to significant slowdown factors, which are already in the order of 200 for the scenarios with a 100 byte packet size, using a BPSK or QPSK modulation and the most simple channel modeling approach. If larger packet sizes are simulated, the slowdown increases further to approx. 4000. The usage of a Rayleigh fading channel is even more demanding and leads to slowdown factors of 7000 and more. However, its is interesting to see that the slowdown factors reach a stable level once the number of nodes is increased to 20. Afterwards, an additional increase has no significant impact anymore.

4.7   GPU-based optimization

Even without a runtime performance evaluation as the one presented in the previous section, it is obvious that the adoption of the time sample as the smallest entity in a network simulation leads to significant slowdowns. Therefore, the question arises whether this slowdown can be reduced, or even eliminated, for instance by advanced simulation and/or signal processing techniques. As previous studies have shown [KCR08, BN09], computationally expensive signal processing algorithms can benefit significantly w.r.t. runtime performance if executed on massive parallel processing units, e.g. on general purpose graphics processing units (GPGPUs). Although GPGPUs operate with clock speeds that are slower than the ones of traditional multi-core central processing units (CPUs), the usage of up to several hundreds or thousands of compute units in parallel can yield speedup factors of 75 and more. A parallel simulation of multiple independent simulation events might also increase the runtime performance even further. In the following, the runtime performance improvement that is offered by GPU-based simulation architectures is evaluated and demonstrated. Note that this evaluation has previously been presented in [AMH11].

In 2006, Perumalla et. al [Per06] presented a first study on whether GPGPUs can improve the runtime performance of discrete-event based simulators. While the special case of fixed-time increment based simulations such as agent-based simulations are well suited for parallelization using GPGPUs, the authors conclude that more generic discrete-event based simulations that do not exhibit fixed-time increments require further research.

The potential of GPGPUs with respect to an improved runtime performance of network simulations has been analysed by Xu et. al in [XB07]. The authors propose a simulation platform that uses the CPU to execute the event scheduler and simulation logic, and GPGPUs to perform computationally intensive signal processing tasks. Hence, they use a hybrid CPU/GPGPU simulation approach. But despite the indication that clear performance benefits can be achieved if the amount of input data is maximised per GPGPU work cycle, the authors conclude that typical signal processing algorithms used for packet encoding and decoding are not well suited for a GPGPU-based approach.

Usually, the maximum speedup that can be achieved by a parallel processing of simulation events is limited by the so called *lookahead* metric. The lookahead denotes the time period during which future events can be processed in parallel without the fear of violating correctness constraints. Consequently, the greater the lookahead, the bigger the potential speedup, since a synchronization among the parallel threads or processes is required less often. Similarly, the computational effort that is spent on each event has an impact on the potential speedup as well: for a fixed lookahead, a higher speedup can be achieved if a lot of computational intensive events (or tasks) have to be completed during the lookahead period — in contrast to very trivial events. In general, the ratio between control (or synchronization) overhead and actual computation efforts determines the maximum speedup. Outside the context of discrete-event based simulations, Amdahl's law [Amd67] describes a boundary that is similar to the above observation: the portion r_p of a program (or code) that can be parallelized, and the portion r_s that can not be parallelized, as well as the number of available processors p determine the maximum speedup s that can be achieved through parallelization, whereas

$$s = \frac{1}{r_s + \frac{r_p}{p}} \tag{4.7}$$

The relevant question within the context of this thesis is therefore: which events of the combined physical layer and network simulator can be parallelized, how much does each of these events contribute to the overall simulation runtime, and how efficient can a parallel version be implemented?

To answer the first two of the three questions raised above, a profiling of the simulator has been performed. For the profiling, an artificial scenario with one transmitting and N receiving nodes was considered. While this does not reflect a realistic scenario setup, it is representative w.r.t. to the scalability of the simulator and the relative efforts spent on each event.

According to the outcome of the profiling, cf. Table 4.2, between 40,4 % to 86,8 % of the computation effort is spent on the processing of EndRx events, whereas most of the work in EndRx is raised by the Viterbi decoder. If a Rayleigh fading channel is considered, a lot of effort is also spent on the computation of the channel coefficients, i.e. 40,9 % of the total runtime in case of one receiver, and 47,8 % of the total runtime in case of 100 receiving nodes. The remaining approx. 10 % - 20 % of the time is either spent on frame construction (cf. a path loss only configuration with 1 receiver), or scattered among all the other less time-consuming signal processing tasks.

Of course, the runtime profile does not state explicitly whether the signal processing algorithms executed at a single event can be parallelized, but considering that

	Path Loss			Rayleigh		
	1	50	100	1	50	100
Transmission	21.1%	0.5%	0.3%	12.7%	0.3%	0.1%
Channel	0.9%	1.1%	1.1%	40.9%	47.6%	47.8%
Reception	76.8%	98.3%	98.5%	45.8%	52.0%	52.1%
StartReceive	6.9%	8.8%	8.9%	4.1%	4.7%	4.7%
EndPreamble	1.6%	2.1%	2.1%	1.0%	1.1%	1.1%
Signal Detection	1.0%	1.4%	1.4%	0.6%	0.7%	0.7%
EndHeader	0.6%	0.7%	0.7%	0.3%	0.4%	0.4%
EndRx	67.7%	86.6%	86.8%	40.4%	45.9%	45.9%
Viterbi Decoding	54.9%	70.5%	70.8%	32.8%	37.3%	37.4%
Demodulation	6.6%	8.2%	8.2%	3.9%	4.4%	4.3%
Other	6.2%	7.9%	7.8%	3.7%	4.2%	4.2%
Other	1.2%	0.1%	0.1%	0.6%	0.1%	0.0%

Table 4.2: Contribution of the physical layer events and their individual contribution to the overall runtime. Depending on the configured channel model and the number of receiving nodes in the network, the relative proportions change significantly.

many of the frame construction and frame reception steps operate on an OFDM symbol basis, a trivial parallelization is always possible: processing multiple OFDM symbols in parallel. Another trivial parallelization approach is the parallel computation of channel effects and packet reception processes for multiple receivers. According to an internal study, the latter one will not violate correctness constraints, since the set of EndPreamble events (in analogy also the set of EndHeader and the set of EndRx events) scheduled at each receiver are separated only slightly in time. Hence this small lookahead is sufficient to allow parallel processing of all these events. Assuming that only these trivial approaches are employed, the portions of the code that contribute to 99.9 % of the total runtime can be executed in parallel, and the maximum speedup that can be obtained, as given by Equation 4.7 with $p \to \infty$, is then 10^3.

To evaluate how much of this maximum speedup can be achieved in reality, the Rayleigh implementation and the Viterbi decoding algorithm have been selected and ported to GPGPUs using the OpenCL standard for parallel programming of heterogeneous systems [ope] as well as the three different GPGPU-based simulation approaches depicted in Figure 4.17. While the first approach uses the GPGPU only as a co-proceesor to speedup the execution of single events, the remaining ones employ the principle of event aggregation to process multiple events in parallel and to reduce the overheads created by CPU/GPU context switches. In addition to that, the third approach employs memory reuse on GPGPUs to minimize overheads due to data transfers between main memory and graphics card. Since the latter two approaches employ mechanisms that are not provided by NS-3, the effectiveness of all approaches has first been evaluated in a standalone implementation that adapts the event scheduling logic of NS-3 but knows only two events: one event responsible for the computation of the Rayleigh fading coefficients, and one event for the Viterbi

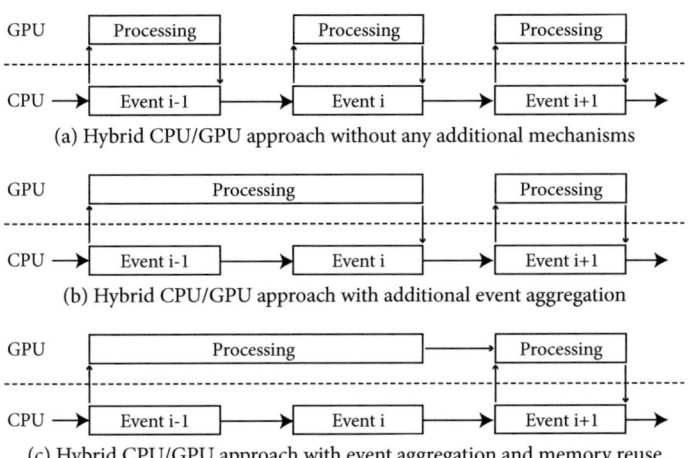

(a) Hybrid CPU/GPU approach without any additional mechanisms

(b) Hybrid CPU/GPU approach with additional event aggregation

(c) Hybrid CPU/GPU approach with event aggregation and memory reuse

Figure 4.17: Three different GPGPU-based simulation approaches to speedup the total simulation runtime.

decoding. Based on this implementation, a synthetic benchmark that reflects the simulation of an event sequence comparable to the transmission of a frame to multiple receivers has been set up. Hence, for N receivers, N Rayleigh events and N Viterbi decoding events are simulated, whereas the output of the Rayleigh events serve as input to the Viterbi decoding event. The input data given to the first event comprised 7120 time samples, which corresponds to 500 bytes of payload per frame at a data rate of 6 Mbps in a 20 MHz channel configuration. The average speedup factors in comparison to a sequential event execution on CPU — which were obtained during 10 simulation runs on a workstation featuring an AMD Phenom II X6 1035T CPU with 8 GB of main memory and an ATI Radeon HD 5870 graphics card with 1600 cores — are shown in Figure 4.18.

When using GPGPUs to speedup only the processing of single events, a maximum speedup factor of 1.5 is achieved. This demonstrates the impact of overheads created by a frequent crossing of the CPU to/from GPU boundary. Additional event aggregation results in a maximum speedup factor of 30.9 for 100 receivers, and if memory reuse is additionally used, the overall speedup factor increases up to a value of 69.6 for 100 receivers. Please note that the speedup will not increase infinitely with the number of receivers processed in parallel, since the number of parallel compute units on the GPU is limited. Despite 1600 cores available on the GPU, the limit of receivers to process in parallel will not be 1600, but significantly less, since multiple cores are used per receiver in order to speedup the processing of each single receiver as well.

Motivated by the results above, the two GPGPU-based signal processing implementations were integrated into NS-3, applying hybrid CPU/GPU simulation with and without event aggregation. The last optimization level that employs memory-

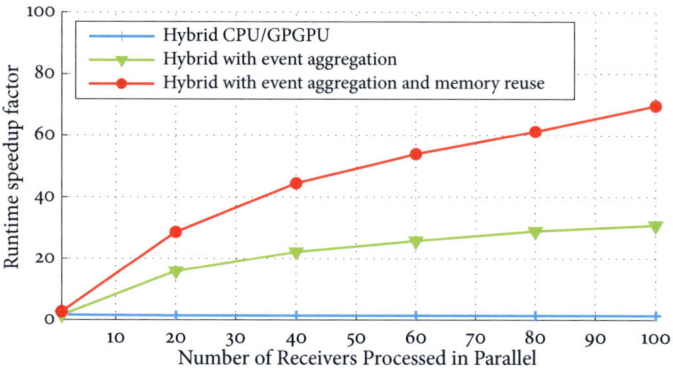

Figure 4.18: Comparison of the speedup factors achieved with the three different GPGPU-based simulation appraches in comparison to a sequential execution on CPU.

reuse was not implemented since a transparent swapping between the host's main memory and the memory on graphics hardware is not supported by the ATI Stream SDK yet and the development of an own memory manager from scratch was out of the context of this thesis. Nevertheless, an average speedup factor of 1.5 for the reference scenario with 100 receivers and Rayleigh fading was achieved when no event aggregation was used. With event aggregation the speedup factor increases further to 4.3. In comparison to the maximum theoretical speedup factor of 6.75 (both signal processing algorithms comprise 85.2 % of the processing time), the obtained speedup reflects already more than 60 % of the maximum. It is expected that even more of the theoretical maximum can be exploited if memory reuse is implemented as well.

Of course, compared to the significant slowdowns reported in Section 4.6 and plotted in Figure 4.16, a speedup factor of 4.3 is only marginal. In order to achieve significant speedups, the work done so far has to be "scaled up" to the remaining signal processing steps such that as many signal processing steps as possible are executed in parallel. Hence, all remaining steps, even those that contribute only marginally to the overall runtime, have to be ported. Considering that the trivial approach is used again in which the reception processes of multiple receivers are executed in parallel, such a "scale up" is assumed to be feasible and the maximum theoretical speedup factor of 10^3 can at least partially be exploited. Assuming that only 60 % of this maximum can be exploited, as before, the slowdown factor of currently 7000 can be reduced substantially down to a value close to 100. With an additional implementation of memory reuse, or an execution of all simulation events on upcoming graphics card that support thread synchronization, the price to pay for an increased accuracy will diminish even more.

To summarize, the above results show that a GPGPU-based optimization of the new simulator using state of the art hardware is feasible, in the sense that the significant slowdowns of a sequential execution can be reduced effectively.

4.8 Conclusions

This chapter identified a gap between the different perspectives taken by experts of the wireless channel, physical layer, and networking domain. Due to the existence of this gap, the corresponding research communities rather co-existed instead of being "in touch" with each other. This observation is emphasized by the fact that no holistic evaluation framework existed that allowed to evaluate the impact of advances or new findings in one field on the conclusions drawn in the other two fields. The strict separation of the different perspectives lead to a usage of inaccurate modeling approaches in the simulators that are typically used by engineers of the networking community, and prevented the solid study of emerging concepts such as cognitive radios, interference cancellation, network coding on physical layer, or multi-antenna systems.

Motivated by the idea to overcome the limitations of state of the art network simulators, a new simulation framework was developed and presented. The proposed simulator integrates the different perspectives within one toolset and adapts the complex time sample as the smallest unit to be simulated. The implemented physical layer was then successfully validated against commercial transceivers operated within a controlled radio propagation environment. Furthermore, the link-layer performance of the implemented IEEE 802.11p based receiver was evaluated within different radio propagation channels and compared to the results obtained using a traditional packet-level simulator. According to the obtained results, significant differences in the frame reception ratios were observed. However, most of these differences can be eliminated through a linear adjustment of the curves, hence, the differences are not fundamental. In a next step, the impact of a time- and frequency-selective channel was analyzed, with the result that the resulting frame reception curves differ from the ones obtained when using a traditional packet-level simulators. But again, the differences were not fundamental and not necessarily worse than the results obtained in a packet-level simulator that is configured to simulate a Rayleigh fading channel. Due to this reason, a consideration of all implemented fast-fading channel models is omitted in the following chapters of this thesis. Instead, a Rayleigh fading based on the Jake's Doppler spectrum is selected as a worst-case scenario in which a distributed coordination mechanisms will be challenged the most.

Since the computational effort to simulate the communication system down to the level of each single time sample is immense, the benefit of GPU-based simulation (or software) architectures was discussed and evaluated in this chapter. According to the obtained results, a large fraction of the introduced runtime slowdowns can be reversed through a GPU-based signal processing if intelligent optimization techniques such as event (or job) aggregation and memory reuse are applied. The development of the proposed simulator therefore represents a prime example of the relatively new discipline called Computational Science and Engineering (CSE), which focuses on the systematic study, creation, application and optimization of computer-based simulation models to understand and analyze complex natural or engineered systems.

5

Characterization of packet collisions in V2V communication networks

Based on the combined physical layer and networking simulator described in Chapter 4, the following sections present an analysis and evaluation of medium access control (MAC) in inter-vehicle communication networks. As the first generation of such networks will be based on the IEEE 802.11p standard specification, the considered coordination mechanism is carrier sense multiple access (CSMA). Hence, the evaluation aims to assess whether CSMA is able to coordinate channel access among neighboring nodes effectively in case of severe fast fading channel conditions — and if not, to answer why this is the case. Recall that an effective coordination is essential in order to avoid simultaneous packet transmissions by multiple nodes and resulting packet collisions at a receiver. As there will not be one true answer to this question — just consider the wide range of scenario and channel conditions — the effectiveness of the coordination is characterized with respect to major influencing factors. Further, the implication of a reduced coordination in the network is described with respect to its significance, and the timing-specific relationship between transmitting and interfering nodes. Such a sensitivity analysis and characterization allows to determine feasibility regions within which performance (or reliability) requirements can be fulfilled by CSMA, and shows how to address situations in which the requirements are not met. However, it is not the objective to actually define such performance or reliability requirements, but to illustrate the fundamental capabilities and limitations of CSMA on the one hand, and to establish an in-depth understanding of a CSMA-based distributed coordination on the other hand. The collected knowledge will later be used in Chapter 6 and Chapter 7 for a discussion of methods which aim to either avoid or overcome the observed weaknesses.

The rest of this chapter is structured as follows: first, existing and relevant work with respect to a performance evaluation of CSMA in inter-vehicle communication scenarios is discussed in Section 5.1 and compared to the characterization that will be presented later on. Section 5.2 then provides a detailed explanation of the applied evaluation methodology by covering aspects such as the general scenario setup, parameter configurations, and the definition of all applied performance metrics. Afterwards, Section 5.3 presents and discusses the obtained simulation results, followed by a summary and conclusion in Section 5.4.

5.1   Related work

The performance of carrier sense based medium access control in broadcast radio channels as well as the hidden terminal problem itself have extensively been studied in the past, either analytically or empirically by means of simulations. Although none of these studies is based on a modeling approach as accurate as the one motivated and presented in Chapter 4, they include several performance metrics which are relevant and applicable for the characterization presented in this chapter. Since it would fill several pages to describe all studies in detail, only the most significant milestones and most relevant studies are covered.

Back in 1975 Tobagi et al. were the first to analyze the hidden terminal problem in CSMA. They concluded that the negative impact of hidden terminals degrades the performance of CSMA significantly due to the resulting packet collisions [TK75]. However, their work was based on assumptions that are either not valid anymore due to technical advances or not applicable to inter-vehicle communication networks. For instance, two packets were considered to be non-decodable if they overlapped in time and the channel was assumed to be noiseless and non-varying.

Based on the IEEE 802.11 standard specification of the distributed coordination function (DCF) Bianchi analyzed the saturation throughput of unicast oriented communication [Bia00]. Bianchi assumed that the transmission queue of each node is never empty in order to keep the network saturated and to obtain the asymptotic throughput performance of the network. Furthermore, ideal and deterministic channel conditions were assumed in his work. The work of Bianchi was later extended by several follow-up studies, e.g. by Gupta and Kumar who addressed the simplifying assumption of an ideal radio propagation channel [Gup03]. But even though these follow-up studies incoorporated additional aspects, most of them considered unicast communication flows, which are not the focus of this thesis.

For that reason Torrent-Moreno et al. carried out a simulation-based evaluation of broadcast reception rates in IEEE 802.11 based vehicular ad-hoc networks [TJH04]. In contrast to previous studies, the authors considered a vehicular scenario that reflected the conditions of a 1.5 km highway with 8 lanes, in which 600 cars were transmitting beacons at a rate of 10 Hz using a transmission power equivalent to a 200 m communication range. In this setting, the probability of successful packet reception with respect to the distance between sender and receiver, and the channel access time have been evaluated, with the apparent conclusion that channel saturation will be the main issue in vehicular networks. Furthermore, the authors state, without explicit proof or quantitative results, that fading channel conditions increase the number of hidden terminal situations, and hence reduces the degree of synchronization.

In two follow-up studies [TMCH05, TCSH06], Torrent-Moreno et al. studied the degree of MAC layer incoordination on a per packet basis. They defined a new metric called *Packet Level Incoordination (PLI)* to quantify the amount of packets that were incoordinated to a given reference packet. Accordingly, a packet p_1 is termed to be incoordinated to a second packet p_2 if the timing between both packet is such that the sender of p_1 could have detected the transmission of p_2 prior to its own transmission, but obviously did not due to a fading channel. Unfortunately, the given definition of incoordination does not include situations in which two nodes have selected the same backoff slot, is therefore tightly coupled to CSMA itself, and consequently not able to quantify the inherent inabilities of the CSMA-based medium access control protocol. In the context of this thesis, the general idea behind PLI is adopted and extended for the evaluation of arbitrary medium access control protocols.

In 2009, Bilstrup et al. evaluated the ability of IEEE 802.11p and Self-Organizing TDMA (STDMA) to support real-time vehicle-to-vehicle communication [BUSB09]. To this purpose, the missed deadline ratio and the probability that two nodes are transmitting at the same time, i.e. their transmissions overlap in time, has been evaluated in a congested highway scenario assuming a data rate of 3 Mbps and non-fading channel conditions. While the first metric is out of context of this thesis and not considered in the remainder, the second metric is highly relevant and adopted in this thesis.

As a follow-up, the same group of authors evaluated the scalability issues of CSMA and STDMA in [BUS10]. Considering only saturated network conditions with channel loads between 80 % to 120 % of the theoretical maximum capacity, the authors evaluated the channel access delay, the probability of concurrent transmissions, and the cumulative distance function of the observed distances between two interfering nodes. Unfortunately, it is not clear from their paper whether deterministic or fading channel conditions are assumed. The evaluation has been continued in [SUS11a, SUS11b], however with a slightly different focus on either MAC-to-MAC delay, on packet error rates, or on a re-definition of the hidden terminal problem under the perspective of safety applications.

Schmidt-Eisenlohr et al. studied the impact of interference in vehicle-to-vehicle communication networks [SE10] as well and developed a metric to characterize the local broadcast capacity of such networks. They further performed a detailed evaluation of the successful packet reception and packet error ratios by distinguishing between packets that are received in the absence of interference, packets that are received despite the presence of interference, as well as between packets being dropped due to channel effects, and packets being dropped due to interference. Although such a differentiation is not the sole objective of the evaluation presented in this chapter, the proposed metrics are adopted and included later on.

To summarize the above work, the following statements can be made. First, existing inter-vehicle communication network performance studies are based on abstract physical layer models or ideal assumptions, neglecting the details of what is happening at the physical layer and during radio propagation. Second, most of the existing work considered performance metrics that are primarily connected to maximum throughput and capacity aspects of a network, e.g. by looking at the average packet reception (or error) ratio, or application relevant aspects such as end-to-end delay. Despite the importance of these metrics, their evaluation is not the focus of this work. To emphasize again, the objective of this work is not only a determination of when and how often CSMA will fail to coordinate concurrent access to the medium (considering a wide range of parameters), but also to understand exactly why it fails, how the resulting situations look like (from the perspective of a single packet), and how such failures can be avoided or dealt with appropriately.

5.2 Methodology

The characterization of packet collisions is performed considering a highway environment with vehicles being placed uniformly on a 5 km long road with 2 lanes per direction, cf. Figure 5.1 for an illustration. The highway environment is chosen since considerably high velocities, and hence pronounced time- and frequency-selective propagation characteristics, can be expected in this setting. A simple broadcast application that is running on each vehicle generates periodic awareness messages at an average rate r (in Hz), whereas the starting time of the application is uniformly distributed over the time interval $1/r$ seconds. In order to introduce a small randomness, a small jitter is applied to the interval between two subsequent awareness messages.

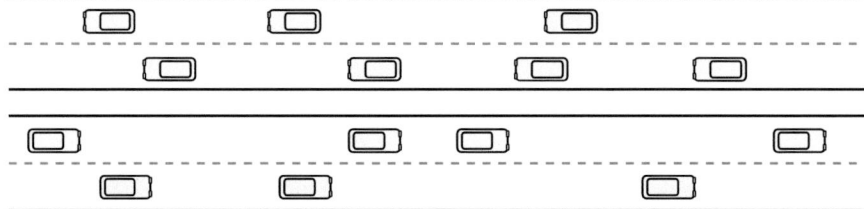

Figure 5.1: Illustration of the considered highway scenario: a 5 km long highway with 4 lanes in total.

To evaluate different network saturation levels, application specific impact factors are varied over a reasonable parameter range, i.e. the beaconing rate is set to either 2 Hz, 5 Hz or 10 Hz, the transmission power is set to either 5 dBm, 10 dBm, 15 dBm or 20 dBm, and the size of an awareness message is set to 200 bytes or 400 bytes. Furthermore, three different average vehicle densities in the range of 40 vehicles to 120 vehicles per highway kilometer are considered to vary the number of transceivers for which concurrent access has to be coordinated. Although mobility is considered in order to simulate fast-fading channel conditions, vehicles are configured to keep their (initial) positions. Since CSMA does not employ any slot reservation technique, and real vehicles do not alter their positions significantly during a few miliseconds

Parameter	Value
Application layer	
Packet size	200 bytes, 400 bytes
Transmission rate	2 Hz, 5 Hz, 10 Hz
Transmission power	5 dBm, 10 dBm, 15 dBm, 20 dBm
Medium access control layer	
Slot time	$13\,\mu s$
Contention window size	15
CCA busy threshold	-91 dBm
Physical layer	
Modulation scheme	QPSK
Coding rate	1/2
Channel bandwidth	10 MHz
Carrier spacing	5.9 GHz
Tx center frequency offset tolerance	20 ppm
Capture threshold	8 dB
Noise level	-99 dBm

Table 5.1: Application layer, medium access control and physical layer parameters and the settings used for the packet collision characterization.

(with respect to the dimension of the network in terms of communication range), the topology of the network can be considered stationary during the channel contention period. This configuration should therefore not affect the relevance of the obtained results. Nevertheless, in order to enable an application of channel fading models, a (fake) mobility of 100 km/h is considered by radio propagation models.

With respect to IEEE 802.11p medium access control, a basic DCF with a CCA busy (i.e. carrier sense) threshold of -91 dBm, a fixed contention window size of 15 slots, and a slot time of $13\mu s$ is used. Further, each vehicle is configured to use a data rate of 6 Mbps in a 10 MHz channel at a carrier frequency of 5.9 GHz. In order to introduce oscillator inaccuracies, a random frequency offset of at most 20ppm is applied (which is the upper limit as defined by the IEEE 802.11p standard specification). Apart from that, each transceiver employs the signal processing algorithms and their respective parametrization as described in Section 4.3. An overview of the most significant configuration parameters is given by Table 5.1. Please note that perfect omni-directional antennas and no antenna gains are considered in this study. The introduction of a positive or negative gain would only affect the maximum distance at which a signal can be received successfully, but not the "essence" of the results.

Most importantly, the radio propagation conditions are varied as well. Initially, only a distance dependent deterministic path loss is considered to study the coordination performance in the absence of any channel fading characteristics. Such a consideration enables the identification of the fundamental CSMA weaknesses, and serves as a reference when analyzing the results of the subsequent simulations in which fading is considered. Thereby it is possible to distinguish between throughput (i.e. packet reception) performance degradations that happen due to insufficient

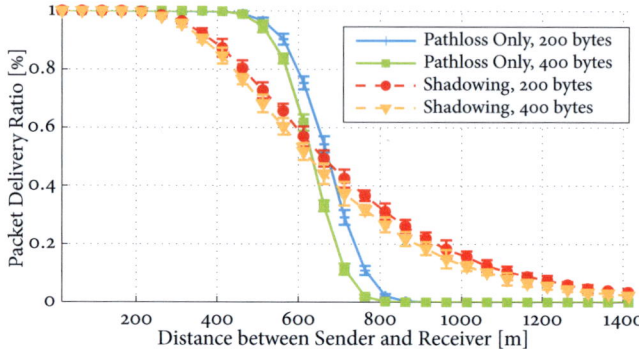

Figure 5.2: Packet delivery ratio w.r.t. distance between sender and receiver in the absence of any interference, for two different packet sizes and either a path loss only channel configuration or a path loss plus normal shadowing configuration.

MAC layer coordination, and throughput performance degradations that happen due to fading channel conditions. As proposed by Kunisch et al. in [KP08], only a power law model with a reference loss of 59.7 dB (at a distance of 1 m) and a path loss exponent of 1.85 is used. Then, large-scale fading characteristics that follow a Log-Normal distribution with $\sigma = 3.2$ dB are introduced. In a last step, the effect of a small-scale fading is analyzed by a simulation of a Rayleigh channel using the Jakes Doppler spectrum (instead of the Normal shadowing).

Figure 5.2 shows the resulting "plain" packet delivery ratios (with respect to the distance between one sender and multiple receivers) for the first two channel configurations described above: a path loss only and a path loss plus Normal shadowing configuration. As illustrated, successful packet receptions are observed up to a distance of approx. 800 m if no shadowing is considered. The introduction of large-scale fading effects using a Normal distribution with $\sigma = 3.2$ dB leads to successful packet receptions at distances even greater than 800 m, but at the expense of successful packet receptions at close distances.

The impact of a Rayleigh fading on the reception performance is illustrated in Figure 5.3. The average packet reception ratios are significantly lower if compared to the first two channel setups. Further, as expected, the packet delivery ratio is reduced at all distances if vehicles are driving in opposite directions. Note that the assumption of a Rayleigh fading even at close distances is very conservative, since a Rayleigh fading does not model any line of sight contribution. This configuration is therefore used to evaluate the MAC layer coordination performance in very challenging conditions, i.e. the worst case.

In total, the combination of all configuration parameters yields a set of 288 different simulation experiments. To achieve statistical significance, each experiment is repeated 20 times, whereas each repetition starts with a different seed for the random number generator, and new controlled but randomly chosen positions for all vehicles.

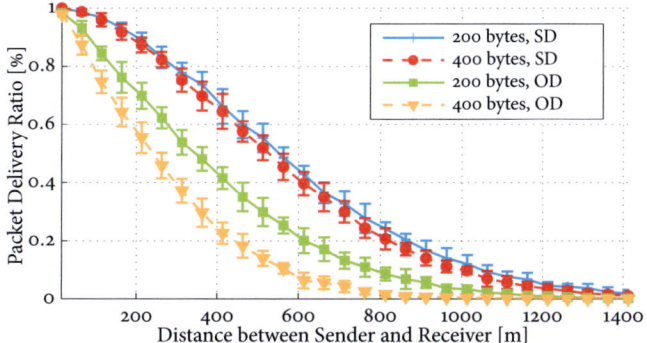

Figure 5.3: Packet delivery ratio with respect to the distance between sender and receiver in case of a Rayleigh fading channel, in the absence of any interference, for two different packet sizes and vehicles driving either in same direction (SD) or opposite direction (OD).

To be precise, only the applied random jitter is re-calculated. The average spacing between two vehicles remains fixed for a given vehicular density. In each experiment, twelve vehicles located in the center of the scenario are selected as reference nodes. During the simlation of an experiment, each packet transmitted by any of these reference nodes is monitored and evaluated with respect to the performance metrics that will be described in Section 5.2.1. Since the experiments differ with respect to the transmission rate used, e.g. some experiments use 2 Hz while others use 10 Hz, the simulated time is chosen such that the same number of packets is transmitted (and evaluated) in each experiment. With respect to computational efforts, a total of 5760 unique simulation runs has to be completed, and more than 238 080 hours (or 27 years) of CPU time has to be spent — considering a minimum runtime of 8 hours per simulation run for a 40 vehicles/km and deterministic pathloss configuration, and a maximum runtime of 72 hours per simulation run for a 120 vehicles/km and Rayleigh fading channel configuration. To cope with that enormous effort, two high performance computing clusters operated by the Steinbuch Centre for Computing at the Karlsruhe Institute of Technology (KIT) are used.

5.2.1 Performance metrics

During each simulation run, the "lifetime" of all packets transmitted by each of the reference nodes is monitored and evaluated with respect to different performance metrics. The applied metrics are classified with respect to receiver and transmitter perspective and are described in the following.

From the perspective of a transmitting (reference) node, the primary metric that describes the coordination efficiency of a MAC protocol is the probability that one or multiple other nodes are incoordinated to an own transmission.

Definition 5.1 (Packet Level Incoordination, PLI) *The packet level incoordination, as observed from the perspective of a node r and one of its generated packets p, describes the probability that at least one node s, s ≠ r, transmitted a packet q during the transmission period of p.*

Compared to the original definition of PLI by Torrent-Moreno et al. in [TCSH06] which is given from a receiver perspective, the above definition is not restricted to CSMA-based mechanisms and includes also the cases in which two nodes start their transmissions exactly at the same point in time. Hence, the above definition includes all possible cases of incoordination. Since it is important to differentiate between an incoordinated node located next to the reference node and an incoordinated node located further away, the PLI is evaluated with respect to the range within which incoordinated nodes are considered.

With respect to the considered scenario in this chapter – each vehicle transmits beacon messages periodically – an upper limit of the expected PLI can be derived analytically. This upper limit is MAC layer independent and only subject to the transmission behavior of all nodes, i.e. their selected transmission power, beaconing rate, and the size of each message. Although any MAC layer procotol will probably perform much better than this uncoordinated case, the following analysis is performed to obtain a first impression on how bad the packet level incoordination can be.

The beaconing rate r determines the beaconing period T during which all nodes will transmit one awareness message each, i.e.

$$T = \frac{1}{r} \tag{5.1}$$

With t_d being the transmit duration of a packet, the number of packets (or "time slots") s that fit into T without any overlap is then given by

$$s = \lfloor \frac{T}{t_d} \rfloor \tag{5.2}$$

and the probability that exactly i out of N nodes start a transmission during one of these time slots is given by

$$P_i = \binom{N}{i} \left(\left(\frac{1}{s}\right)^i \left(1 - \frac{1}{s}\right)^{N-i} \right) \tag{5.3}$$

By summing up the probabilities of all P_i with $0 < i \le N$, the overall probability P that at least one out of N considered nodes starts a transmission during one of the available time slots is obtained, i.e.

$$P = \sum_{i=1}^{N} P_i \tag{5.4}$$

Of course, the above derivation is based on the assumption that the transmission times of the nodes are uniformly distributed. Assuming that this is the case and packets account to 400 bytes, a PLI as illustrated in Figure 5.4 has to be expected. As illustrated, the PLI increases with the beaconing rate used, the range in which vehicles are

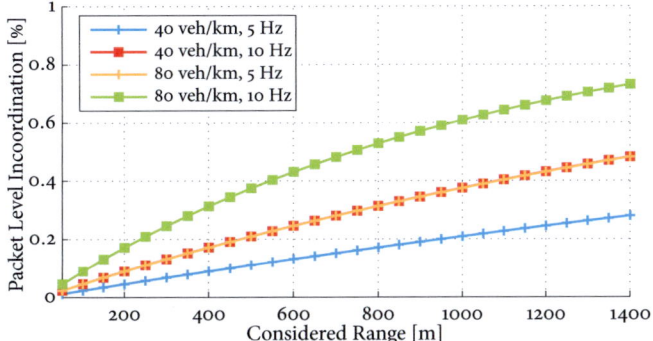

Figure 5.4: Probability of incoordination w.r.t. the considered range around the transmitting node, a packet size of 400 bytes, CSMA being disabled, two different vehicle densities and beaconing rates.

considered, and the number of vehicles that are located within that range. Please recall that no MAC layer coordination is considered above. In a CSMA enabled setup, a significantly lower PLI is expected for all ranges smaller than the carrier sense range, hence, the PLI of approx. 40 %, as shown in Figure 5.4 for a 10 Hz beaconing rate, a range of 600 m, and 80 vehicles/km, is way too large for a real system.

Apart from the quantification of the PLI, it is also important to resolve the type of incoordination. With respect to CSMA, the reason for an incoordination could be that either both nodes started their transmission at exactly the same points in time, e.g. due to simultaneous expiration of backoff timers, or that the incoordinated node did not sense the reference transmission, e.g. due to shadowing or fading channel characteristics. To distinguish between both cases, the time difference between both transmissions has to be evaluated, which leads to the definition of the *Incoordination Delay Profile*.

Definition 5.2 (Incoordination Delay Profile, IDP) *The incoordination delay profile describes the probability distribution of the starting time differences between a set of packet transmissions $P = \{p_1, ..., p_n\}$ and each packet's corresponding set of incoordinated transmissions $Q_i = \{q_{i1}, ..., q_{ij}\}$, with $1 \leq i \leq n$, and j being the number of packets interfering with p_i.*

In case of CSMA and distance decaying deterministic channel conditions, the IDP should indicate that all incoordinated nodes located within the carrier sense range — the range within which the received signal will exceed the CCA busy threshold — transmit more or less simultaneously[1] with the reference node. Only incoordinated nodes outside the carrier sense range should show significantly greater delays. To

---

[1]Due to the delay of the signal propagation process and the carrier sensing itself, the latter one typically being at the order of one OFDM symbol, hence $8\mu s$ when using IEEE 802.11p, very small delays have to be expected.

determine the effectivness of CSMA with respect to this controlled spatial reuse of the channel, the IDP is evaluated with respect to the distance between sender and incoordinated node in the following.

To quantify the negative impact of existing incoordination from a receiver perspective, the packet delivery and the packet error ratios are evaluated with respect to the distance between the transmitting node and each potential receiver. While doing this, the packet error ratio (PER) is distinguished with respect to the primary error reason, being either the channel effects or interfering packet transmissions. Interference is allowed to be present in the first case as well, i.e. an error belongs to the first case only if the packet was even then undecodable when present interference is "ignored". Due to a simulation based approach such a check is easily possible.

5.2.2 Characterization of packet collisions

The performance metrics described in the previous section are suitable to quantify the coordination and throughput performance of an inter-vehicle communication network. However, these metrics do not characterize the situations which are created by incoordinated transmissions, which is required to identify possible solutions that aim to avoide or repair them.

First, it is interesting to determine the intensity of interfering packets with respect to their received signal strength. The evaluation of this aspect leads to the definition of the *Interference Intensity Profile*.

Definition 5.3 (Interference Intensity Profile) *From the perspective of a node n, the interference intensity profile of a set of packets $P = \{p_1, ..., p_i\}$ describes the probability distribution of the average received signal strengths contributed by the set of packets that interfere with any of the packets in P at n.*

Another important aspect is the number of transmissions that interfere with a given packet. In particular for the design of solutions that aim to repair existing incoordination it is important to know whether only one, two or even more packets are interfering. For instance in the case of a cross-layer optimization based on multi-antenna systems, cf. the example of Tan et. al described in Section 4.1, the exact number of packets is decisive. To this purpose an *Interference Count Profile*, which is defined as follows, is rendered after each simulation.

Definition 5.4 (Interference Count Profile) *From the perspective of a node n, the interference count profile of a set of packets $P = \{p_1, ..., p_i\}$ with respect to a signal strength threshold S describes the probability distribution of the number of packets c_i that interfere with p_i at node n and arrive with a signal strength greater than S.*

As emphasized in the definition, the profile is based on a filter that ignores all interfering packets that arrive with a signal strength below a given threshold S. The rationale for such a filtering is simply the removal of irrelevant packets which have no impact on the successful reception of the reference packet. For instance, by setting S to -99 dBm, only interfering packets that are stronger than the background noise level and that may significantly cause a packet drop are counted.

5.3 Results

The following two sections present and discuss a representative subset of the obtained results. This subset is sufficient in order to illustrate the fundamental findings and to demonstrate the conclusions that are eventually drawn. In particular, only the 80 vehicles/km and 120 vehicles/km scenarios with a 400 bytes packet size configuration are considered in the following. The reader who wishes to evaluate and screen the complete set of results is able to access the results as well as the full source code of all experiments online [Mit12].

5.3.1 Transmitter perspective

Figure 5.5 illustrates the observed packet level incoordination (with respect to the range in which incoordination is considered) using three different packet generation rates, the two selected vehicle densities of 80 vehicles/km and 120 vehicles/km, and three different channel configurations, i.e. a deterministic path loss only setup, a setup with additional Log-Normal shadowing, and a setup with additional Rayleigh fading. As illustrated, almost no incoordination is observed within a range of approx. 700 m for most scenario configurations that exhibit only a deterministic path loss, cf. Figure 5.5(a) and Figure 5.5(b). This is an expected result, since the range of 700 m reflects the area within which the received signal strength stays above the configured -91 dBm CCA busy threshold. CSMA can therefore be certified to achieve its design goal in such an environment and setup. Only if the number of contending vehicles and the packet generation rate is increased, e.g. to 120 vehicles/km and a 10 Hz generation rate, a small amount of incoordinated transmissions can also be observed within a range of 700 m. Yet, in comparison to the analytical PLI curves presented in Section 5.2.1, this incoordination level is still quite low.

If a large-scale fading based on a Log-Normal shadowing is assumed, the corresponding PLI curves are slightly increased in comparison to the deterministic path loss setup, cf. Figure 5.5(c) versus Figure 5.5(a) and Figure 5.5(d) versus Figure 5.5(b). Particularly for ranges slightly below and above the deterministic carrier sense range of 700 m a noticeable increase of the PLI can be observed. This is also expected, since the large-scale fading leads to situations in which a vehicle located within the deterministic carrier sense range experiences received signal strengths below the -91 dBm CCA busy threshold, hence these vehicles will not block their MAC layer and might interfere with one of the reference transmissions. This phenomenon is even worse if a Rayleigh fading channel is considered, cf. Figure 5.5(e) and Figure 5.5(f), however, the PLI is still significantly lower than the values that were obtained analytically for a setup in which no MAC layer coordination is assumed. For instance, even in a setup with 120 vehicles/km and a 10 Hz beaconing rate, close to zero interference is introduced by vehicles located within a range of 200 m. Whether this is sufficiently low can not be answered at this point, since no statement about the resulting packet delivery ratios is made. In general terms, an additional evaluation of the MAC layer performance from a receiver perspective is required in order to answer the question whether a small increase of the PLI is significant or not.

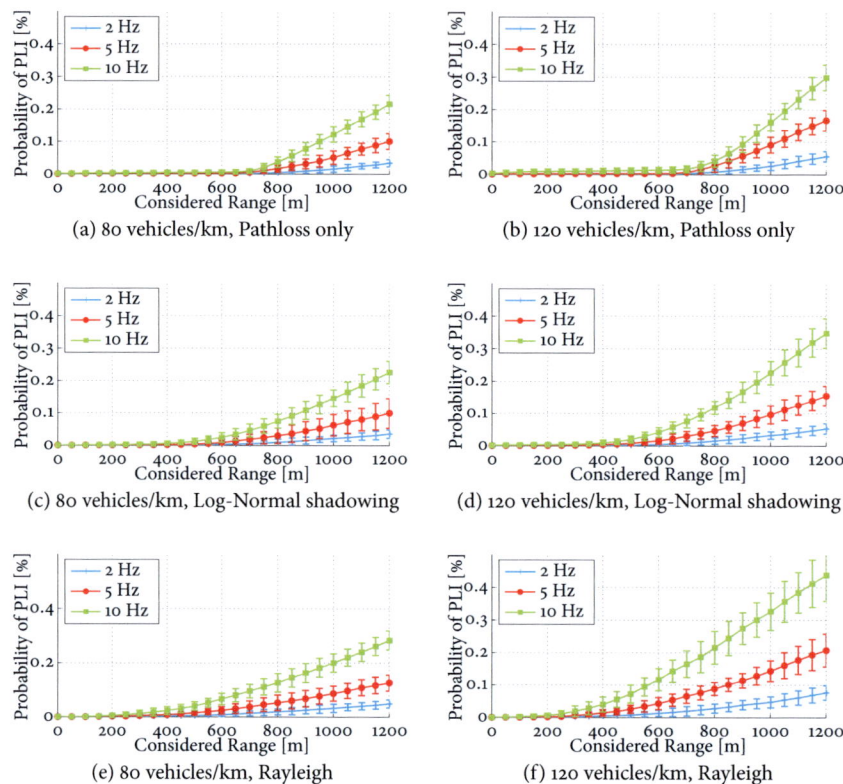

(a) 80 vehicles/km, Pathloss only

(b) 120 vehicles/km, Pathloss only

(c) 80 vehicles/km, Log-Normal shadowing

(d) 120 vehicles/km, Log-Normal shadowing

(e) 80 vehicles/km, Rayleigh

(f) 120 vehicles/km, Rayleigh

Figure 5.5: Probability of PLI with respect to the range within which incoordination is considered. Scenarios with 80 vehicles/km, a 20 dBm transmit power and different channel configurations are illustrated on the left side. On the right side: scenarios with 120 vehicles/km, a 20 dBm transmit power and different channel configurations.

As shown in Figure 5.5(b), a small amount of incoordinated transmissions is observed within the deterministic carrier sense range despite the absence of any signal fading. According to the design of CSMA, such an incoordination should only occur if the transmitting vehicle (i.e. the reference node) and the interfering vehicle start to transmit at (more or less) the same point in time. In such a situation, the interfering node is inherently not able to sense the signal of the reference node prior to its own transmission. In order to evaluate this aspect, the observed IDPs with respect to the distance between the reference node and a potentially interfering node are discussed in the following. Since the benefit of showing results for multiple scenarios is marginal, two setups with 80 vehicles/km and 120 vehicles/km, a 20 dBm transmit power, a 10 Hz beaconing rate and a packet size of 400 bytes is considered in the following.

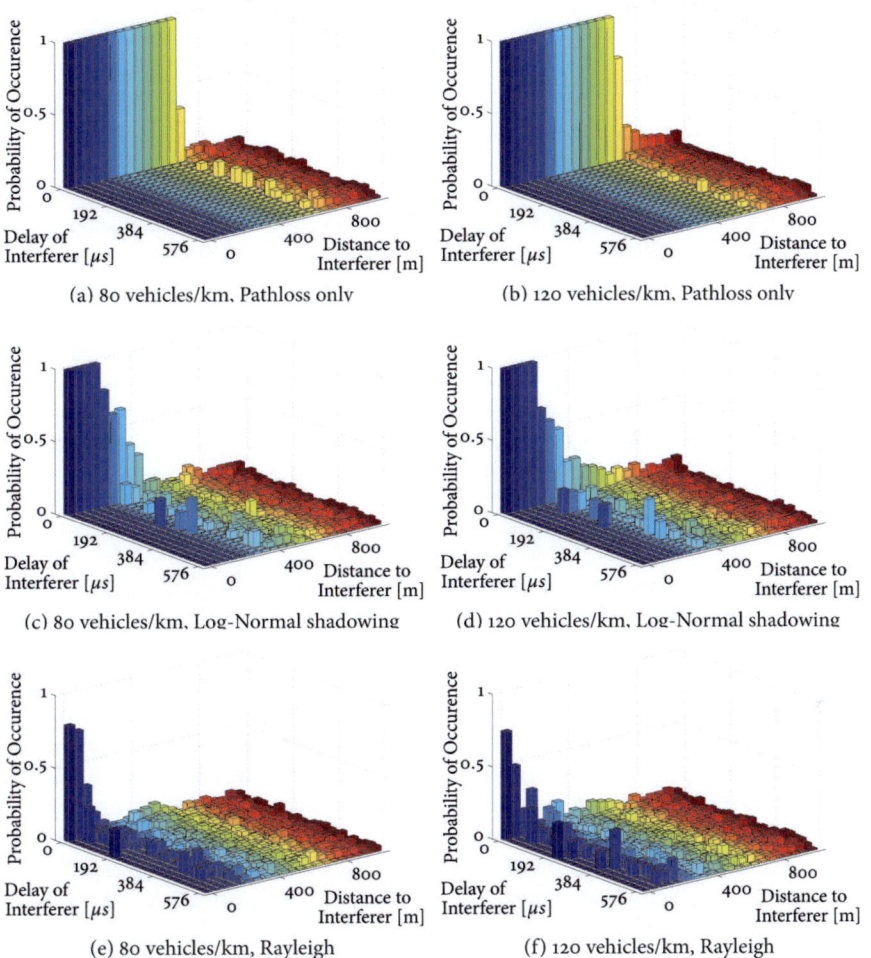

(a) 80 vehicles/km, Pathloss only

(b) 120 vehicles/km, Pathloss only

(c) 80 vehicles/km, Log-Normal shadowing

(d) 120 vehicles/km, Log-Normal shadowing

(e) 80 vehicles/km, Rayleigh

(f) 120 vehicles/km, Rayleigh

Figure 5.6: Observed incoordination delay profiles with respect to the distance between reference and incoordinated nodes.

Figure 5.6(a) and Figure 5.6(b) illustrate the observed IDPs with respect to the distance between a reference node and interfering nodes for the deterministic channel configuration and the 10 Hz beaconing rate setup. Since the length of a 400 byte packet is equal to $576\mu s$ in the time domain, the time difference between the transmission of a reference node and the transmission of an incoordinated node can be at most $576\mu s$. This maximum value is however not observed for interferers located within a range of 700 m. Indeed, as expected in this setup, incoordination from vehicles located within the carrier sense range occurs only if interfering vehicles transmit exactly at the same point in time as the reference node. Hence, CSMA can again be certified to fulfill its objective. Please note that a more or less uniform distribution of the incoordination delay is observed for all distances greater than the carrier sense range.

Unsurprisingly, the situation changes if fading characteristics are introduced. As shown in Figure 5.6(b) and Figure 5.6(c), which plots the IDPs under a Log-Normal shadowing configuration, the range within which incoordination occurs only due to identical transmission times decreases to approx. 300 m. For greater distances, the IDP tends towards a uniform distribution of the incoordination delays. A similar but more intense effect can be observed in the Rayleigh fading channel configuration, cf. Figure 5.6(d) and Figure 5.6(e). In such an environment, the principle of CSMA has its difficulties to avoid incoordination that is not caused by identical transmission times. Recall that incoordination is still less likely to occur at such close distances (in comparison to remote distances). Only the time domain characteristic of incoordinated transmissions at close distances has changed, and is not fundamentally different from incoordinated transmissions at remote distances anymore (as it was in the deterministic path loss only channel configuration).

5.3.2 Receiver perspective

In the previous section, the performance of CSMA was evaluated from the perspective of the transmitting vehicle, with the conclusion that the coordination effectiveness of CSMA decreases if the wireless channel exhibits signal fading and if the intensity of this fading increases. The questions that will be answered in this section are now: how significant is a small increase of the packet level incoordination with respect to the successful reception of a transmitted message? What is the primary reason for reception errors – incoordination or channel effects? How do transmitted and interfering messages relate to each other, in terms of signal strength and the number of incoordinated transmissions?

Figure 5.7(a) and Figure 5.7(b) start with the evaluation of the packet delivery ratio in non-fading scenarios by using the same configuration already used for the illustration of the packet level incoordination. As expected, the highest PDRs are achieved (at all distances and independent of the number of vehicles) if a beaconing rate of 2 Hz is configured (in comparison to 5 Hz and 10 Hz). However, depending on the distance of interest, this difference can be marginal or as large as 70 %. For instance, the PDR at 400 m is only 2 % in the 120 vehicles/km case for a 10 Hz beaconing rate, but increases to a PDR of 72 % if the beaconing rate is throttled to 2 Hz. At the same time, the PDRs at 100 m are almost equal for all shown scenarios and beaconing rates. Hence, depending on whether safety applications are interested in packets transmitted from remote distances or close distances, there is a clear benefit in reducing the beacon generation rate.

An increase of the incoordination level due to an additional Log-Normal shadowing or Rayleigh fading effect leads to lower PDRs at close distances and increased PDRs at remote distances. The slope of each curve is simply flattened. Whereas the

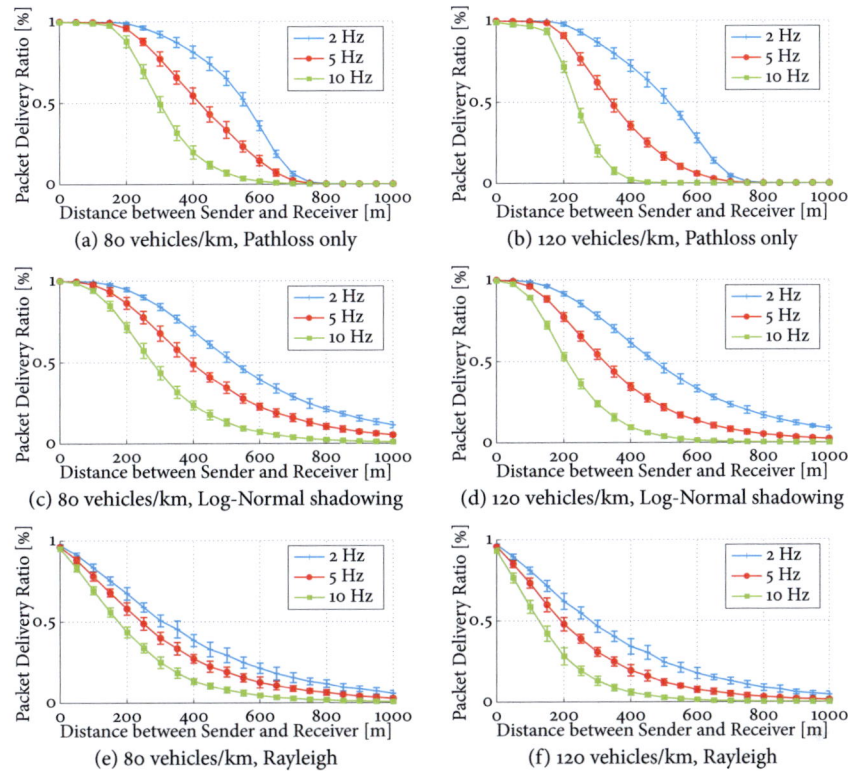

(a) 80 vehicles/km, Pathloss only

(b) 120 vehicles/km, Pathloss only

(c) 80 vehicles/km, Log-Normal shadowing

(d) 120 vehicles/km, Log-Normal shadowing

(e) 80 vehicles/km, Rayleigh

(f) 120 vehicles/km, Rayleigh

Figure 5.7: Illustration of the packet delivery ratio with respect to the distance between sender and receiver, and different channel configurations. All curves are based on a 20 dBm transmit power, a 10 Hz beaconing rate and a 400 byte packet size.

drop at close distances is noticable but not substantial in case of a Log-Normal shadowing, cf. Figures5.7(c) versus Figure 5.7(a) and Figure 5.7(d) versus Figure 5.7(b), a Rayleigh fading channel leads to a substantial increase of the number of packet errors, cf. Figure 5.7(e) versus Figure 5.7(a) and Figure 5.7(f) versus Figure 5.7(b). For instance, the PDR of the 80 vehicles/km and 10 Hz setup at a distance of 200 m drops from initially 90 % down to approx. 73 % if Normal shadowing is assumed – that is a 17 percentage points difference. In contrast, the PDR experiences a drop by 45 percentage points down to a value of 45 % if the channel is assumed to incoorporate a Rayleigh fading on top of the deterministic path loss. Similar observations can be made in the 120 vehicles/km scenario.

Figure 5.7 illustrates also a second observation: the introduction of fading effects reduces the impact of an increased incoordination. Whereas a small difference in the PLI leads to significantly different PDR curves in the non-fading case, the difference between the PDR curves diminishes if fading is considered. This is attributed to

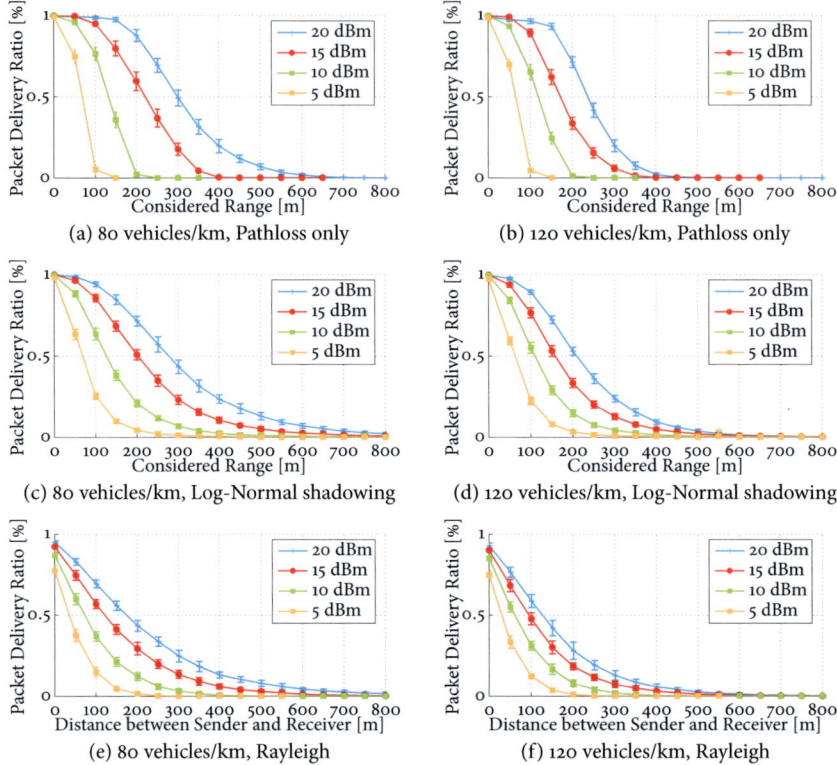

Figure 5.8: Illustration of the packet delivery ratio with respect to the distance between sender and receiver. On the left side: scenarios with 80 vehicles/km, a 10 Hz beaconing rate and different channel configurations. On the right side: scenarios with 120 vehicles/km, a 10 Hz beaconing rate and different channel configurations.

the fact that incoordination is now only one source for packet reception errors. The second source is the fading channel itself, which leads to failed packet receptions at close distances even in the absence of interference. Whether one source is more dominant than the other will be analyzed and discussed later.

So far, the packet delivery ratio was evaluated for a fixed transmission power setting and three different beaconing rates. It was concluded that a lower beacon generation rate decreases the incoordination level, which in turn increases the packet delivery ratio. Hence, lower beaconing rates are to be preferred, although their benefit is reduced as soon as fading effects are introduced. Can this observation be transferred to transmission power adjustments as well, in the sense that a lower transmit power increases the packet delivery ratio, at least at close distances? To answer this question, Figure 5.8 plots the obtained packet delivery ratios for a packet size of 400 bytes, a fixed beacon generation rate of 10 Hz and four different transmit power settings, namely 5 dBm, 10 dBm, 15 dBm and 20 dBm. According to the obtained results, the usage of a reduced transmit power is only beneficial if the generated data traffic of all nodes within the carrier sense range is close to or above the capacity limit of the channel. For instance, a small benefit at close distances can only be observed in the 120 vehicles/km scenario within which a channel load of 5.76 Mbps is generated at a 20 dBm transmit power setting, cf. Figure 5.8(b). This is attributed to the high reference path loss and the small path loss exponent of the propagation environment, which account to 59.7 dB at 1 m and a value of 1.85. As a result, an incoordinated transmission is irrelevant only if the distance between incoordinated and receiving node is greater by at least 350 m than the distance between reference and receiving node. If this condition is not met, the resulting signal-to-interference ratio is smaller than 8 dB, which, however, is the minimum ratio that needs to be fulfilled in oder to have a chance to successfully decode the reference signal at all. If now a reduced transmit power is used, the range within which CSMA suppresses incoordination is reduced as well and the number of hidden terminals increases – but that is not exactly what helps to achieve the above signal-to-interference ratio condition. In addition to this observation, the benefit of a reduced transmit power is only noticable under deterministic channel conditions. As soon as fading effects are added, the already small benefit vanishes. This leads to the conclusion that a reduced transmission power alone has no positive effect on the packet delivery ratio, not even at close distances, if the network is operated within its theoretical limit. The situation usually changes if a significantly higher load level is offered to the channel, for instance if all nodes within each others carrier sense range generate a load of 9 Mbps.

The next aspect that needs to be discussed is the question of whether existing incoordination or fading channel effects are the primary source for packet reception errors. As stated earlier, the benefit of a reduced beaconing rate diminishes if the fading intensity of the channel increases. This could be attributed to the fact that the channel can cause reception errors in such a setup as well. Whether this fact plays a dominant role is answered by Figure 5.9, which plots the packet reception error due to interference ratios. To make sure that the illustrated values are interpreted correctly in the following: a ratio of one states that all failed packet receptions occur due to interference; similarly, a ratio of 0.3 indicates that only 30 percent of all packet reception errors are caused by interference and the remaining 70 percent happen either due to channel effects or the receiver being in transmission state. Hence, the ratio is given with respect to all failed packet receptions, and not with respect to the total number of transmitted packets. As before, two different vehicle densities are considered, 80 vehicles/km and 120 vehicles/km, as well as a packet size of 400 bytes and a transmission power setting of 20 dBm. The beaconing rate is set to either 2 Hz, 5 Hz or 10 Hz.

If a deterministic path loss only channel configuration is simulated, as shown in Figure 5.9(a) and Figure 5.9(b), the packet reception error due to interference ratio is (more or less) equal to one for all distances smaller than approx. 500 m. Beyond a distance of 500 m, the ratio begins to decrease steadily until it reaches a value of zero at a distance of 800 m. This is an expected result, since this kind of shape looks

93

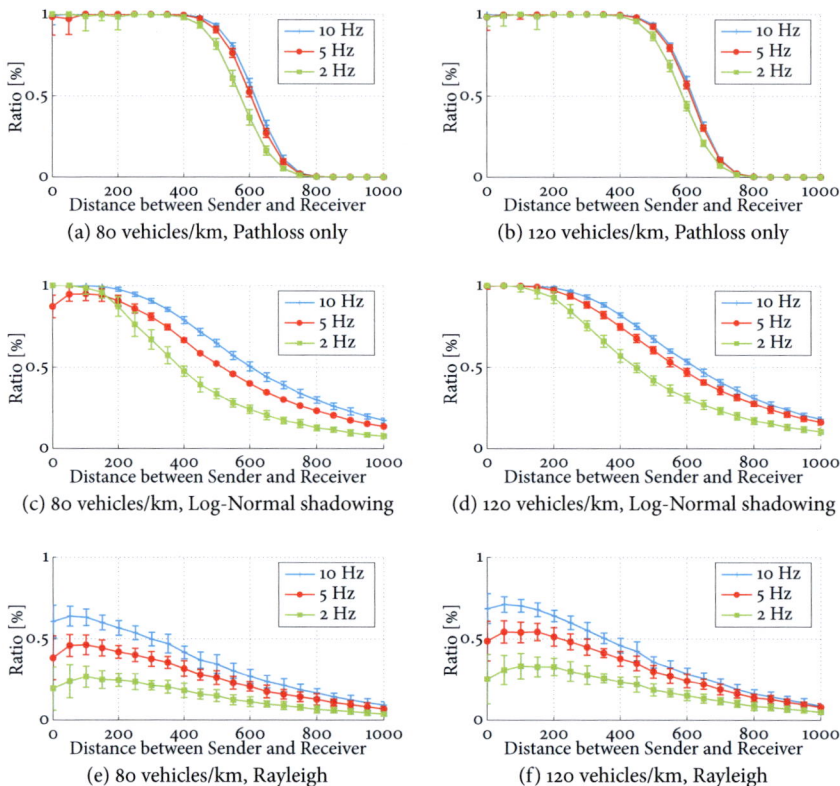

(a) 80 vehicles/km, Pathloss only

(b) 120 vehicles/km, Pathloss only

(c) 80 vehicles/km, Log-Normal shadowing

(d) 120 vehicles/km, Log-Normal shadowing

(e) 80 vehicles/km, Rayleigh

(f) 120 vehicles/km, Rayleigh

Figure 5.9: Illustration of the packet error due to interference ratio with respect to the distance between sender and receiver. On the left side: scenarios with 80 vehicles/km, a 20 dBm transmit power and different channel configurations. On the right side: scenarios with 120 vehicles/km, a 20 dBm transmit power and different channel configurations.

like the shape of the one sender one receiver reception curves shown in Figure 5.2 of Section 5.2, i.e. the distance decaying path loss starts to become responsible for decoding errors once the distance is greater than 500 m. Since some packets are not successfully decoded due to the receiver being in transmission state, the reception error due to interference is only close but not equal to one for some distances smaller than 500 m. This is an unavoidable side effect since the packet reception error ratio is close to zero at those distances, i.e. only a very small number of packets is not received successfully at all, which leads to an increased significance of the actually rare event that a packet is dropped due to the transceiver being in transmission state.

The packet reception error due to interference ratio is reduced if the path loss only channel setup is replaced by a Log-Normal shadowing effect, c.f. Figure 5.9(c)

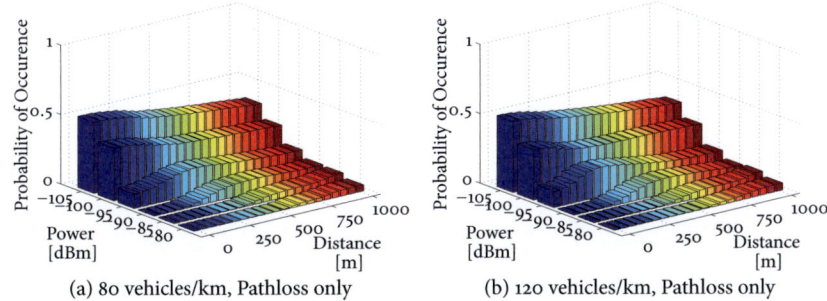

(a) 80 vehicles/km, Pathloss only   (b) 120 vehicles/km, Pathloss only

Figure 5.10: Illustration of the interference intensity profile with respect to the distance between sender and receiver. On the left side: a setup with 80 vehicles/km. On the right side: a setup with 120 vehicles/km. Further, a 20 dBm transmit power, a 10 Hz beaconing rate and 400 byte packets were configured.

and Figure 5.9(d). Similar to the PDR curves presented before, the shape of the curve flattens, hence, the negative impact of interference is slightly relaxed. However, interference still is the primary error reason for packets being dropped over small distances. The situation changes if a Rayleigh fading of the channel is considered: as shown in Figure 5.9(e) for a 80 vehicles/km setup, interference is only responsible for more than 50 % of the reception errors if short distances up to 300 m and a 10 Hz beaconing rate are considered. In all other cases, interference causes less than 50 % of all observed packet reception failures. A similar observation can be made in the 120 vehicles/km scenario which is illustrated in Figure 5.9(f). The above observations lead to the conclusion that the negative impact of incoordination becomes less important if the fading intensity of the channel increases.

Apart from a quantization of the incoordination levels, its impact on the successful reception of packets, and the identification of the primary error reason, it is also interesting to characterize incoordination with respect to the interference level (in terms of signal strength) that an incoordinated (or interfering) packet transmission introduces at a receiver. Figure 5.10 plots the interference intensity profiles of the 80 vehicles/km and the 120 vehicles/km scenario (w.r.t. the distance between the sender and the transmitter) using the deterministic channel setup.

In such a setup, it is no surprise that most of the incoordinated packet transmissions arrive with only very low signal strengths, c.f. Figure 5.10(a) and Figure 5.10(b). For instance, approx. 80 % to 90 % of the interfering packets arrive with a signal strength that is either lower or only slightly higher than the background noise level of -99 dBm. It is also observed that almost zero packets arrive with a signal strength greater than -80 dBm. Further, only a small ratio of interfering packets arrive with a signal strength greater than -90 dBm.

No fundamental change in the shape of the profiles can be observed if a Log-Normal shadowing or Rayleigh fading is considered instead of a deterministic path

95

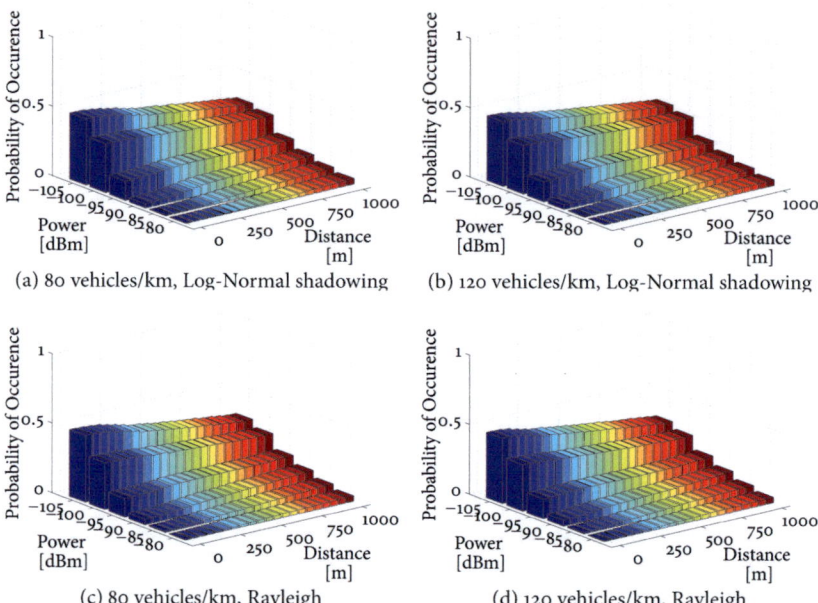

(a) 80 vehicles/km, Log-Normal shadowing

(b) 120 vehicles/km, Log-Normal shadowing

(c) 80 vehicles/km, Rayleigh

(d) 120 vehicles/km, Rayleigh

Figure 5.11: Illustration of the interference intensity profile with respect to the distance between sender and receiver. On the left side: a setup with 80 vehicles/km. On the right side: a setup with 120 vehicles/km. Further, a 20 dBm transmit power, a 10 Hz beaconing rate and 400 byte packets were configured.

loss only, as shown in Figure 5.11(a), Figure 5.11(b), Figure 5.11(c) and Figure 5.11(d). Only minor variations in the probability distribution are noticable, which can be interpreted as follows: if interfering transmissions are present, the intensity of each does not depend on the actual channel characteristics. Or, to state it the other way round: a change of the channel characteristics does not influence the intensity of an interfering packet transmission significantly. It may of course originate from a different vehicle located at a different location, but in terms of signal strength, the differences are marginal. Does this also apply to the number of interfering packet transmissions?

To answer this question, Figure 5.12 plots the number of interfering packet transmissions that are stronger than the background noise, i.e. stronger than -99 dBm. As shown for the case of a distance decaying path loss only channel configuration, cf. Figure 5.12(a) and Figure 5.12(b), the probability that only one packet interfers is relatively high at close distances in the 80 vehicles/km setup, i.e. approx. 73 %. This probability decreases to a level of 35 % at a distance of 1000 m. In contrast to this decrease, the probability of two (or three) interfering packets increases from approx. 20 % (or 1 %) at close distances to a value of 45 % (or 16 %) at a distance of 1000 m.

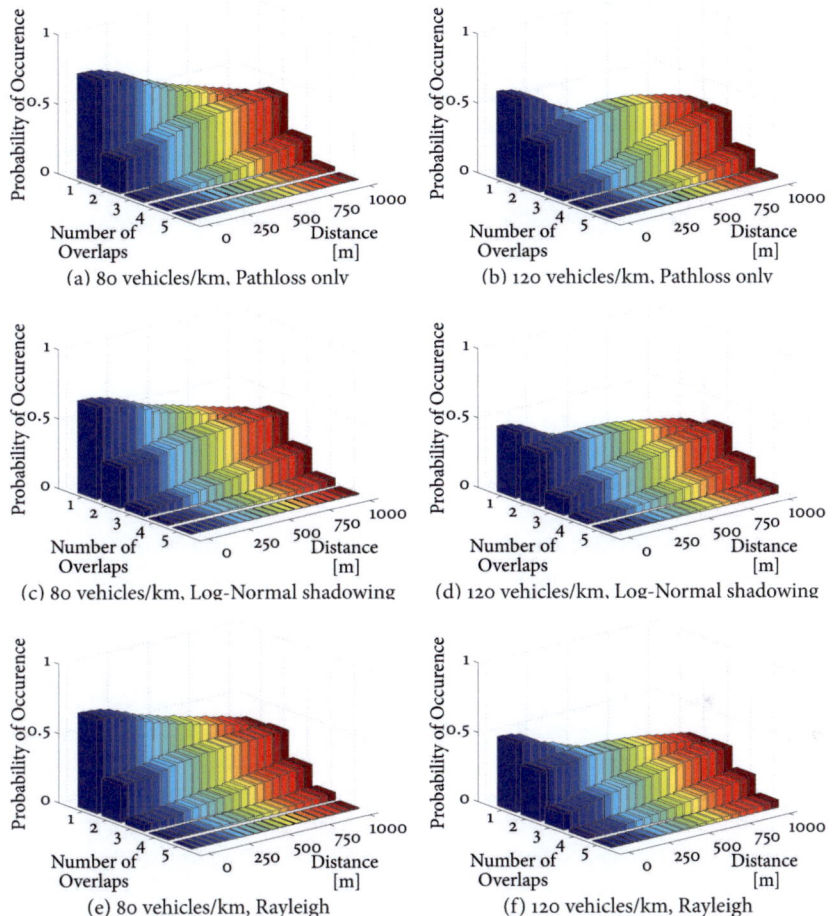

(a) 80 vehicles/km, Pathloss only

(b) 120 vehicles/km, Pathloss only

(c) 80 vehicles/km, Log-Normal shadowing

(d) 120 vehicles/km, Log-Normal shadowing

(e) 80 vehicles/km, Rayleigh

(f) 120 vehicles/km, Rayleigh

Figure 5.12: Illustration of the observed interference count profiles with respect to the distance between sender and receiver. On the left side: a setup with 80 vehicles/km. On the right side: a setup with 120 vehicles/km. Further, a 20 dBm transmit power, a 10 Hz beaconing rate and 400 byte packets were configured.

More than three overlapping packets are only very rarely observed. Similar observations can be made in the 120 vehicles/km scenario as well, with the difference that the probability values are different (due to the higher congestion level of the network) and that four overlapping transmissions begin to occur at an increasing rate at distances greater than 250 m. If a fading of the channel is added, for instance in terms of a Log-Normal shadowing as in Figure 5.12(b) and Figure 5.12(b), the shape of the interference intensity profiles is flattened over the distance that is considered. For instance, whereas the difference between the maximum and minimum probability of one overlapping packet (in the 80 vehicles/km scenario with a distance decaying path loss) accounts to 38 percentage points, the difference between the maximum and minimum probability of one overlapping packet (in the 80 vehicles/km scenario with a Normal shadowing) accounts only to 25 percentage points. The consideration of a Rayleigh fading channel leads to similar results, cf. Figure 5.12(e) and Figure 5.12(f).

To summarize, the observed interference count profiles indicate that a change of the channel characteristics does not influence the shape of the interference count profile in a fundamental way, although the probability values do change.

5.4 Conclusions

In this chapter, the performance of the IEEE 802.11p based MAC layer, which uses CSMA to coordination concurrent access to the wireless channel, was evaluated from two different perspectives and with respect to a wide range of scenario configurations as well as three different radio propagation characteristics.

From the perspective of a transmitter, the probability of incoodination was analyzed with respect to the range within which potential incoordination is considered. According to the obtained results, **the CSMA mechanism can be certified to successfully suppress interfering transmissions from within the carrier sense range** of the transmitter if only a distance decaying path loss is simulated, i.e. if the assumptions made by the protocol are met. **If additional fading effects are present**, either by means of a Log-Normal shadowing or a Rayleigh fading, CSMA begins to experience difficulties in suppressing interfering transmissions from within the carrier sense range. However, this is an expected result, and **the amount of incoordinated transmissions from within the carrier sense range remains on a low level**. In addition, the reasons for incoordination were analyzed. The obtained incoordination delay profiles show that incoordinated transmissions from within the carrier sense range occur only due to identical transmission times as longs as only a distance decaying path loss is simulated. Hence, CSMA fulfills its objective. In case of fading channel conditions, hidden terminal situations are introduced within the (formerly deterministic) carrier sense range, with the result that incoordinated transmissions from within the carrier sense range emerge during the whole transmission period – which, however, is also no surprise and an expected result.

From the perspective of a receiver, the packet delivery and the packet reception error due to interference ratios were evaluated. In general, it was observed that **a reduced beacon generation rate, and hence a slightly reduced incoordination level, leads to significantly increased packet delivery ratios** if only a distance decaying path loss is considered. Depending on the considered scenario, such a reduction is able to increase the packet delivery ratio by up to 70 percentage points. In contrast to this observation, **a reduction of the transmit power did not help to improve the packet delivery ratios significantly**. This is attributed to the high reference path loss and the small path loss exponent of the propagation environment. Despite the **introduction of fading channel effects the benefit of a reduced beacon generation rate**

is still noticably, although it is not as significant as in a non-fading environment.
On the contrary, the already small benefit of a reduced transmit power vanished completely. The reason for both observations is the fact that the negative impact of incoordination, and thereby the issue of a congested channel, becomes less important if the fading intensity of the channel increases.

In a last step, the characteristics of occuring packet collisions were analyzed, with the conclusion that the **majority of incoordinated packet transmissions arrives with a signal strength close to the background noise level**. Hence, interference is primarily generated by nodes located close to the border of the (deterministic) carrier sense range. It was further observed, that fading channel effects did not affect these characteristics in a fundamental way, i.e. the majority of all interfering packet transmissions still arrives with a signal strength close to the background noise level. The evaluated interference count profiles further showed that in most of the cases only one to three packets interfered at all.

In the beginning of this thesis, the question was raised whether a time- and frequency-selective channel has a significant impact on the performance of an inter-vehicle communication network based on IEEE 802.11p, in particular on the coordination of concurrent access by multiple nodes. According to the results presented in Section 4.5 and Section 5.3, fast-fading characteristics affect the reception and coordination performance noticeably. But, in comparison to previous work, **there is no fundamental difference between the results obtained with simulators that employ simplified physical layer and channel models, and the results obtained with a simulator as used in this thesis**. That does not imply that there is no difference, but the existing differences can easily be addressed through curve shifting if one is interested in the average performance only.

6
Avoidance of packet collisions in V2V communication networks

The characterization of packet collisions in Chapter 5 showed that the amount of packet collisions increases significantly once the load offered to the channel increases beyond a given threshold. Hence, a possible solution to avoid or at least reduce the probability of packet collisions could be an adaptation of the transmit power and the beaconing rate whenever the load is close to this threshold. While the adjustment of the beaconing rate leads to a lower update rate, a lower transmission power restricts the geographical area in which interference has a negative impact, increases the spatial reuse of the channel, and thus favors reception from vehicles in the close surrounding. The advantage of such a solution is the full compatibility with the IEEE 802.11p standard specification, hence no modifications on physical or medium access control layer are required. Alternatively, the CSMA-based medium access control can be adapted or even completely replaced by a fundamentally different coordination mechanism.

In this chapter, the two options are explored and discussed with respect to their effectiveness. First, Section 6.1 studies existing proposals in the field of congestion control for safety-related beaconing in vehicular networks from a control theory perspective. Afterwards, Section 6.2 surveys alternative MAC protocols and analyzes their advantages and disadvantages in comparison to the distributed coordination function in IEEE 802.11p. Concluding remarks and a brief summary is given in Section 6.3.

6.1   Congestion control

In the following, rate and transmit power based congestion control mechanisms that aim to limit the load generated solely by cooperative awareness messages are evaluated from a control theory perspective. Since the term "control" is taken literally in this work, existing proposals that are based on either a prioritization of safety messages or on a dropping of messages whenever internal transmission queues are congested, are not considered. The same argumentation applies to studies that aim to optimize message inter-reception times and tracking accuracies, or which adjust the transmission rate and power with respect to the current velocity. Hence, studies such as [XMKS04, ARP05, EGH+06, ZSC+07, RSK+10] are skipped in the following.

6.1.1   Control theory

The process of restricting the load on the wireless channel, and thereby reducing the number of packet collisions in the network, is fundamentally related to traditional control theory. In particular, since no central coordination entity is available and each node that contributes to congestion should help to reduce it, congestion control mechanisms belong to the distributed control discipline.

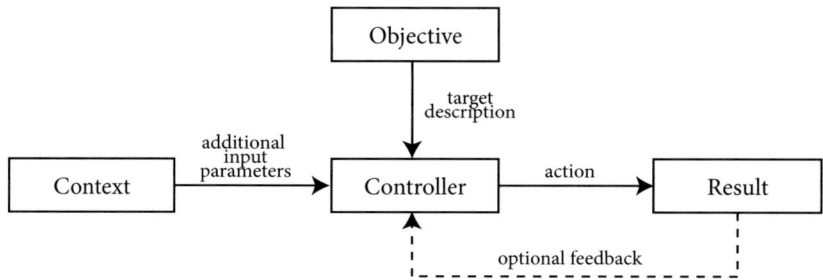

Figure 6.1: The structure of a generic control unit that aims to satisfy a given objective based on the context of the system and optional feedback about the result of its action.

Figure 6.1 illustrates the structure of a generic control unit: the core is the *controller* itself, which aims to keep the system close to a given *objective*. The controller typically receives additional input parameters that describe the *context* in which the system is currently in and takes actions that influence the state of the system in order to fulfill the given objective. Depending on the type of controller, optional feedback about the actual state of the system is provided to evaluate whether the taken action yielded the expected *result*.

With respect to congestion control, the objective is clearly a restriction of the channel load. The specific limit could be given in terms of the maximum amount of data that may be offered to the channel by neighboring nodes per unit of time, or as the maximum fraction of time during which the channel may be sensed busy. On the one hand, a limitation of the offered load, in the following termed *Beaconing Load*, is to be desired since it accounts for potential transmission overlaps and is therefore

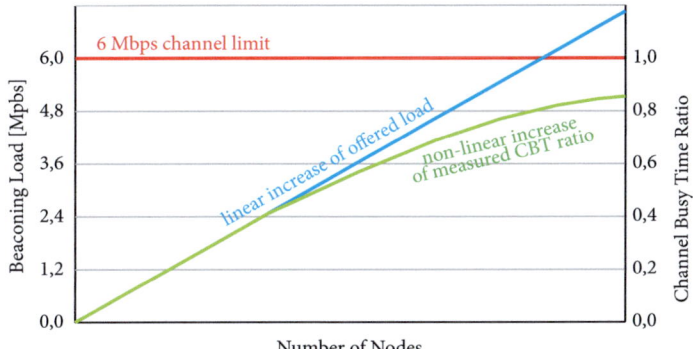

Figure 6.2: Illustration of the relationship between the offered load and the channel busy time ratio.

more accurate. However, the amount of data that is currently offered is difficult to measure by transceivers which simply can not determine whether there are currently one, two or more packets in the air. On the other hand, the fraction of time during which the channel is sensed busy, in the following termed *Channel Busy Time* (CBT) ratio, can easily be determined by a transceiver, yet with the drawback that the obtained measure does not match with the real congestion level if saturated network conditions are considered. This fundamental difference is illustrated in Figure 6.2 which plots both metrics for an increasing number of nodes. While the amount of data that is offered to the channel increases linearly with the number of nodes that contribute to congestion, the resulting channel busy time ratio continues to increase only slightly once a saturation point has been reached. Hence, the channel busy time ratio is not an optimal measure to describe the congestion that is present in high channel load situations.

From a control theory perspective, a controller that employs feedback is typically called *closed-loop controller*. In contrast to a closed-loop controller, a controller that does not make use of feedback is called *open-loop controller*. In general, the availability and usage of feedback is desired since it helps to increase the robustness, accuracy and effectiveness of a controller. If no feedback is used, the performance of a controller depends significantly on the underlying system model. Although the usage of feedback is therefore prefered, the provisioning of feedback may lead to additional communication overhead. As the impact of a vehicle's action, e.g. the reduction of the transmit power or beaconing rate, can not be be sensed by the vehicle itself, neighboring vehicles are the only source of feedback. Hence, such a feedback has to be communicated and introduces additional control overhead.

Detached from the terminology used in control theory, effective congestion control solutions have to master two aspects: *congestion detection* and *congestion control*. To detect a congestion in the network each node needs to monitor relevant status properties of the network, e.g. the number of neighboring vehicles or the conges-

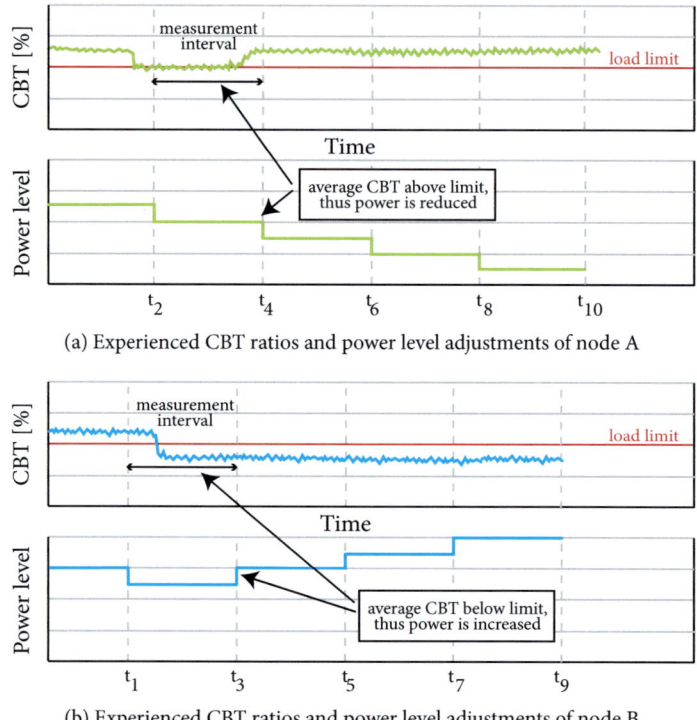

(a) Experienced CBT ratios and power level adjustments of node A

(b) Experienced CBT ratios and power level adjustments of node B

Figure 6.3: Illustration of what can go wrong if congestion control is performed in a non-cooperative or uncoordinated manner: if no feedback about the own congestion measurement is given, or no mutual knowledge about each others transmit parameters is available, situations can occur in which wrong actions are taken. In the above example, node A further decreases its transmit power level and B does the opposite, although it should be the other way round.

tion level itself. If these properties indicate a congestion, a profound action has to be derived by each node. In the given context, it is generally desired that all nodes that contribute to a congestion of the network help to reduce it, and that nodes that are contributing most to the congestion reduce their amount of offered data prior to nodes that already have a small contribution. Within the research community, these two aspects are commonly referred to as the principles of *participation* and *fairness*. To ensure that these principles are implemented, feedback among nodes is inevitable. What can happen if no feedback is employed is illustrated in Figure 6.3 which plots the measured CBT ratios and the transmit power adjustments over time out of the perspective of two nodes A and B that use only locally available information[1]. Initially,

---

[1] Without loss of generality, the following examples neglects the actions taken by other nodes in the network to ease comprehensibility.

both nodes measure CBT ratios greater than the desired load limit, whereas node A uses a slightly lower power level than node B. At the end of the first measurement interval of node B, i.e. at t_1, node B reduces its power level by one step since the average CBT ratio (w.r.t. the measurement interval) is above the limit. Assuming that this reduction then leads to the fact that node B does not affect the load experienced by node A anymore, the result of this action is a drop of the measured CBT ratio at node A, as shown in Figure 6.3a slightly before t_2. However, since the average CBT ratio in the first measurement period of node A is still greater than the load limit, node A also decreases its power level by one step at t_2. If this reduction now also leads to the fact that the congestion level at node B is not affected by node A anymore, the CBT ratio at B decreases as well, cf. Figure 6.3b slightly after t_1. At t_3, node B then checks the average CBT ratio again, and since it is now below the desired load limit, node B increases the power level again. Consequently, node A is affected by node B again and observes an increase in the measured CBT ratio. The significance of this increase is evaluated by node A at the end of its second measurement interval, i.e. at t_4. Since the average CBT ratio during the measurement interval still exceeds the load limit, node A decreases its transmit power level. In the following, node A continues to consider congested channel conditions and decreases its transmit power even further. In contrast to node A, node B continues to measure an average CBT ratio below the load limit, considers the channel to be free, and continues to increase its power level. By looking back at the example above, two fundamental issues can be identified:

1. Both nodes have a different perspective on the congestion level in the network,

   (a) with respect to the geographic location, and

   (b) with respect to the period of time during which the congestion level was measured.

2. The actions that are taken by both nodes are not coordinated,

   (a) neither w.r.t. the direction of the transmit power adjustment,

   (b) nor w.r.t. the time at which the actions are taken.

These issue become even more significant if a scenario with two approaching groups of nodes is considered. In case that both groups experience significantly different congestion conditions, the objective should be that the initially different transmission parameters used in both groups converge to a common value the closer they get to each other. Without a solution to the above issues, this objective is difficult to achieve in a controlled way. In the following, we refer to the above issues using the terms *improper congestion detection* and *incoordinated reaction policy*.

The first issue can obviously be avoided if a closed-loop controller that considers not only the local congestion level, but also the congestion level of neighboring nodes is employed. For instance, if node B would have known that node A experiences congested channel conditions, it could have acted differently. A synchronization of the measurement periods would further improve the cooperative detection of congested channel conditions. In addition to a feedback about channel congestion states, the second issue requires feedback about the current transmit power settings used by neighboring nodes, and a strict decoupling of the measurement period from the point in time at which adjustments are performed. In particular, it has to be guaranteed that every node in the network had the chance to react to a given congestion level before further reactions may be carried out by individual nodes. Alternatively, a hysteresis or the principle of additive increase, multiplicative decrease (AIMD) can be used to favor power level reductions over power level increases. Depending on the selected approach and its implementation (or parametrization), the intensity of the oscillation and the reaction time may vary. Please note that similar considerations apply if congestion control based on beaconing rate adaptation is employed.

In the following sections, congestion control methods that have been proposed in the past are surveyed, and evaluated with respect to the structure of a generic controller. Further, existing solutions are analyzed with respect to the principles of participation and fairness, as well as with respect to the two fundamental issues described avove: *improper congestion detection* and *incoordinated reaction policy*. To differentiate between solutions that are inherently vulnerable to oscillation problems, and solutions that are not, all methods are further classified into *proactive* and *reactive control* protocols.

6.1.2   Proactive control

Torrent-Moreno et al. were among the first to work on a solution that limits the load generated by cooperative awareness messages. Initially, their solution was completely centralized and aimed to determine a transmission power assignment under which the congestion level at each node stays below a so called *Maximum Beaconing Load* (MBL) limit [TMSH05]. Their idea is based on the following consideration: under the assumption that channel conditions are known, the usage of a fixed packet size, fixed beaconing rate and equal transmission powers for all nodes, the sum of packets that would lead to a MAC busy state can be calculated for each individual node. Through an estimation of this sum (i.e. the amount of load that is being offered to each node) for all possible power levels, it is then possible to determine the maximum power level that can be used by all nodes without violating the desired load limit. In a follow-up work, Torrent-Moreno et al. presented a distributed version of their algorithm called *Distributed Fair Power Adjustment for Vehicular Environments* (D-FPAV) that can be implemented in a decentralized network [TMSH06]. In order to maintain an effective control, each node has to broadcast a list of all known neighbors every now and then, for instance once per second. This kind of feedback is required to assist the fundamental load estimation process. If this feedback would not be provided, the estimation of the load experienced by a node located close to the border of the own communication range may be wrong, since the contribution by nodes that are located outside the own communication range (and therefore unknown) is then not considered. This issue gains importance whenever non-uniform node distributions are considered.

Obviously, the dissemination of neighbor tables that list all known nodes creates a significant overhead. As has been shown by Mittag et al. in [MSEK$^+$08], this overhead can be as much as 40 % of the load that is generated by cooperative awareness messages themselves. In order to address this issue at least slightly, Torrent-Moreno et al. relaxed the neighbor table exchange such that only the subset of nodes located close to oneself is included in the disseminated neighbor table [TMSH09]. A further reduction of the communication overhead was achieved by Mittag et al. in [MSEK$^+$08] through the exchange and usage of node density measurements instead of individual node positions. Since the employed histograms describe the vehicle density in the surrounding of each vehicle and are therefore more compact than a list of all neighbors, the overhead could be reduced from 40% down to less than 1 %.

A proactive control algorithm that adjusts the transmission power, beaconing rate, or both, is presented by Baldessari et al. in [BSL$^+$10]. Their solution takes the CBT ratio $CBT_j(t_{i-1}, t_i)$ observed by a node j during the time interval $[t_{i-1}, t_i)$ and the average beaconing rate r_{avg} (used by neighboring nodes) as an indicator of the number of vehicles $N_j(t_{i-1}, t_i)$ that affected the congestion level at node j. In particular, $N_j(t_{i-1}, t_i)$ is computed as follows:

$$N_j(t_{i-1}, t_i) = \frac{CBT_j(t_{i-1}, t_i)}{r_{avg}} \cdot \frac{C}{s} - 1 \qquad (6.1)$$

whereas C is the capacity of the channel and s the size of a single packet. This is a valid approximation if uniform transmission power levels, uniform channel conditions and a uniform node distribution is considered. Assuming that this is the case, their rate only control then determines the beaconing rate $r_j(t_i, t_{i+1})$ that shall be applied to subsequent transmissions as follows:

$$r_j(t_i, t_{i+1}) = \frac{CBT_{th}}{N_j(t_{i-1}, t_i) + 1} \cdot \frac{C}{s} \qquad (6.2)$$

whereas CBT_{th} is the CBT ratio limit, C, s, and $N_j(t_{i-1}, t_i)$ as described or defined before. While this approach works as long as uniform channel conditions and node distributions are considered, it breaks in non-uniform scenarios due to a fundamental issue in the design of the control algorithm: the algorithm uses the locally observed CBT ratio to derive the beaconing rate for future packet transmissions, despite the fact that only neighboring nodes have the potential to influence the own CBT ratio. To correct this issue, at least the computed $r_j(t_i, t_{i+1})$ needs to be fed back (as a suggestion) to neighboring nodes. Since the same issues apply also to the transmit power and the combined power-rate control algorithm, further explanations are skipped.

In comparison to reactive control approaches, proactive control mechanisms are not vulnerable to oscillation issues and come with the benefit of being able to adapt the transmission parameters prior to an excess of a given load limit. Hence, they are able to literally avoid congested channel conditions. However, proactive approaches come with one major drawback: in order to estimate the expected load generated by neighboring vehicles, such approaches require a communication model that maps individual transmission power levels to deterministic carrier sense ranges.

Unfortunately, this mapping is reasonable only as long as it reflects the average propagation conditions of the wireless channel. Thus, propagation conditions should be either dynamically estimated as nodes move, which is very difficult to do in a practical scenario, or they should be statistically estimated to build specific profiles for different environments, e.g., urban and highway.

6.1.3   Reactive control

In the beginning of 2008, Khorakhun et al. presented a CBT-based congestion control mechanism that uses either the transmit power or the beaconing rate to control the load in the network [KBR08]. In their basic mode of operation each node continuously increases or decreases the transmission power (or beacon generation rate) by one step, depending on whether the local CBT ratio obtained during the previous measurement period was below or above a pre-defined threshold. As discussed in Section 6.1.1, this proposal does not lead to a stable and fair controller. With the objective to address this issue, Khorakhun et al. suggested to employ feedback w.r.t. measured CBT ratios, used transmit powers and employed beacon generation rates, and to allow an increase of the power (or rate) only if the locally used value is below the average power (or rate) configuration used by neighboring nodes. However, this change is not sufficient to ensure stable operation in all situations, in particular due to the fact that actions are not coordinated w.r.t. time.

The work by Kohorakhun et al. has been continued and improved by two follow-up proposals [BKR09, BKR10]. Similar to their proposal in 2008, the updated algorithm is based on an exchange of the locally measured CBT ratio, and an exchange of the locally used transmit power (or rate). However, the previous lack of a coordination action plan and time schedule is solved by incooporating a hysteresis, i.e. the usage of two different CBT thresholds for increase and decrease operations, as well as a synchronization of measurement intervals among neighboring nodes.

Another reactive congestion control approach was recently proposed by Huang et al. in [HFSK10], where the authors adaptively change both beacon generation rate and transmission power with the goal of reducing channel congestion, and consequently improving a vehicle's ability to accurately track the position of surrounding vehicles. Whereas the transmission rate is adjusted independently of the congestion level, but such that the position tracking error stays within a given limit, transmission power control is applied with respect to the locally observed CBT ratio. However, since only locally available information (i.e., direct observations) is used, the issue of improper congestion detection is not addressed at all.

An adoption of the principles employed by the Transmission Control Protocol (TCP) is proposed by He et al. in [HCCC10]. Based on an exchange of locally obtained CBT ratios, the network is considered to be congested if at least one neighboring node indicates a congestion. In analogy to previous proposals, the beaconing rate is then increased stepwise as long as no congestion is present. But, as soon as a congestion of the channel is detected, the rate is set back to its initial (e.g. lowest) value and increased stepwise again until a rate value equivalent to 50 % of the rate at which congestion was observed is reached. Afterwards, a congestion avoidance is initiated by increasing the time period between further subsequent rate increments. Despite the fact that the proposed controller seems to solve all fundamental issues, it is probably suboptimal with respect to convergence time.

The issue of stability and convergence time of rate control based congestion control has been studied by Kenney et al. in [KBR11]. Under the assumption that no hidden terminals are present, and that each node knows which common maximum beaconing rate still adheres to a given load limit, the authors propose a controller that is optimal with respect to stability and convergence time. It further solves all fundamental control issues described in Section 6.1.1 as long as the assumptions are met. However, perfect knowledge is difficult to provide in distributed systems, and hidden terminals have to be expected. Hence, the fundamental challenges within a distributed system are not addressed.

In [TJC+11] Tielert et al. present a congestion control mechanism called *PULSAR* which is based on CBT measurements and an adaptation of the beaconing rate. Their approach employs fixed length measurement intervals of 250 ms duration during which the current congestion level is determined. To reduce measurement noise, a first-order digital low-pass filter is employed in addition. Further, the measurement periods are synchronized using GPS in order to ensure that all nodes derive their action with respect to the same point in time. With respect to congestion detection, PULSAR provides feedback of the current congestion level over 2-hops. Based on the maximum congestion level that is observed either locally or by a neighboring node, the rate is then either increased or decreased using the principle of additive increase and multiplicative decrease.

6.1.4 Standardization

In Europe, congestion control in vehicular communications is considered to be a building block and seen as mandatory in order to guarantee a reliable communication performance for safety-related applications. This was acknowledged by the Car-2-Car Communication Consortium (C2C-CC) as early as in 2009 through the establishment of a task force on transmit power control that was initiated by the author of this thesis. The results from this task force have helped to persuade the European Commission to establish a Specialist Task Force (STF) on the configuration and validation of decentralized congestion control methods for Intelligent Transportation Systems (ITS) within the European Telecommunications Standard Institute (ETSI). From March 2010 until October 2010, the STF with its six experts from industry and the research community has been working on a technical specification for a standardized congestion control to be used by ITS. The result of their work lead to the ETSI Technical Specification 102 687 which was approved in the beginning of 2011.

The ETSI specification defines a decentralized congestion control framework on physical and medium access layer that allows to implement most of the solutions discussed in the previous sections. Since the specification focuses only on information available on these two layers, the included mechanisms do not incorporate aspects such as the geographic position of individual nodes or distances between nodes. Such additional information will be introduced on network layer, and expected to be used by congestion control mechanisms that reside on network layer. Out of this reason, the mandatory basic control algorithm defined by TS 102 687 is based on an open-loop controller that uses only locally available information about channel congestion. In addition, an enhanced but optional control algorithm that makes use of feedback provided by neighboring nodes, e.g. their observed congestion level and their currently used transmit power or beaconing rate, is included. Both approaches will use the channel busy time metric to define the congestion limit, since it can be implemented by the hardware.

A standardization of congestion control has not yet started in the United States. However, the Vehicle-to-Vehicle Interoperability (V2VI) project that is being carried out by the U.S. Department of Transportation (DoT) is currently implementing, testing and evaluating several congestion control protocols, i.e. the solutions proposed by Kenney et al. and Tielert et al. The results of this effort are envisioned to lead towards a standardization of congestion control within the Vehicle Safety Communications Consortium (VSCC) of the Crash Avoidance Metrics Partnership (CAMP).

6.2   Alternative MAC layer protocols

Various medium access control approaches were proposed, analyzed, modified and extended for use in V2V communication networks. This section presents a survey on alternative MAC approaches, describes their basic ideas and discusses their advantages and respective disadvantages over CSMA with respect to an inter-vehicle communication scenario. Please note that the following survey is based on portions of the work already presented in [MSEK+10].

6.2.1   Time division multiple access based approaches

With time-division multiple access (TDMA), the available frequency band is slotted in time. Ideally, each time slot is used by a single sender only to avoid packet collisions. In ad hoc networks, however, the lack of centralized control leads to challenges of how to assign time slots to senders, of how to perform slot synchronization and of how to deal with hidden and exposed nodes.

In [CRW+81] the Reservation-ALOHA (R-ALOHA) protocol was proposed to improve the throughput of the purely contention based protocol slotted ALOHA. Though it was initially developed for satellite communication, it has been extended and analyzed by [MR88, ZHW91, LSP95, MHRY05] for the use in inter-vehicle communication or distributed packet radio networks in general.

In R-ALOHA, the channel is divided into frames, and frames themselves are subdivided into N consecutive slots. In addition R-ALOHA requires sufficiently large dimensioned time slots to cover the transmission of a single data packet and to dominate the maximum channel propagation delay. By using a simple sensing, each station should be able to determine whether a slot is *unused* or *used*. A slot is declared unused if no packet has been transmitted or if a collision has been detected. Contrary, a slot is declared used if exactly one packet was transmitted in this slot and was successfully received. Consequently, if a station wants to transmit a packet, it randomly selects an unused slot and contends for it, as it would do in slotted ALOHA. If the initial transmission attempt in the unused slot succeeded, i.e. no other station selected the same slot, the station will become the owner of the slot and can use it as long as needed. However, in case a collision with another station occurred, a different random unused slot will be probed during the next frame.

[MR88] extended R-ALOHA to account for the mobility of stations in vehicular environments. They propose the Concurrent Slot Assignment Protocol (CSAP) for traffic information exchange to take care of the hidden terminal problem and the fact that stations can not detect collisions they are involved in. They divide each frame into N data slots and N collision slots, whereas data slot i corresponds to collision slot i. A station which is currently the owner of a slot i uses collision slot i to broadcast its perspective, as a bitmap vector, on the reservation status of all other slots. Since every station that owns a slot is broadcasting such a bitmap vector, each station is able to merge the vectors and obtain a slot assignment in the 2-hop neighborhood. The authors state that CSAP is suited for limited mobility in the system and suggest to use a purely contention based solution if mobility is unlimited.

Based on CSAP, [ZHW91] propose a similar approach called DCAP, which further divides the channel according to the movement direction of vehicles and includes a fast channel handover in case of increasing co-channel interference. Due to the mobility it can happen that an initially unused slot is interfered by other stations. If packet loss ratio increases above a specific threshold, the station initiates a handover request and switches to the new logical channel once it has been established. An analysis and simulation of the protocol states that handovers are performed very quickly and collision probabilities are significantly small.

The performance of R-ALOHA for inter-vehicle communications has been evaluated using a discrete Markov chain by Liu et al. in [LSP95] and Ma et al. in [MHRY05]. [LSP95] use a metric called *deadline failure probability* (DFP) to describe the reliability of R-ALOHA. They state that the probability of not receiving a status update from a station within a specific time, e.g. within the next 4 frames, decreases with an increasing number of stations or error rates. [MHRY05] investigate also the impact of multipath and shadowing, including the near-far and capture effects, on the performance of R-ALOHA. They state that capturing can significantly improve the stability of R-ALOHA.

The hybrid approach of [LHSR01], which uses TDMA and CDMA, is a carry on of the DCAP proposal by [ZHW91]. Compared to DCAP they do not only distinguish between used and unused slots, but also between slots that cannot be used due to an existing reservation and slots that cannot be used due to interference. This distinction is used to implicitly signal negative acknowledgements within the slot assignment bitmap vector. For instance, in the case a vehicle can not decode a packet successfully, it will indicate this fact by tagging the slots as being interfered and thereby telling the sender that it did not receive the packet.

Recently, [BUSB09] evaluated the ability of Self-Organizing TDMA (STDMA) to support inter-vehicle communication. Similar to the proposals described above STDMA applies the principle of R-ALOHA, but, since it has been developed and standardized for the automatic identification system (AIS) for communication between ships and is part of the ITU-R Recommendation M.1371-1 [[ITU98]], with the focus on broadcast communication. In AIS, each ship transmits periodic heartbeat messages, which for instance contain information about its current position and heading, to establish a similar mutual awareness as envisioned by inter-vehicle communication. To support this objective, STDMA divides time into frames with fixed duration and frames themselves further into equally sized slots. However, no global frame synchronization is required and only time slots have to be aligned. Based on this definition, each ship performs the following steps to determine the time slots within a frame for the transmission of its heartbeat messages: (i) directly after joining the network, each ship monitors the channel for the duration of at least one frame to determine the current reservation and usage of slots; (ii) given the heartbeat rate r per frame, each ship then selects r "random" slots per frame, such that the slots are equally distributed in time and, if possible, unused. If there are no unused slots available, slots which are used by the ship located furthest away will be selected; (iii) each reserved slot is used during the following 3 to 8 frames and has to be reselected afterwards using the same reservation scheme again. According to Bilstrup et al. STDMA is able to support safety-related inter-vehicle communication if no channel fading is considered. However, the channel characteristics of the allocated frequency spectrum for inter-vehicle communication will be subject to severe fading and whether STDMA remains robust or not in such an environment is an open question.

At the time of writing, a specialist task force of the European Telecommunications Standard Institute (ETSI) studies the applicability of STDMA in vehicular environments, with the objective to determine whether STDMA outperforms CSMA and whether it should be considered in a second generation of wireless communication technology for ITS. In comparison to CSMA, STDMA introduces controlled collisions if the network is saturated and the capacity of the channel is approached or even exceeded. As a result, packet transmissions from close distances are favored over transmissions from distances further away — without the need to perform any distributed congestion control. Whether this advantage can be exploited sufficiently well in a fast-fading channel environment is still under discussion within the research community. Further, if mobility and frequent topology changes are considered, the reservation of slots may also lead to a sequence of repeated packet collisions simply due to the fact that two nodes that initially do not interfer with each other may enter each others communication (or interference) range. The benefit of slot reservation is then converted into a significant drawback. The usage of a slot-based scheme also limits the flexibility with respect to the usage of different packet sizes, since each potential message needs to fit into one time slot. If varying packet sizes have to be supported, a TDMA based approach will be less bandwidth efficient.

6.2.2 Space division multiple access based approaches

With space-division multiple access (SDMA), access to the medium is controlled dependent on the current location of a vehicle. Instead of a distributed assignment of spreading codes or time slots among vehicles, the specific time-slot, the to be used frequency or spreading code of a transmission is derived from the geographical position of a vehicle. Of course such a scheme relies on the availability of user location information such as provided by GPS or magnetic positioning systems. Note, that the accuracy of the location information provided by GPS or magnetic positioning systems might not be sufficient to enable an effective SDMA-based medium access control scheme.

[BV01] introduced the first SDMA-based system model in which the geographical space and the available bandwidth are partitioned into N divisions, for instance equally sized cells for space division and N TDMA-, CDMA- or FDMA-channels for bandwidth division. By using a 1:1 map between the space and bandwidth divisions and by obtaining its current location on the road, a vehicle is then able to determine its channel assignment. They claim to provide delay-bounded access, since vehicles are mobile and changing their location over time. Further, the bandwidth assignment is fair as long as channels are of equal size. However, this scheme is static and inefficient. Since their model requires a space partitioning in which only one vehicle per division is allowed, a great amount of channels is left unused if not all divisions are occupied. To account this issue, the authors propose to allow more than one vehicle per space division and use a contention-based scheme within a space division.

A similar idea has been published by [KGMRR+03]. Their Location-based Channel Access (LCA) protocol is very similar to the proposal of [BV01] in the sense that space is divided into cells and mapped to channels. They also discuss the tradeoff between cell size, the corresponding time for which a cell-to-channel mapping can be used and the efficiency in case of a small number of vehicles. They conclude that it is necessary to allow more than one vehicle per cell and use a CSMA/CA or approach inside each cell.

6.2.3 Code division multiple access based approaches

In a code-divison multiple access (CDMA) based system, concurrent access to the wireless medium is provided by the usage of different spreading codes among several senders. In principle, each sender multiplies its data signal with a spreading code before transmitting the signal to the wireless channel, thereby increasing the transmitted signal bandwidth. In order to successfully decode the signal, a receiver has to perform the reverse process and 'divide' the received signal by the spreading code. With this technique, it is possible to decode multiple incoming transmissions simultaneously, given that the individual streams arrive with equal signal strengths. In a distributed CDMA system, the challenging task is then (i) how to assign spreading codes to stations, such that codes are not used by two senders at the same time, and (ii) how to equalize the received signal strengths to mitigate the well known near-far problem.

A promising study that considered CDMA for inter-vehicle communication has been published by [NH98]. They propose a multicode sense (MCS)/CDMA system in which each vehicle senses the currently used spreading codes in the network in order to determine unused codes. For this to work, they assume the usage of equal transmission powers by all vehicles and the capability to demodulate all possible spreading codes in parallel. The challenge of equalizing the received powers is then simply ignored by arguing that low received signal strengths will correspond to packets from far distances and high signal strengths will correspond to packets from close distances. Since packets originated from close distances are of greater importance, this may be tolerated.

In [LHSR01] the adoption of UTRA-TDD was investigated regarding its suitability for vehicle-to-vehicle communications. UTRA-TDD incorporates elements of code-division multiple access (CDMA) and of time-division multiple access (TDMA). It was observed that transmit power control represents a challenging problem when applying CDMA in ad hoc networks due to the variety of senders and receivers and their respective locations. The authors of [LHSR01] concluded that the different codes can not be used for multiple access but could allow a single sender to transmit independently to various receivers simultaneously. However, for one-hop broadcast communication, this feature might be of less importance, although it could be used to make transmissions robust against noise and interferences.

6.3 Conclusions

In this chapter, several methods that aim to avoid packet collisions have been analyzed and discussed. First, the challenge of decentralized congestion control in inter-vehicle communication networks was studied from the perspective of distributed control theory. The collected observations in this first step lead to the **development of critical design requirements that need to be met by any congestion control algorithm that intends to be effective and robust**. In principle, those requirements belong to the disciplines termed **cooperative detection of** and **cooperative reaction to congestion in the network**. Despite the impression that the established design requirements are more or less intuitive, the subsequent survey of recently proposed distributed congestion control algorithms showed that this is not the case: **a majority of the existing work does not fulfill all of the establishes requirements**, no matter whether a saturation of the network is approached through an adaptation of the transmit power or the beacon generation rate. However, it is crucial to implement all requirements since the distributed control issue is very sensitive to oscillations.

A lack of this awareness could also be noticed in the respective standardization bodies and consortia. For instance, prior to the work presented in this thesis, neither the Car-2-Car Communication Consortium (C2C-CC) nor the European Telecommunications Standard Institute (ETSI) acknowledged the necessity of cooperative congestion control. Eventually, **the results of this work have helped to establish a C2C-CC task force on transmit power control, which in turn helped to persuade the European Commission to fund an ETSI specialist task force (STF) on the con-**

figuration and validation of decentralized congestion control methods. Furthermore, the analysis and design requirements presented in this chapter have been contributed to the STF and can be considered to be one of the reasons why the relevance and importance of cooperative congestion control is today recognized by the industry and research community.

As an alternative to distributed congestion control, various medium access control protocols have been studied with respect to the question whether they are able to avoid packet collisions much better than CSMA. Based on a qualitative assessment, **one alternative to IEEE 802.11p was identified as a potential replacement for the coordination of periodic broadcast messages: Self-Organizing TDMA.** Since the evaluation of a second MAC protocol is out of scope of this thesis, a quantitative assessment is skipped at this point. However, it should be pointed out that the MAC evaluation methodology presented in Section 5 is well suited to characterize the packet collision probability and coordination performance of STDMA in vehicular environments.

7

Repair of packet collisions in V2V communication networks

The characterization of packet collisions in Chapter 5 showed that the amount of packet collisions increases if the load offered to the channel increases. The previous chapter therefore analyzed and evaluated distributed congestion control methods which aim to reduce the load offered to the channel by adjusting either the transmission power or the beacon generation rate. In the following, a different approach is considered in order to deal with packet collisions: successive interference cancellation. From information theory it is known that two overlapping signals can be decoded and successfully received if they satisfy certain conditions with respect to their relative signal strength. In particular, if one signal is stronger than the other such that it can be decoded successfully by the receiver, an estimate of how it arrived at the receiver can be calculated (e.g. based on an estimation of the channel coefficients) and substracted from the cumulation of both signals and the background noise. The result is a "cleaned up" version of the weaker signal and the background noise. If the weaker signal is then sufficiently stronger than the background noise, it can also be decoded successfully. In the context of this thesis, the principle of successive interference cancellation is considered to be a mechanism that might be able to repair packet collisions instead of avoiding them. Whether these expectations are justified and whether successive interference cancellation can increase the capacity of an IEEE 802.11p based communication network is the focus of this chapter.

The rest of this chapter is structured as follows: first, Section 7.1 provides a brief overview on the history of successive interference cancellation and surveys existing work in which interference cancellation was used to improve the performance of IEEE 802.11 based networks. Section 7.2 then describes the setup of the simulation experiments which are used to determine the maximum benefit that can be achieved using successive interference cancellation. The results of these simulations are afterwards presented and discussed in Section 7.3. A summary and conclusion is given in Section 7.4.

7.1 Related work

Medium access control protocols usually aim to isolate transmissions of different users, either in space, frequency, time or code domain. However, in a distributed system it is nearly impossible to guarantee such an isolation, due to hidden terminals and fading channel conditions. In case of random access, time division or code division multiple access, it is therefore possible that transmissions of two or more stations overlap in time and frequency, i.e. they interfere with each other. This effect is commonly called *multiple access interference* (MAI) and has a negative impact on the reception performance in terms of bit error rate and successful packet error rate.

In the context of direct sequence code division multiple access (DS-CDMA), *multi-user detection* is a widely used technique to encounter the negative impact of MAI [Vit95, Ver98]. In the case of orthogonal codes, a simple (or conventional) matched filter detector is sufficient to decode each users signal: the cumulative signal of all users is fed into N matched filters, each of which tries to correlate the signal with a fixed code sequence. Since all codes are orthogonal to each other, the performance of each filter is only affected by the noise component of the channel, i.e. each filter has to distinguish between the noise $n(t)$ and the signal $s_i(t)$ that has been generated by a station using code i. If however code orthogonality is not given, a conventional matched filter detector will treat the multiple access interference as noise and therefore introduce a non-zero probability of bit errors (even if there would not be any noise at all). Hence, an optimal receiver should consider the distortions that are introduced by multiple users, and cancel out the MAI contributions during the decoding process, i.e. before matching the signal against a fixed code sequence [Ver86].

Obviously, the performance of an interference cancellation based multi-user detection mechanism depends on the performance of the employed sequence (or channel) estimator. For instance, Verdu et al. could show that a maximum likelihood sequence estimator (MLSE) achieves optimality for an additive white gaussian noise channel [Ver86]. As an alternative to interference cancellation based multi-user detection, several approaches that apply linear detection have been proposed. Lupas et al. for instance proposed to multiply the matched filter outputs by the inverse of the cross-correlation matrix instead of cancelling out the interference directly [LV89, LV90]. Their approach has been further optimized by Zheng et al. [ZB95, ZF97]. Another alternative that models the multiple access interference as colored noise has been proposed by Monk et al. for decentralized linear detectors [MDMH94]. The reader who wishes to learn more details on interference cancellation in CDMA based communication systems is referred to the surveys and overviews given in [Oja97, Pap00].

More recently, Halperin et al. proposed to employ interference cancellation in IEEE 802.11 based wireless LANs to improve the capacity of the channel and to possibly simplify higher layer protocols [Hal07]. Their idea is based on the observation that concurrent transmissions do not necesarily lead to reception failures of all frames involved. As experimental studies have shown, frames can successfully be received even if the transceiver is already decoding a different but weaker frame [LKL+07]. This phenomenon is called *capture effect* and usually leads to a reception failure of the weaker packet. In order to recover the loss of the weaker frame, Halperin et al. make use of successive interference cancellation: after a successful decoding of the captured packet, the receiver reconstructs the signal of the packet (based on channel estimation) and substracts it from the cumulative signal; afterwards, the receiver attempts to decode the weaker signal by using the "cleaned up" version of the cumulative signal. Apparently, the performance is again dependent on the accuracy of the channel estimation technique used. Yet, according to several studies significant benefits are achievable. For instance Moscibodra et al. showed that throughput gains of up to 2 x the theoretical single-transmitter limit and nearly 3 x over traditional CSMA can be achieved [MWW06].

In contrast to the work cited above, safety-related inter-vehicle communication networks primarily implement a one-to-many addressing scheme. For instance, it is desired that the own message is received by as many neighbors as possible. This is not the case in the work of Moscibodra et al. which assumes that only unicast flows are present in the network. As a result, a throughput improvement can already be achieved if a transmission schedule is found that "creates" packet transmission constellations under which the conditions for a successful interference cancellation are met and under which as many relevant packets as possible are received by each network node. Whether similar performance gains can be achieved if every node is potentially interested in every single packet is not obvious.

7.2 Experiment setup

The evaluation of the benefit of successive interference cancellation is based on the same simulation scenarios and parameters that were already used in Chapter 5, their description is therefore skipped in this section. Further, instead of simply implementing a successive interference algorithm and then finding out how much it brings in the considered scenario, an upper limit of the number of packets that can be recovered using successive interference cancellation is determined. This upper limit can easily be obtained with te help of the network simulator, which posseses the perfect knowledge about each single transmission, how the corresponding signals look like, and how the signals arrived at the receiver after the channel has altered them. Hence, an evaluation of each packet's "circumstances" can be performed during each simulation run, which in turn allows to identify all packets that can be repaired if a perfect interference cancellation is applied. For instance, it is easily possible to perform a "what if" analysis: would a packet have been decoded successfully if one of the interfering packets had not been present? This approach leads to a performance metric termed *Maximum Packet Recovery Ratio* in the following.

Definition 7.1 (Maximum Packet Recovery Ratio, MPRR) *The maximum packet recovery ratio describes the probability at which a packet p can be recovered using the principle of successive interference cancellation. A packet p is considered to be recoverable, only if*

1. *it has not been received successfully*

2. *the reception failed due to an overlap with a second packet q,*

3. *the overlapping packet q was successfully received, and*

4. *packet p can be decoded successfully in the absence of q.*

Following the characterization of packet collisions in Chapter 5, the maximum packet recovery ratio is evaluated with respect to the distance between sender and receiver again.

7.3 Results

In the following, the observed benefit of successive interference cancellation is illustrated using two different vehicle densities, three different beaconing rates, three different channel setups, and a packet size of 400 bytes. Figure 7.1(a) and Figure 7.1(b) start with the results of the distance decaying path loss only setup, and show that only up to 1 % of all transmitted packets qualify for a "recovery" using successive interference cancellation. This is a quite disappointing result, in particular if compared to the significant throughput gains that have been reported by Moscibodra et al. in [MWW06] for unicast oriented communications. A significantly increased benefit can also not be observed if a fading of the channel is assumed. Despite the observation that an increase is noticable, as depicted by Figure 7.1(c) and Figure 7.1(d) for a Log-Normal shadowing configuration, the overall benefit remains smaller than 2 %. The same applies to the results obtained within a Rayleigh fading channel, cf. Figure 7.1(e) and Figure 7.1(f). According to the interference intensity profiles presented in Section 5.3.2, the very small benefit is a direct result of the carrier sense mechanism used by IEEE 802.11p which aims to prevent incoordinated packet transmissions from areas that are too close to the transmitter. While this is clearly the objective of the MAC layer, it does not help to increase the probability that two packets arrive at a receiver with a signal strength that is great enough in order to be decodable.

The obvious question arises: can the deployed MAC protocol be modified such that the benefit of successive interference cancellation is increased in an inter-vehicle communication scenario? In particular, would such a modification help to achieve the same performance gains that have been reported by previous work? The answer is given by a comparison of the considered scenarios. In a safety-oriented inter-vehicle communications setup, one generally aims to deliver as many packets to as many neighboring vehicles as possible. Hence, each neighbor is considered to be potentially interested in the transmitted packet and it is more or less impossible to optimize the transmission parameters for a single receiver without sacrificing the performance at another. On the contrary, nodes in the scenarios considered by previous

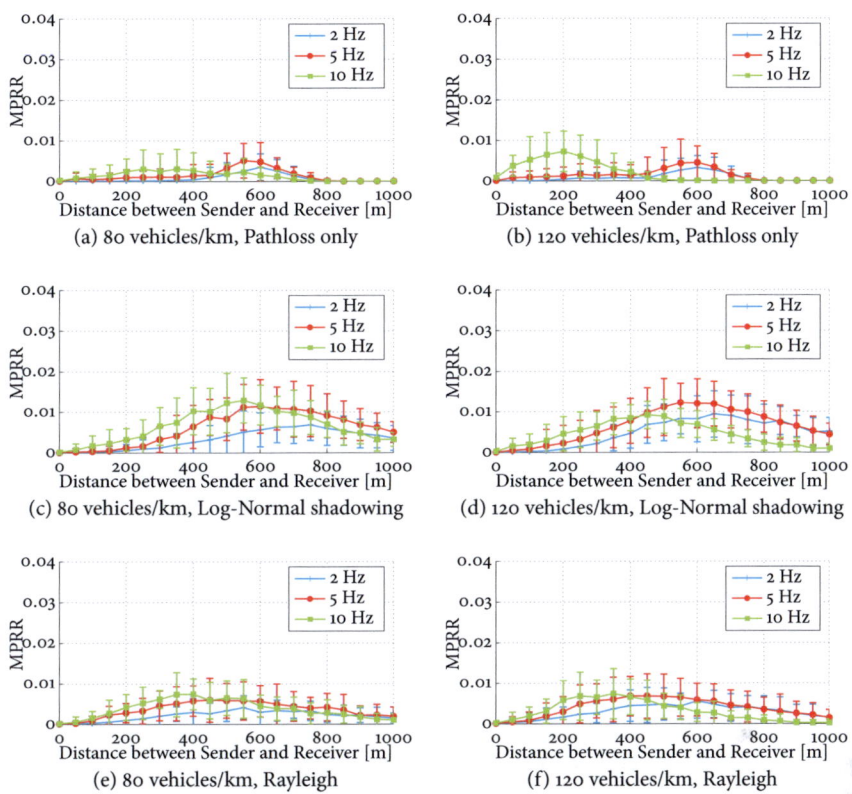

(a) 80 vehicles/km, Pathloss only

(b) 120 vehicles/km, Pathloss only

(c) 80 vehicles/km, Log-Normal shadowing

(d) 120 vehicles/km, Log-Normal shadowing

(e) 80 vehicles/km, Rayleigh

(f) 120 vehicles/km, Rayleigh

Figure 7.1: Illustration of the observed maximum packet recovery ratio with respect to the distance between sender and receiver. On the left side: a setup with 80 vehicles/km. On the right side: a setup with 120 vehicles/km. Both setups further used a 20 dBm transmit power and 400 bytes packets.

work aim (from the perspective of a single node) to transmit as many packets as possible to one single node. Hence, a packet is targeted at one neighboring node only, not at all. As a result, it is much more easy to find "successive interference cancellation friendly" network topologies and data flows in such unicast oriented networks. Most importantly, the transmit power can be tuned individually on a per node basis such that the conditions that allow a successful application of successive interference cancellation at a receiving node are met often enough. Additional support is given by the small amount of contending nodes that generate continuous bursts of data traffic. This leads to regular packet collisions by nodes that relate to each other perfectly with respect to their distance to the receiver and therefore also with respect to the received signal strength of their transmitted packets. If a safety-oriented beaconing in an inter-vehicle communication network is considered, all the above characteristics do not exist: (i) instead of only a few nodes, the network consists of up to 100 or 200 nodes that are within each others carrier sensing and communication range; (ii) it is difficult (if not impossible) to tune the transmit power of all nodes such that the required received signal strength relationship between two overlapping packets is fulfilled equally well at all receivers. In fact, while the adjustment may improve the benefit of successive interference cancellation at one receiver, it might introduce reception errors at other receivers that did not occur prior to the adjustment; (iii) instead of a continuous generation of data packets, each node is generating data packets only a few times per second, hence even if a transmit constellation occurs that allows to apply successive interference cancellation, it is not very likely to exploit this constellation in the next packet transmission again.

According to the obtained simulation results and the above discussion, it is concluded that successive interference cancellation can be applied in inter-vehicle communication networks, but only with a marginal benefit in terms of an increased packet delivery ratio. Since the observed recovery ratios represent an upper bound that assumes a perfect cancellation of the stronger signal, the performance of a practical successive interference algorithm is probably even smaller. Consequently, the effort to implement such an algorithm is considered not to be worthwile, and hence is skipped in this thesis.

7.4 Conclusions

In this chapter, the idea of a receiver based solution to the coordination problem at medium access layer was evaluated. In particular, the benefit of a successive interference cancellation based approach was analyzed, which allows to decode not only the stronger but also the weaker packet being involved in a collision. However, instead of actually implementing an interference cancellation algorithm, the upper bound has been identified over a wide range of scenario parameters and channel conditions using the developed simulator presented in Section 4. The results of these simulations state that successive interference cancellation can improve the packet delivery ratio by only up to 2 percentage points – significantly less than the throughput gains reported in previous studies that considered unicast oriented communications scenarios. The difference in the considered scenarios and the impact on the obtained performance gains was subsequently discussed, with the final conclusion that **successive interference cancellation** in a broadcast oriented network – such as the one considered in this thesis – **is not considered to be significantly worthwile**.

Despite this negative outcome of the evaluation, this chapter demonstrates a benefit that is probably more important than the specific simulation results: **the ability to actually study advanced cross-layer optimizations in a controlled, repeatable and flexible way, and to accurately quantify the performance of mechanisms that combine physical layer and network level aspects**. In particular the perfect knowledge about each network node, about each packet, about each packet's lifetime and each packet's signal representation allows to approach new ideas using simple "what if..." type of research questions. As a result, a rapid development of new protocols, ideas, and mechanisms, as well as a flexible, easy to handle, and controlled evaluation of their applicability is enabled.

8
Conclusions

The improvement of safety on the road based on a wireless periodic exchange of mobility and status related information between vehicles has motivated this thesis to study the robustness of the envisioned communication technology IEEE 802.11p. As a prime example of upcoming ubiquitious systems, such inter-vehicle communication networks demonstrate the necessity to perform a joint optimization of all layers that contribute to the overall system performance. For instance, a separate optimization of each layer, as it has been done in the past, is not going to succeed if devices, i.e. vehicles in the considered scenario, are supposed to operate in a "self-organized" and "intelligent" manner. In order to ensure that such ubiquitous systems are robust and provide a reliable service to its users, all possible effects that can occur on each layer as well as their implications on other layers have to be well understood. Hence, an expertise across multiple research domains is required, in particular from engineers that design such networks.

In the context of IEEE 802.11p based inter-vehicle communication networks, one major challenge is the coordination of concurrent medium access by neighboring vehicles. Since no central coordination entity is expected to be available in such a system, access to the medium is scheduled in a distributed manner using the well-known and widely studied Carrier Sense Multiple Access (CSMA) mechanism. Yet, in contrast to existing network deployments and research studies that consider static environments, the wireless channel of an inter-vehicle communications scenario exhibits severe time- and frequency-selective characteristics, which lead to a small-scale fading of the transmitted signals. According to recent channel measurement campaigns that have been carried out by experts of the channel modeling domain, the intensity of that fading is expected to have a significant impact on the performance of the physical layer and the coordination effectiveness of medium access control. However, since network engineers are usually no experts of the lower layers of the protocol stack, their physical layer and channel models are based on too simplifying assumptions and are not able to reflect these fading characteristics sufficiently well. Hence, channel modeling experts raised the concern that the lack of a proper modeling approach in the evaluation tools of the networking community might lead to false conclusions. Likewise, since channel modeling experts lack an expertise in higher layers, they were also not able to answer whether their observations actually have a significant impact or not.

The gap between the perspectives taken by experts of the radio propagation channel, by experts of the physical layer, and by experts of the networking domain lead to a set of incompatible modeling approaches and evaluation (or simulation) frameworks used within each of the co-existing research communities. Whereas highly accurate channel simulators operate on complex time samples with a duration of only a few nanoseconds each, state of the art network simulators abstract all these details and assume only an average signal strength that remains constant over the whole transmit duration of a single packet. Hence, the direct coupling of a highly accurate channel simulator and a network simulator is not easily possible and challenges an evaluation of the impacts of a time- and frequency-selective channel on the performance of IEEE 802.11p based inter-vehicle communication networks.

Motivated to overcome the co-existence of the different research communities and to foster a better cooperation between them, this thesis presented a **combined wireless channel, physical layer and networking simulator**, which enables the usage of detailed and accurate models at all layers. The developed simulation framework has been **validated against commercial transceivers** in a controlled and emulated radio environment. Further, in order to be able to assess the impact of a time- and frequency-selective channel, **two different channel modeling approaches have been implemented**: first, six tapped-delay line channel models were added to the simulator, and second, a geometry-based stochastic channel model was implemented that takes the number of surrounding vehicles as well as the existence of randomly placed scatterers located at the side of the road into account. The resulting evaluation framework is suited to answer the question whether time- and frequency-selective channel conditions have a significant impact on the performance of the network, **breaks up with the co-existence of** incompatible evaluation approaches used by the respective **research communities**, and serves as a **foundation for future research studies** that advance into areas that could not be entered without the proposed framework.

Since the computational effort required to run a simulation experiment with this new simulator is raised by several orders of magnitude, **the benefit of GPU-based architectures to speedup the runtime performance** has been evaluated in this thesis. The obtained results showed that significant runtime speedups can be achieved if the employed models and signal processing algorithms are implemented according to state of the art software development paradigms. For instance, the runtime performance evaluation carried out in this thesis showed that concepts such as memory reuse on the GPU, transparent caching, and task (or event) aggregation are crucial in order exploit the existing potential. **The presented simulator is therefore** a prime example of the relatively new discpline called **Computational Science and Engineering (CSE)** which focuses on the systematic study, creation and application of computer-based simulation models in order to understand and analyze complex natural or engineered systems. CSE combines multiple disciplines – computer science, mathematics, and engineering – and makes use of high-performance computing in order to cope with the immense computational efforts that are required to simulate such complex systems.

In a next step, and based on the developed network simulator, the reception and coordination performance of the IEEE 802.11p MAC layer was analyzed. With respect to the reception performance, the following conclusions could be drawn from the obtained results:

1. Time- and frequency-selective channel characteristics have a significant impact on the reception performance of IEEE 802.11p.

2. The packet reception ratio curves that were observed in such channels differ from the curves that are obtained when using a simplifying packet-level model.

3. However, this difference is not fundamental, i.e. it can be eliminated through a linear adjustment of the bit error rate curves employed by traditional packet-level simulators.

In reference to the analyzed coordination performance, the obtained results also state that

1. CSMA is able to suppress interfering transmissions from within the carrier sense range if a distance decaying path loss only channel is considered, i.e. if the assumptions made by the protocol are met.

2. CSMA begins to allow incoordinated transmissions from within the carrier sense range if fading channel effects are considered, however, this incoordination remains on a relatively small level.

3. A small increase of the incoordination level can cause a significant deterioration of the packet delivery ratio as experienced from the perspective of a receiver.

4. The usage of a reduced beacon generation rate leads to significantly increased packet delivery ratios in a distance decaying path loss only channel. In comparison, the benefit of a reduced transmit power is marginal.

5. The benefit of a reduced transmit power or beaconing rate is reduced if a fading of the channel is considered.

6. In the majority of all cases, interfering packet transmissions arrive with a signal strength that is close to the background noise level, independent of the considered channel configuration.

7. The number of interfering packet transmissions that arrive with a signal strength greater than the background noise is also independent of the considered channel configuration and is rarely greater than three packets.

8. While fading channel effects reduce the level of coordination in the network, they also reduce the severity of the resulting interference. Hence, the negative impact of incoordination is reduced as well.

In addition to the characterization of the performance that can be expected in IEEE 802.11p based inter-vehicle communication networks, the **question of how effective and robust congestion control mechanisms should look like** was discussed. Therefore, the underlying distributed control problem was analyzed from a control theory perspective. Based on the microscopic inspection of a small-scale scenario, fundamental problems were identified and resulting requirements with respect to the design of an effective controller were established: **cooperative detection of congested channel conditions**, and **cooperative as well as synchronized reaction to congested channel conditions**. Existing congestion control proposals were evaluated with respect to these requirements, and classified into proactive and reactive, as well as open-loop and closed-loop controllers. The established set of design requirements was also contributed to the standardization efforts lead by the European Telecommunications Standard Institute (ETSI). Further, **alternative medium access control protocols were discussed** with the conclusion that **Self-organizing Time-division Multiplex (STDMA) is the most promising candidate that could perform as well or even better as CSMA.**

As an alternative to congestion control, a receiver based approach using **successive interference cancellation was considered as a potential solution that mitigates the negative impact of incoordination**. In contrast to the adjustment of each node's transmission behavior, successive interference cancellation adds the ability to successfully decode two overlapping packets one after the other if certain requirements are met. However, according to the obtained results, **the benefit of successive interference cancellation is only marginal and increases the probability of successful packet reception at most by only a few percentage points**. Despite this negative outcome, the presented analysis of successive interference cancellation demonstrated how easily the presented network simulator can be used to evaluate novel cross-layer optimization strategies or emerging concepts that originate from information theory.

As pointed out above, the combined wireless channel, pyhsical layer and network simulator allows to study emerging concepts and ideas that could not be evaluated before. For instance, research questions that relate to multi-antenna systems, beamforming techniques, network coding, or cognitive radio concepts can easily be approached with the help of this new simulator. While these techniques are already known to the majority of the research community, even upcoming concepts and ideas can be addressed by this simulator, e.g. ideas that are based on the assumption that even very expensive signal processing algorithms will eventually find their way into future transceivers. For instance, many new possibilities emerge if unlimited computing (or signal processing) capabilities are assumed.

With respect to a distributed coordination of concurrent access to the wireless channel, the potential of a STDMA-based medium access control should be evaluated in the future. Whereas CSMA is probably going to be the used in a first generation of inter-vehicle communication networks, it is conceivable that a second genera-tion will employ a STDMA based solution, for instance if a fair comparison between CSMA and STDMA indicates that STDMA achieves a better coordination among network nodes in vehicular environments. If this turns out to be the case, additional research that explores potential migration paths from a CSMA-based operation to a STDMA-based operation will also be necessary.

A
Flow diagrams of the physical layer implementation

The logic of the state machine presented in Section 4.3.2 is implemented within the physical layer *SendPacket* function and the event handlers that are responsible for the four different events of the frame/packet reception process: *StartReceive*, *EndPreamble*, *EndHeader*, and *EndRx*. The following flow diagrams illustrate the steps that are processed upon expiration of the four events.

Upon the arrival of a new incoming signal, i.e. when a StartReceive event expires, it is first checked whether the signal strength of the signal is greater than a configurable energy detection threshold, cf. Figure A.1. This threshold is typically configured to reflect the Johnson-Nyquist noise (or thermal noise) level, which is frequency and bandwidth dependent and accounts to -104 dBm for a 10 MHz channel configuration at 5.9 GHz. If the signal strength is less than the thermal noise, the packet is discarded since it will not contribute significantly to the interference level at the receiver. If it is stronger than thermal noise, the packet is added to the interference manager which will keep track of the signal and consider it during cumulative signal computations. What happens then depends on the current state of the physical layer: 1. if the physical layer is currently in transmission state, the packet is dropped and not considered for reception; 2. if the state is either idle or CCA busy, an EndPreamble event is scheduled; 3. if the physical layer is synchronized to a packet or even already decoding the data symbols of it, an additional check is performed: is the SINR of the packet greater than the capture threshold CP_{th}? If yes, the current packet is dropped, i.e. its running EndHeader or EndRx event is canceled, and an EndPreamble event is scheduled for the captured packet. If not, the incoming packet is dropped. A final check handles carrier sense related activities and depending on its output, the physical layer state is either changed to CCA busy or idle.

The handler of an EndPreamble event already branches w.r.t. the physical layer state in the beginning: 1. if the physical layer is in transmission state the packet is dropped; 2. if the physical layer is in reception state, it is checked whether the capture threshold is satisfied and if the preamble can be detected successfully: if not, the packet is dropped, if yes, the already running EndRx event is cancelled, the state is changed to SYNC, frequency offset estimation is performed and an EndHeader event is scheduled; 3. if the physical layer is in SYNC state, it is checked whether the SINR of the packet is greater than 4 dB and whether the preamble is detected successfully: if not, the packet is dropped, if yes, the already running EndHeader event is cancelled, the state is kept at SYNC, frequency offset estimation is performed and an EndHeader event is scheduled; 4. if the physical layer is either in idle or CCA busy state, it is checked whether the SINR of the packet is greater than 4 dB and whether the preamble is detected successfully: if not, the packet is dropped, if yes, the state is changed to SYNC, frequency offset estimation is performed and an EndHeader event is scheduled.

One might wonder why an extra 4 dB check is introduced in the synchronized, idle, and CCA busy branches of the EndPreamble handler. The reason is simple and a workaround to properly model the system in a discrete event-based simulator: since the EndPreamble event (as all other events) relates to a specific packet, it can happen that the correlation output of the preamble detector signals a successful detection, although this indication may result from a stronger packet that arrived nearly at the same point in time. In such a situation, the preamble portions of both packets will overlap significantly, and the correlator won't be able to distinguish between both packets. Whereas a real system would implicitly make a distinction between both packets by synchronizing to the stronger packet (without knowing about the existance of a weaker one), this implicit distinction has to be made explicit in a discrete event-based simulator. Hence the additional 4 dB SINR check.

Upon expiration of an EndHeader event, it is first checked whether the current physical layer state is equal to synchronized or not. If not, a fatal error is thrown and the simulation is aborted since the handler will check whether to switch to receiving state or not and such a transition is only allowed from the synchronized state. If the physical layer is currently synchronized, the signal header portion is decoded and the parity bit is checked for correctness. If the check is positive, the frame length and datarate of the packet are determined, and EndRx event is scheduled and the state is switched to RX. If the parity check is negative, the packet is dropped and the state is changed to either idle or CCA busy.

The final EndRx event handler is less complex than the previous ones: upon expiration the data bits are decoded and compared to the original bit sequence that was used by the transmitter during frame construction. If the bit sequences are identical, the packet is given up to the MAC layer, if not, it is dropped. Finally, the physical layer state is changed to either idle or CCA busy.

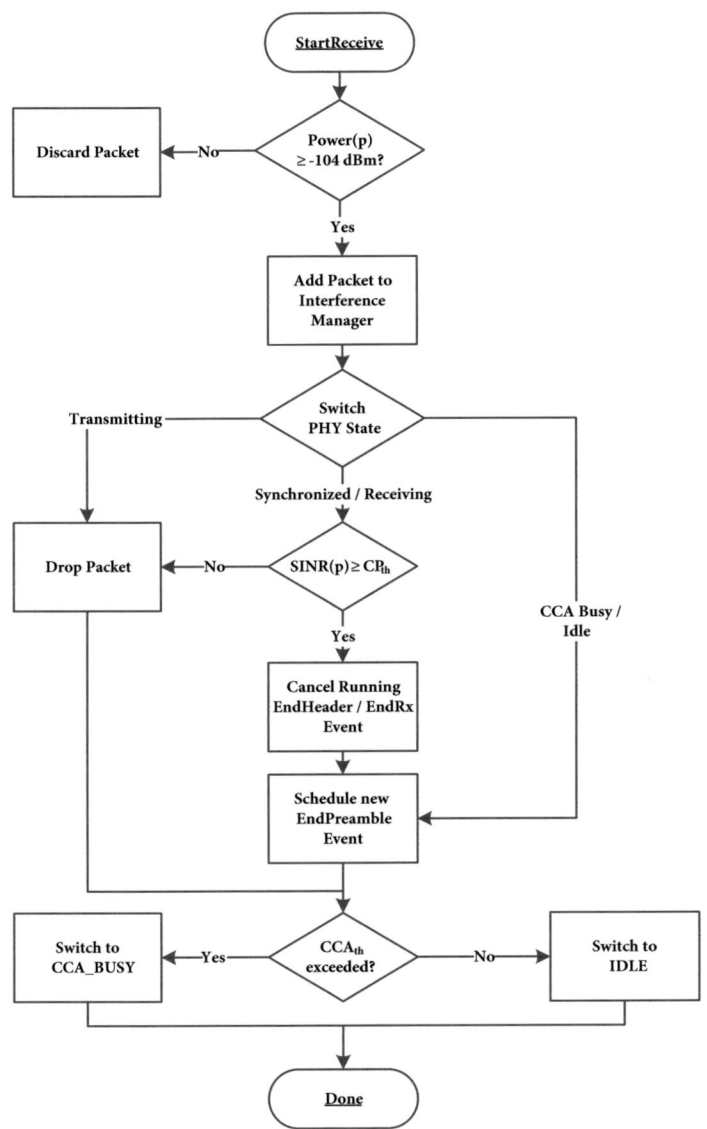

Figure A.1: Illustration of the processing steps that are executed whenever new complex time samples that represent a packet "arrive" at the antenna of a receiver.

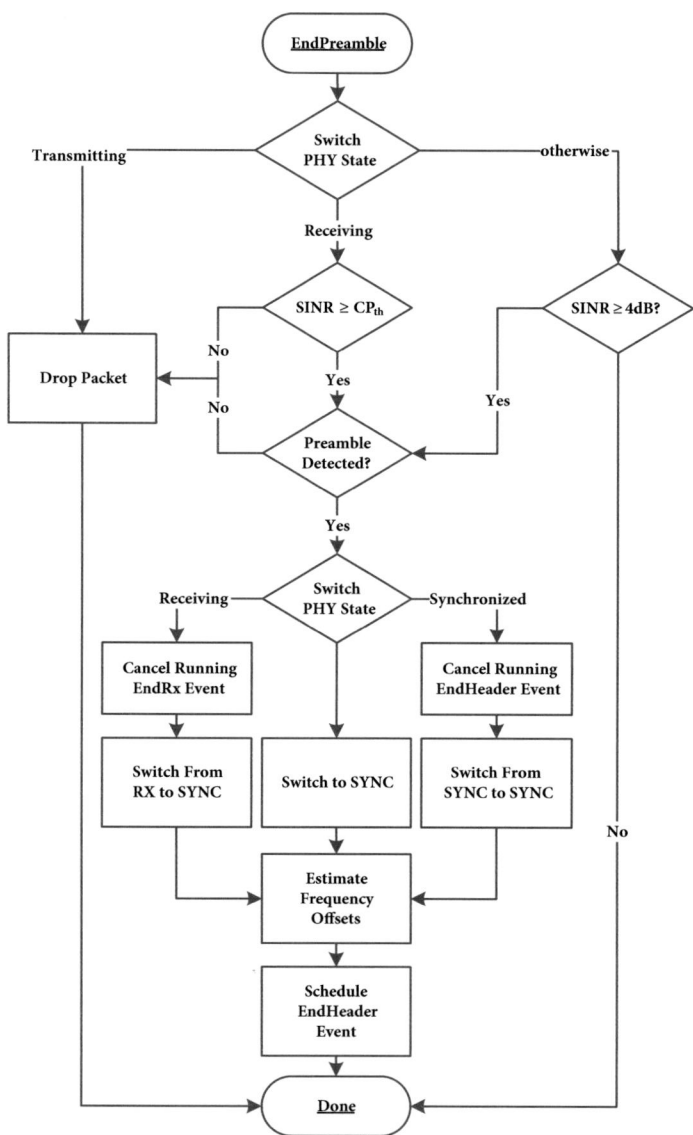

Figure A.2: Illustration of the processing steps that are executed whenever the End-Preamble event of a packet expires.

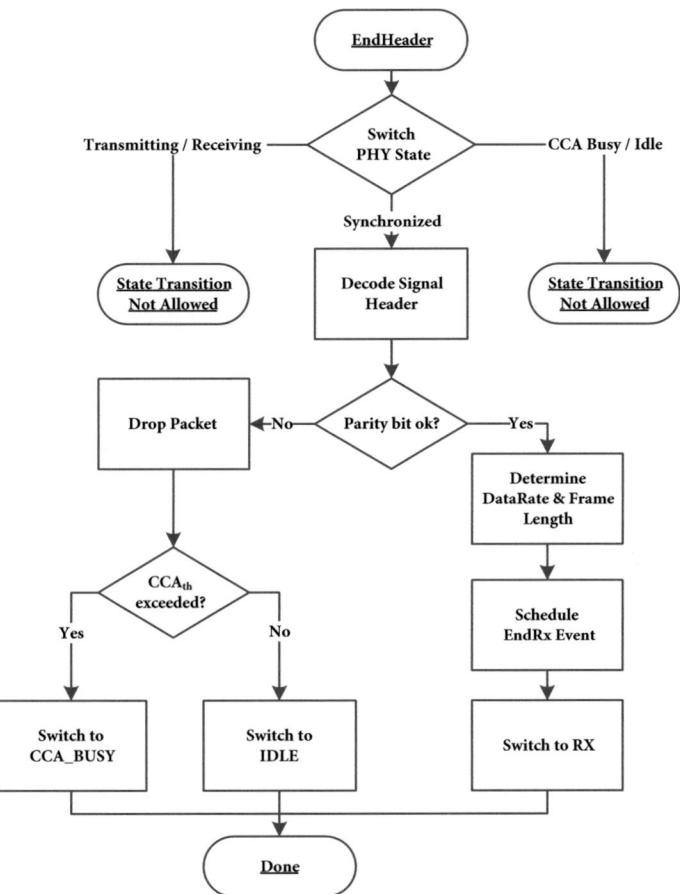

Figure A.3: Illustration of the processing steps that are executed whenever the End-Header event of a packet expires.

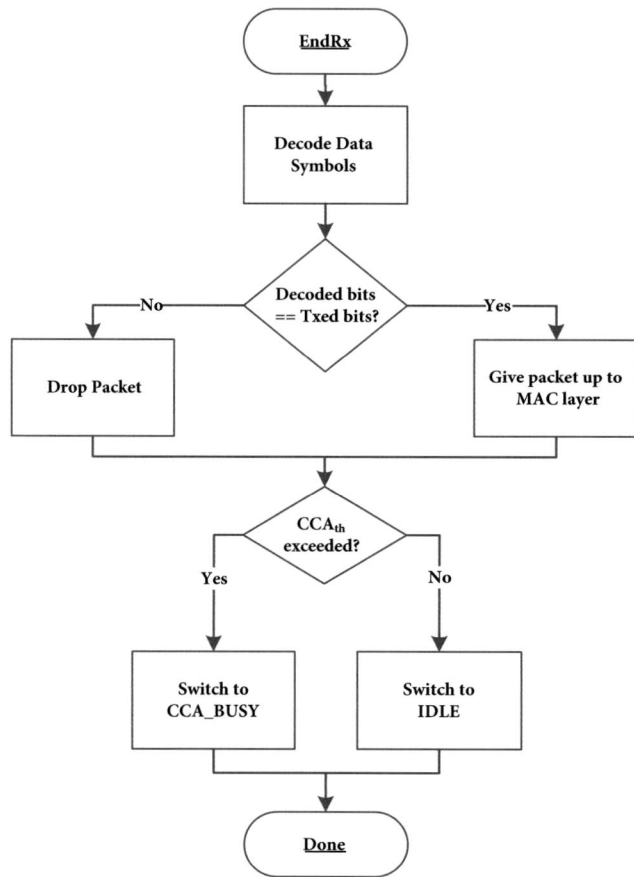

Figure A.4: Illustration of the processing steps that are executed whenever the EndRx event of a packet expires.

B
Optimization of signal detector auto-correlation threshold

As pointed out in Section 4.3.4, the autocorrelation threshold of the signal detector is an important parameter that can and has to be optimized. While a low threshold leads to an increased preamble detection and acceptance rate, it also leads to reception attempts that eventually fail due to insufficient SNR levels. Such attempts should be avoided, since they lead to unnecessary reception states and unneeded blocking periods at higher layers – which might have a negative impact on medium access control and network performance since inadequate feedback is provided. On the other hand, a threshold that is set too high leads to declined packets that could have been decoded without errors successfully. It is therefore important to configure a threshold that is high enough to filter out all false negatives, but also low enough to accept all successfully decodable packets.

Figure B.1 illustrates the differing preamble acceptance and packet reception ratios with respect to the observed signal-to-interference noise (SINR) ratio when using four different auto-correlation thresholds, namely 0.82, 0.84, 0.86, and 0.88. As can be seen in Figure B.1(a), the preamble acceptance ratio curves shift to the right if the correlation threshold is increased. Unlike the preamble acceptance ratio curves, the packet reception ratio curves differ only marginally, cf. Figure B.1(b), whereas an increasing portion of successfully decodable packets is ignored if a threshold of 0.86 or higher is used. Out of this reason, an auto-correlation threshold of 0.85 was used in the thesis.

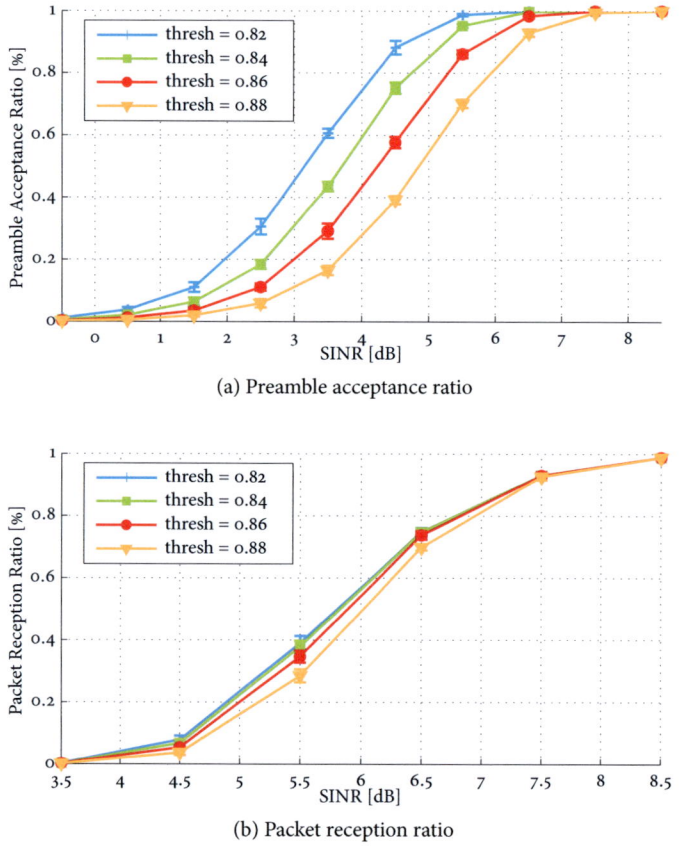

(a) Preamble acceptance ratio

(b) Packet reception ratio

Figure B.1: Obtained preamble acceptance and resulting packet reception ratios with respect to the observed SINR level and four different auto-correlation thresholds in the signal detector implementation.

Bibliography

[AH86]   A. S. Akki and F. Haber. A statistical model of mobile-to-mobile land communication channel. *IEEE Transactions on Vehicular Technology*, 35(1):2– 7, February 1986.

[AI07]   G. Acosta-Marum and M.A. Ingram.   Six time- and Frequency-Selective empirical channel models for vehicular wireless LANs. *Vehicular Technology Magazine, IEEE*, 2(4):4–11, 2007.

[Amd67]   G. M. Amdahl. Validity of the Single Processor Approach to Achieving Large Scale Computing Capabilities. In *Proceedings of AFIPS Spring Joint Conference*, 1967.

[AMH11]   P. Andelfinger, J. Mittag, and H. Hartenstein.   GPU-Based Architectures and Their Benefit for Accurate and Efficient Wireless Network Simulations. In *Modeling, Analysis Simulation of Computer and Telecommunication Systems (MASCOTS), 2011 IEEE 19th International Symposium on*, pages 421 –424, July 2011.

[ARP05]   M. Artimy, W. Robertson, and W. Phillips. Assignment of Dynamic Transmission Range Based on Estimation of Vehicle Density.   In *Proceedings of the ACM International Workshop on Vehicular Inter-Networking (VANET)*, pages 40–48, Cologne, Germany, September 2005.

[Bel63]   P. Bello.   Characterization of randomly Time-Variant linear channels. *IEEE Transactions on Communications Systems*, 11(4):360–393, December 1963.

[Bia00]   G. Bianchi. Performance Analysis of the IEEE 802.11 Distributed Coordination Function. *IEEE Journal on Selected Areas in Communications*, 18(3):535–547, March 2000.

[BKR09]   H. Busche, C. Khorakhun, and H. Rohling. Self-Organized Update Rate Control for Inter-Vehicle Networks. In *Proceedings of the International Workshop on Intelligent Transportation (WIT)*, Hamburg, Germany, March 2009.

[BKR10] H. Busche, C. Khorakhun, and H. Rohling. Congestion Control in a Self-Organized Car-to-Car Radio Network. In *Proceedings of the International Workshop on Intelligent Transportation (WIT)*, Hamburg, Germany, March 2010.

[BN09] S. Bai and D.M. Nicol. GPU Coprocessing for Wireless Network Simulation. Technical report, University of Illinois at Urbana-Champaign, 2009.

[BSL+10] R. Baldessaro, D. Scanferla, L. Le, W. Zhang, and A. Festag. Joining Forces for VANETs: A Combined Transmit Power and Rate Control Algorithm. In *Proceedings of the International Workshop on Intelligent Transportation (WIT)*, Hamburg, Germany, March 2010.

[BUS10] K. Bilstrup, E. Uhlemann, and E. G. Ström. Scalability issues of the MAC methods STDMA and CSMA of IEEE 802.11p when used in VANETs. In *2010 IEEE International Conference on Communications Workshops (ICC)*, pages 1–5. IEEE, May 2010.

[BUSB09] K. Bilstrup, E. Uhlemann, E. G. Ström, and U. Bilstrup. On the ability of the 802.11p MAC method and STDMA to support real-time vehicle-to-vehicle communication. *EURASIP Journal on Wireless Communication Networks*, 2009, January 2009.

[BV01] S.V. Bana and P. Varaiya. Space Division Multiple Access (SDMA) for Robust Ad-hoc Vehicle Communication Networks. *Intelligent Transportation Systems, 2001. Proceedings. 2001 IEEE*, pages 962–967, 2001.

[CH99] M. Cummings and S. Haruyama. FPGA in the Software Radio. *IEEE Communications Magazine*, 37(2):108–112, 1999.

[CHBS08] L. Cheng, B. E Henty, F. Bai, and D. Stancil. Highway and rural propagation channel modeling for vehicle-to-vehicle communications at 5.9 GHz. In *IEEE Antennas and Propagation Society International Symposium, 2008. AP-S 2008*, pages 1–4. IEEE, July 2008.

[CHC+08] L. Cheng, B. Henty, R. Cooper, D. Stancil, and F. Bai. Multi-Path propagation measurements for vehicular networks at 5.9 GHz. In *IEEE Wireless Communications and Networking Conference, 2008. WCNC 2008*, pages 1239–1244. IEEE, April 2008.

[CHS+07] L. Cheng, B. E Henty, D. Stancil, F. Bai, and P. Mudalige. Mobile Vehicle-to-Vehicle Narrow-Band channel measurement and characterization of the 5.9 GHz dedicated short range communication (DSRC) frequency band. *IEEE Journal on Selected Areas in Communications*, 25(8):1501–1516, October 2007.

[CJTD06] Q. Chen, D. Jiang, V. Taliwal, and L. Delgrossi. IEEE 802.11 based Vehicular Communication Simulation Design for NS-2. In *Proceedings of the 3rd International Workshop on Vehicular Ad Hoc Networks*, pages 50–56, Los Angeles, CA, USA, 2006. ACM.

[CKZ+10] N. Czink, F. Kaltenberger, Y. Zhou, L. Bernado, T. Zemen, and X. Yin. Low-complexity geometry-based modeling of diffuse scattering. In *2010 Proceedings of the Fourth European Conference on Antennas and Propagation (EuCAP)*, pages 1–4. IEEE, April 2010.

[CRW+81] W. Crowther, R. Rettberg, D. Walden, S. Ornstein, and F. Heart. A System for Broadcast Communications: Reservation-ALOHA. *Proceedings of the 6th Hawaii International Conference on System Sciences*, page 373, 1981.

[CSJ+07] Q. Chen, F. Schmidt-Eisenlohr, D. Jiang, M. Torrent-Moreno, L. Delgrossi, and H. Hartenstein. Overhaul of IEEE 802.11 Modeling and Simulation in ns-2. In *Proceedings of the 10th ACM Symposium on Modeling, Analysis, and Simulation of Wireless and Mobile Systems*, pages 159–168, Chania, Crete Island, Greece, 2007. ACM.

[CWL09a] X. Cheng, C.-X. Wang, and D. I. Laurenson. A Geometry-Based stochastic model for wideband MIMO Mobile-to-Mobile channels. In *IEEE Global Telecommunications Conference, 2009. GLOBECOM 2009*, pages 1–6. IEEE, December 2009.

[CWL+09b] X. Cheng, C.-X. Wang, D. I. Laurenson, S. Salous, and A. V. Vasilakos. An adaptive geometry-based stochastic model for non-isotropic MIMO mobile-to-mobile channels. *IEEE Transactions on Wireless Communications*, 8(9):4824–4835, September 2009.

[Eato2] J. W. Eaton. *GNU Octave Manual*. Network Theory Limited, 2002.

[EGH+06] T. ElBatt, S. K. Goel, G. Holland, H. Krishnan, and J. Parikh. Cooperative Collision Warning Using Dedicated Short Range Wireless Communications. In *Proceedings of the ACM International Workshop on Vehicular Inter-Networking (VANET)*, pages 1–9, Los Angeles, CA, USA, September 2006.

[FHM05] W. Franz, H. Hartenstein, and M. Mauve. *Inter-Vehicle Communications Based On Ad Hoc Networking Principles - the FleetNet Project*. Universitätsverlag Karlsruhe, 2005.

[Gas02] M. S. Gast. *802.11 Wireless Networks: The Definitive Guide*. O'Reilly Media, 1 edition, April 2002.

[Ged40] N. B. Geddes. *Magic Motorways*. Random House, 1940.

[glo] GloMoSim — Global Mobile Information Systems Simulation Library. http://pcl.cs.ucla.edu/projects/glomosim/.

[Gup03] N. Gupta. A Performance Analysis of the 802.11 Wireless Lan Medium Access Control. *Communications in Information & Systems*, 3(4):479–304, 2003.

[Hal07] D. Halperin. Interference cancellation: Better receivers for a new wireless MAC. In *Proceedings of the 6th workshop on Hot Topics in Networks*, Atlanta, GA, November 2007.

[HAW08] D. Halperin, T. Anderson, and D. Wetherall. Taking the sting out of carrier sense: Interference cancellation for wireless LANs. In *Proceedings of the 14th ACM international conference on Mobile computing and networking*, pages 339–350, San Francisco, California, USA, 2008. ACM.

[HBSG06] L. Hogie, P. Bouvry, M. Seredynski, and F. Guinand. A Bandwidth-Efficient Broadcasting Protocol for Mobile Multi-hop Ad hoc Networks. In *Proc. of the Int'l Conference on Systems, Mobile Communications and Learning Technologies*, pages 71–71, April 2006.

[HCCC10] J. He, H.-W. Chen, T. M. Chen, and W. Cheng. Adaptive congestion control for DSRC vehicle networks. *Comm. Letters.*, 14:127–129, February 2010.

[HFSK10] C.-L. Huang, Y.P. Fallah, R. Sengupta, and H. Krishnan. Adaptive Intervehicle Communication Control for Cooperative Safety Systems. *IEEE Network*, 24(1):6–13, January 2010.

[HL10] H. Hartenstein and K. P. Laberteaux. *VANET - Vehicular Applications and Inter-Networking Technologies*. Wiley, 2010.

[HS05] K. Hartman and J. Strasser. Saving lives through advanced vehicle safety technology: Intelligent vehicle initiative final report. Technical report, FHWA-JPO-05-057, 2005.

[HYW+09] T. Hwang, C. Yang, G. Wu, S. Li, and G. Ye Li. OFDM and Its Wireless Applications: A Survey. *Vehicular Technology, IEEE Transactions on*, 58(4):1673 –1694, May 2009.

[IEE07] IEEE Standards Association. IEEE Standard for Information technology – Telecommunications and information exchange between systems – Local and metropolitan area networks – Specific requirements – Part 11: Wireless LAN Medium Access Control (MAC) and Physical Layer (PHY) Specifications. http://standards.ieee.org/getieee802/802.11.html, 2007.

[IEE10] IEEE Standards Association. IEEE Standard for information technology – Telecommunications and information exchange between systems – Local and metropolitan area networks – Specific requirements Part 11: Wireless LAN Medium Access Control (MAC) and Physical Layer (PHY) Specifications - Amendment 6: Wireless Access in Vehicular Environments. http://standards.ieee.org/getieee802/802.11.html, 2010.

[Int] International Organisation for Standardisation. Information technology – Open Systems Interconnection – Basic Reference Model: The Basic Model (ISO/IEC 7498-1:1994). http://standards.iso.org/ittf/PubliclyAvailableStandards/index.html. 1994.

[ITP] The IT++ library. http://sourceforge.net/apps/wordpress/itpp/.

[ITU98] ITU-R Recommendation M.1371-1. *Technical Characteristics for a Universal Shipborne Automatic Identification System Using Time Division Multiple Access in the Maritime Mobile Band*, 1998.

[Jak75] W. C. Jakes. *Microwave Mobile Communications*. John Wiley & Sons Inc., February 1975.

[JC08] Y. Jian and S. Chen. Can CSMA/CA networks be made fair? In *Proceedings of the 14th ACM international conference on Mobile computing and networking*, pages 235–246, San Francisco, California, USA, 2008. ACM.

[jis] SWANS — Scalable Wireless Ad hoc Network Simulator. http://jist.ece.cornell.edu/.

[JS04] G. Judd and P. Steenkiste. Repeatable and Realistic Wireless Experimentation Through Physical Emulation. *SIGCOMM Comput. Commun. Rev.*, 34(1):63–68, 2004.

[KBR08] C. Khorakhun, H. Busche, and H. Rohling. Congestion Control for VANETs based on Power or Rate Adaptation. In *Proceedings of the International Workshop on Intelligent Transportation (WIT)*, Hamburg, Germany, March 2008.

[KBR11] J. B. Kenney, G. Bansal, and C. E. Rohrs. LIMERIC: a linear message rate control algorithm for vehicular DSRC systems. In *Proceedings of the Eighth ACM international workshop on Vehicular inter-networking*, VANET '11, pages 21–30, New York, NY, USA, 2011. ACM.

[KCP+11] J. Karedal, N. Czink, A. Paier, F. Tufvesson, and A. F Molisch. Path loss modeling for Vehicle-to-Vehicle communications. *IEEE Transactions on Vehicular Technology*, 60(1):323–328, January 2011.

[KCR08] A. Kerr, D. Campbell, and M. Richards. GPU VSIPL: High-Performance VSIPL Implementation for GPUs. In *High Performance Embedded Computing Workshop*, September 2008.

[KGMRR+03] S. Katragadda, C.N.S. Ganesh Murthy, M.S. Ranga Rao, S. Mohan Kumar, and R. Sachin. A Decentralized Location-Based Channel Access Protocol for Inter-Vehicle Communication. *Vehicular Technology Conference, 2003. VTC 2003-Spring. The 57th IEEE Semiannual*, 3:1831–1835, April 2003.

[KP08] J. Kunisch and J. Pamp. Wideband Car-to-Car radio channel measurements and model at 5.9 GHz. In *Vehicular Technology Conference, 2008. VTC 2008-Fall. IEEE 68th*, pages 1–5. IEEE, September 2008.

[KSG+08] A. Kuntz, F. Schmidt-Eisenlohr, O. Graute, H. Hartenstein, and M. Zitterbart. Introducing Probabilistic Radio Propagation Models in OMNeT++ Mobility Framework and Cross Validation Check with NS-2. In *Proceedings of the 1st International Conference on Simulation Tools and Techniques for Communications, Networks and Systems & Workshops*, pages 1–7. ICST, 2008.

[KTC+09] J. Karedal, F. Tufvesson, N. Czink, A. Paier, C. Dumard, T. Zemen, C. F Mecklenbräuker, and A. F Molisch. A geometry-based stochastic MIMO model for vehicle-to-vehicle communications. *IEEE Transactions on Wireless Communications*, 8(7):3646–3657, July 2009.

[KWA09] W. Kasch, J. Ward, and J. Andrusenko. Wireless network modeling and simulation tools for designers and developers. *Communications Magazine, IEEE*, 47(3):120–127, March 2009.

[Lee90] W. Lee. *Mobile Cellular Telecommunications Systems*. McGraw-Hill, Inc., New York, NY, USA, 1990.

[LHSR01] M. Lott, R. Halfmann, E. Schultz, and M. Radimirsch. Medium Access and Radio Resource Management for Ad hoc Networks Based on UTRA TDD. In *MobiHoc '01: Proceedings of the 2nd ACM international symposium on Mobile ad hoc networking & computing*, pages 76–86, New York, NY, USA, 2001. ACM.

[Liu03] C.-H. Liu. On the design of OFDM signal detection algorithms for hardware implementation. In *Global Telecommunications Conference, 2003. GLOBECOM '03. IEEE*, volume 2, pages 596–599, 2003.

[LKL+07] J. Lee, W. Kim, S.-J. Lee, D. Jo, J. Ryu, T. Kwon, and Y. Choi. An experimental study on the capture effect in 802.11a networks. In *Proceedings of the second ACM international workshop on Wireless network testbeds, experimental evaluation and characterization*, pages 19–26, Montreal, Quebec, Canada, 2007. ACM.

[LSP95] T.-K. Liu, J.A. Silvester, and A. Polydoros. Performance Evaluation of R-ALOHA in Distributed Packet Radio Networks with Hard Real-Time Communications. *Vehicular Technology Conference, 1995 IEEE 45th*, 2:554–558, Jul 1995.

[LV89] R. Lupas and S. Verdú. Linear multiuser detectors for synchronous code-division multiple-access channels. *IEEE Transactions on Information Theory*, 35(1):123–136, January 1989.

[LV90] R. Lupas and S. Verdú. Near-far resistance of multiuser detectors in asynchronous channels. *IEEE Transactions on Communications*, 38(4):496–508, April 1990.

[MAT] MATLAB high-level language and interactive environment. http://www.mathworks.com/products/matlab/.

[Mat08] D. W. Matolak. Channel modeling for Vehicle-To-Vehicle communications. *IEEE Communications Magazine*, 46(5):76–83, May 2008.

[MDMH94] A. M. Monk, M. Davis, L. B. Milstein, and C. W. Helstrom. A Noise-whitening Approach to Multiple Access Noise Rejection – Part I: Theory and Background. *IEEE Journal on Selected Areas in Communications*, 12(5):817–827, June 1994.

[MFSW04] J. Maurer, T. Fügen, T. Schäfer, and W. Wiesbeck. A new inter-vehicle communications (IVC) channel model. In *Vehicular Technology Conference, 2004. VTC2004-Fall. 2004 IEEE 60th*, volume 1, pages 9–13. IEEE, September 2004.

[MFW02] J. Maurer, T. Fügen, and W. Wiesbeck. Narrow-band measurement and analysis of the inter-vehicle transmission channel at 5.2 GHz. In *Vehicular Technology Conference, 2002. VTC Spring 2002. IEEE 55th*, volume 3, pages 1274–1278. IEEE, 2002.

[MHRY05] X. Ma, P. Hrubik, H. Refai, and S. Yang. Capture Effect on R-ALOHA Protocol for Inter-Vehicle Communications. *Vehicular Technology Conference, 2005. VTC-2005-Fall. 2005 IEEE 62nd*, 4:2547–2550, Sept. 2005.

[Mit12] J. Mittag. Characterization, Avoidance and Repair of Packet Collisions in Inter-Vehicle Communication Networks: The Complete Set of Results, February 2012. http://dsn.tm.kit.edu/download/ns3-physim/results.html.

[MLBLMF10] R. Massin, C. Lamy-Bergot, C. J. Le Martret, and R. Fracchia. Omnet++-based cross-layer simulator for content transmission over wireless ad hoc networks. *EURASIP J. Wirel. Commun. Netw.*, 2010:14:1–14:12, April 2010.

[MMK+11] C.F. Mecklenbräuker, A.F. Molisch, J. Karedal, F. Tufvesson, A. Paier, L. Bernado, T. Zemen, O. Klemp, and N. Czink. Vehicular Channel Characterization and Its Implications for Wireless System Design and Performance. *Proceedings of the IEEE*, 99(7):1189–1212, July 2011.

[MOL07] M.N. Mariyasagayam, T. Osafune, and M. Lenardi. Enhanced Multi-Hop vehicular broadcast (MHVB) for active safety applications. In *Telecommunications, 2007. ITST '07. 7th International Conference on ITS*, pages 1–6, 2007.

[MPHS11] J. Mittag, S. Papanastasiou, H. Hartenstein, and E.G. Ström. Enabling Accurate Cross-Layer PHY/MAC/NET Simulation Studies of Vehicular Communication Networks. *Proceedings of the IEEE*, 99(7):1311–1326, July 2011.

[MR88] A. Mann and J. Rückert. A New Concurrent Slot Assignment Protocol for Traffic Information Exchange. *Vehicular Technology Conference, 1988, 38th IEEE*, pages 503–508, June 1988.

[MSEK+08] J. Mittag, F. Schmidt-Eisenlohr, M. Killat, J. Härri, and H. Hartenstein. Analysis and design of effective and low-overhead transmission power control for vanets. In *Proceedings of the fifth ACM international workshop on VehiculAr Inter-NETworking*, VANET '08, pages 39–48, New York, NY, USA, 2008. ACM.

[MSEK+10] J. Mittag, F. Schmidt-Eisenlohr, M. Killat, M. Torrent Moreno, and H. Hartenstein. *VANET – Vehicular Applications and Inter-Networking Technologies*, chapter 7: MAC Layer and Scalability Aspects of Vehicular Communication Networks, pages 219–272. John Wiley & Sons Inc., 2010.

[MSW01] J. Maurer, T. M. Schäfer, and W. Wiesbeck. A realistic description of the environment for inter-vehicle wave propagation modelling. In *Vehicular Technology Conference, 2001. VTC 2001 Fall. IEEE VTS 54th*, volume 3, pages 1437–1441. IEEE, 2001.

[MTKM09] A. F. Molisch, F. Tufvesson, J. Karedal, and C. F. Mecklenbräuker. A Survey On Vehicle-to-Vehicle Propagation Channels. *IEEE Wireless Communications*, 2009, December 2009.

[MWW06] T. Moscibroda, R. Wattenhofer, and Y. Weber. Protocol Design Beyond Graph-based Models. *ACM HotNets*, 2006.

[NH98] T. Nagaosa and T. Hasegawa. Code Assignment and the Multicode Sense Scheme in an Inter-Vehicle CDMA Communication Network (Special Section on Spread Spectrum Techniques and Applications). *IEICE Transactions on Fundamentals of Electronics, Communications and Computer Sciences*, 81(11):2327–2333, 1998.

[NS2] Network Simulator ns-2. http://www.isi.edu/nsnam/ns/.

[ns3] The NS-3 Network Simulator. http://www.nsnam.org/.

[Oja97] T. Ojanpera. Overview of multiuser detection/interference cancellation for DS-CDMA. In *1997 IEEE International Conference on Personal Wireless Communications*, pages 115–119. IEEE, December 1997.

[ope] OpenCL – the open standard for parallel programming of heterogeneous systems. http://www.khronos.org/opencl/.

[Pap00] A. Papasakellariou. Overview of interference cancellation for CDMA wireless systems. In *International Conference on Information Technology: Coding and Computing, 2000. Proceedings*, pages 86–91. IEEE, 2000.

[PC07] J. Peng and L. Cheng. A Distributed MAC Scheme for Emergency Message Dissemination in Vehicular Ad Hoc Networks. *Vehicular Technology, IEEE Transactions on*, 56(6):3300–3308, Nov. 2007.

[Per06] K. S. Perumalla. Discrete-event Execution Alternatives on General Purpose Graphical Processing Units (GPGPUs). In *Proceedings of the 20th Workshop on Principles of Advanced and Distributed Simulation*, PADS '06, pages 74–81, Washington, DC, USA, 2006. IEEE Computer Society.

[PKC+07] A. Paier, J. Karedal, N. Czink, H. Hofstetter, C. Dumard, T. Zemen, F. Tufvesson, A. F Molisch, and C. F Mecklenbräuker. Car-to-car radio channel measurements at 5 GHz: pathloss, power-delay profile, and delay-Doppler spectrum. In *4th International Symposium on Wireless Communication Systems, 2007. ISWCS 2007*, pages 224–228. IEEE, October 2007.

[PNS00] R.J. Punnoose, P.V. Nikitin, and D.D. Stancil. Efficient simulation of ricean fading within a packet simulator. In *Vehicular Technology Conference, 2000. IEEE VTS-Fall VTC 2000. 52nd*, volume 2, pages 764–767 vol.2, 2000.

[Pro01] J. G. Proakis. *Digital Communications*. in Electrical and Computer Engineering. McGraw-Hill, 4 edition, 2001.

[Rap09] T. S. Rappaport. *Wireless communications : principles and practice*. Prentice Hall communications engineering and emerging technologies series. Prentice Hall, Upper Saddle River, NJ [u.a.], 2. ed., 18. print. edition, 2009.

[RKVO08] O. Renaudin, V. Kolmonen, P. Vainikainen, and C. Oestges. Wideband MIMO Car-to-Car radio channel measurements at 5.3 GHz.

In *Vehicular Technology Conference, 2008. VTC 2008-Fall. IEEE 68th*, pages 1–5. IEEE, September 2008.

[RKVO09] O. Renaudin, V. Kolmonen, P. Vainikainen, and C. Oestges. Car-to-car channel models based on wideband MIMO measurements at 5.3 GHz. In *3rd European Conference on Antennas and Propagation, 2009. EuCAP 2009*, pages 635–639. IEEE, March 2009.

[RLLK08] J. Ryu, J. Lee, S.-J. Lee, and T. Kwon. Revamping the IEEE 802.11a PHY simulation models. In *Proceedings of the 11th International Symposium on Modeling, Analysis and Simulation of Wireless and Mobile Systems*, pages 28–36, Vancouver, British Columbia, Canada, 2008. ACM.

[RSK+10] S. Rezaei, R. Sengupta, H. Krishnan, X. Guan, and R. Bhatia. Tracking the position of neighboring vehicles using wireless communications. *Transportation Research Part C: Emerging Technologies*, 18(3):335–350, June 2010.

[SE10] F. Schmidt-Eisenlohr. *Interference in Vehicle-to-Vehicle Communication Networks: Analysis, Modeling, Simulation and Assessment*. PhD thesis, Karlsruhe Institute of Technology (KIT), Karlsruhe, 2010.

[SEM04] E. Sourour, H. El-Ghoroury, and D. McNeill. Frequency offset estimation and correction in the IEEE 802.11a WLAN. In *IEEE 60th Vehicular Technology Conference*, pages 4923–4927, Los Angeles, CA, USA, 2004.

[SLI] Simulink simulation and model-based design. http://www.mathworks.com/products/simulink/.

[SM08] I. Sen and D. W Matolak. Vehicle–Vehicle channel models for the 5-GHz band. *IEEE Transactions on Intelligent Transportation Systems*, 9(2):235–245, June 2008.

[SMS+11] M. Sepulcre, J. Mittag, P. Santi, H. Hartenstein, and J. Gozalvez. Congestion and awareness control in cooperative vehicular systems. *Proceedings of the IEEE*, 99:1260 – 1279, July 2011.

[SSIC04] K. Sundaresan, R. Sivakumar, M.A. Ingram, and T.-Y. Chang. Medium Access Control in Ad-hoc Networks with MIMO Links: Optimization Considerations and Algorithms. *IEEE Transactions on Mobile Computing*, 3(4):350–365, 2004.

[SUS11a] K. Sjöberg, E. Uhlemann, and E. G. Ström. Delay and interference comparison of CSMA and self-organizing TDMA when used in VANETs. In *Wireless Communications and Mobile Computing Conference (IWCMC), 2011 7th International*, pages 1488–1493. IEEE, July 2011.

[SUS11b] K. Sjöberg, E. Uhlemann, and E. G. Ström. How severe is the hidden terminal problem in VANETs when using CSMA and STDMA? In *2011 IEEE Vehicular Technology Conference (VTC Fall)*, pages 1–5. IEEE, September 2011.

[TB10] I. Tan and A. Bahai. *VANET – Vehicular Applications and Inter-Networking Technologies*, chapter 6: Physical Layer Considerations for Vehicular Communications, pages 157–215. John Wiley & Sons Inc., 2010.

[TCSH06] M. Torrent-Moreno, S. Corroy, F. Schmidt-Eisenlohr, and H. Hartenstein. IEEE 802.11-based One-hop Broadcast Communications: Understanding Transmission Success And Failure Under Different Radio Propagation Environments. In *Proceedings of the 9th ACM international symposium on Modeling analysis and simulation of wireless and mobile systems*, MSWiM '06, pages 68–77, New York, NY, USA, 2006. ACM.

[TJC+11] T. Tielert, D. Jiang, Q. Chen, L. Delgrossi, and H. Hartenstein. Design methodology and evaluation of rate adaptation based congestion control for vehicle safety communications. In *Proceedings of the 3rd IEEE Vehicular Networking Conference (VNC 2011)*, Amsterdam, Netherlands, November 2011.

[TJH04] M. Torrent-Moreno, D. Jiang, and H. Hartenstein. Broadcast reception rates and effects of priority access in 802.11-based vehicular ad-hoc networks. In *Proceedings of the 1st ACM international workshop on Vehicular ad hoc networks*, VANET '04, pages 10–18, New York, NY, USA, 2004. ACM.

[TK75] F. Tobagi and L. Kleinrock. Packet Switching in Radio Channels: Part II–The Hidden Terminal Problem in Carrier Sense Multiple-Access and the Busy-Tone Solution. *IEEE Transactions on Communications*, 23(12):1417– 1433, December 1975.

[TLF+09] K. Tan, H. Liu, J. Fang, W. Wang, J. Zhang, M. Chen, and G. M. Völker. SAM: enabling practical spatial multiple access in wireless LAN. In *Proceedings of the 15th annual international conference on Mobile computing and networking*, pages 49–60, Beijing, China, 2009. ACM.

[TMCH05] M. Torrent-Moreno, S. Corroy, and H. Hartenstein. Poster abstract: Formalizing packet level incoordination in IEEE 802.11 ad hoc networks: 1-Hop broadcast performance analysis. In *ACM International Conference on Mobile Computing and Networking (MOBICOM)*, Cologne, Germany, August 2005.

[TMSH05] M. Torrent-Moreno, P. Santi, and H. Hartenstein. Fair sharing of bandwidth in vanets. In *Proceedings of the 2nd ACM international workshop on Vehicular ad hoc networks*, VANET '05, pages 49–58, New York, NY, USA, 2005. ACM.

[TMSH06] M. Torrent-Moreno, P. Santi, and H. Hartenstein. Distributed fair transmit power adjustment for vehicular ad hoc networks. In *Sensor and Ad Hoc Communications and Networks, 2006. SECON '06. 2006 3rd Annual IEEE Communications Society on*, volume 2, pages 479–488, September 2006.

[TMSH09] M. Torrent-Moreno, J. Mittag, P. Santi, and H. Hartenstein. Vehicle-to-Vehicle communication: Fair transmit power control for Safety-Critical information. *IEEE Transactions on Vehicular Technology*, 58(7):3684–3703, 2009.

[TS111] ETSI TS 102 687 v1.1.1: Intelligent Transport Systems (ITS); Decentralized Congestion Control Mechanisms for Intelligent Transport Systems operating in the 5 GHz range; Access layer part. http://www.etsi.org/deliver/etsi_ts/102600_102699/102687/01.01.01_60/ts_102687v010101p.pdf, July 2011.

[TSH05] M. Torrent-Moreno, P. Santi, and H. Hartenstein. Fair sharing of bandwidth in VANETs. In *Proceedings of the 2nd ACM international workshop on Vehicular ad hoc networks*, pages 49–58, Cologne, Germany, 2005. ACM.

[TTLB08] I. Tan, W. Tang, K. Laberteaux, and A. Bahai. Measurement and analysis of wireless channel impairments in DSRC vehicular communications. In *IEEE International Conference on Communications, 2008. ICC '08*, pages 4882–4888. IEEE, May 2008.

[TV05] D. Tse and P. Viswanath. *Fundamentals of Wireless Communication*. Cambridge University Press, New York, NY, 1 edition, July 2005.

[TZF+09] K. Tan, J. Zhang, J. Fang, H. Liu, Y. Ye, S. Wang, Y. Zhang, H. Wu, W. Wang, and G. M. Völker. Sora: High Performance Software Radio Using General Purpose Multi-core Processors. In *Proceedings of the 6th USENIX Symposium on Networked Systems Design and Implementation*, pages 75–90, Berkeley, CA, USA, 2009. USENIX Association.

[Ver86] S. Verdú. Minimum probability of error for asynchronous gaussian multiple-access channels. *IEEE Transactions on Information Theory*, 32(1):85–96, January 1986.

[Ver98] S. Verdú. *Multiuser detection*. Cambridge University Press, 1998.

[Vit95] A.J. Viterbi. *CDMA: principles of spread spectrum communication.* Addison-Wesley wireless communications series. Addison-Wesley Pub. Co., 1995.

[VO79] A. J. Viterbi and J. K. Omura. *Principles of Digital Communication and Coding.* Mcgraw-Hill College, 1979.

[Wal92] J. Walker. Drive, Prometheus & GSM. In *Proceedings of the Mobile Radio Technology, Marketing and Management Conference*, London, UK, 1992.

[war] WARP: Wireless Open Access Research Platform. http://warp.rice.edu/trac/.

[WCL09] C.-X. Wang, X. Cheng, and D. Laurenson. Vehicle-to-vehicle channel modeling and measurements: recent advances and future challenges. *IEEE Communications Magazine*, 47(11):96–103, November 2009.

[WK07] T. Wu and C.-M. Kuo. 3-D Space-Time-Frequency correlation functions of Mobile-to-Mobile radio channels. In *Vehicular Technology Conference, 2007. VTC2007-Spring. IEEE 65th*, pages 334–338. IEEE, April 2007.

[Wu07] Y. Wu. Network coding for wireless networks. Technical report, Microsoft Research, 2007.

[XB07] Z. Xu and R. Bagrodia. GPU-Accelerated Evaluation Platform for High Fidelity Network Modeling. In *Proceedings of the 21st International Workshop on Principles of Advanced and Distributed Simulation*, PADS '07, pages 131–140, Washington, DC, USA, 2007. IEEE Computer Society.

[XMKS04] Q. Xu, T. Mak, J. Ko, and R. Sengupta. Vehicle-to-Vehicle Safety Messaging in DSRC. In *Proceedings of the ACM International Workshop on Vehicular Inter-Networking (VANET)*, pages 19–28, Philadelphia, PA, USA, October 2004.

[YHE+06] J. Yin, G. Holland, T. ElBatt, F. Bai, and H. Krishnan. DSRC channel fading analysis from empirical measurement. In *First International Conference on Communications and Networking in China, 2006. ChinaCom '06*, pages 1–5. IEEE, October 2006.

[ZB95] F.-C. Zheng and S. K. Barton. On the performance of near-far resistant CDMA detectors in the presence of synchronization errors. *IEEE Transactions on Communications*, 43(12):3037–3045, December 1995.

[ZF97] F.-C. Zheng and M. Faulkner. Power control requirements in linear decorrelating detectors for CDMA. In *Vehicular Technology Conference, 1997, IEEE 47th*, volume 1, pages 213–217 vol.1. IEEE, May 1997.

[ZHW91] W. Zhu, T. Hellmich, and B. Walke. DCAP, A Decentral Channel Access Protocol: Performance Analysis. *Vehicular Technology Conference, 1991. Gateway to the Future Technology in Motion., 41st IEEE*, pages 463–468, May 1991.

[ZS08a] A. G. Zajic and G. L. Stubber. Space-Time correlated Mobile-to-Mobile channels: Modelling and simulation. *IEEE Transactions on Vehicular Technology*, 57(2):715–726, March 2008.

[ZS08b] A. G. Zajic and G. L. Stuber. Statistical properties of wideband MIMO Mobile-to-Mobile channels (Special paper). In *IEEE Wireless Communications and Networking Conference, 2008. WCNC 2008*, pages 763–768. IEEE, April 2008.

[ZS09] A. G. Zajic and G. L. Stuber. Three-dimensional modeling and simulation of wideband MIMO mobile-to-mobile channels. *IEEE Transactions on Wireless Communications*, 8(3):1260–1275, March 2009.

[ZSC+07] Y. Zang, L. Stibor, X. Cheng, H.-J. Reumerman, A. Paruzel, and A. Barroso. Congestion control in wireless networks for vehicular safety applications. In *Proceedings of The 8th European Wireless Conference*, page 7, Paris, France, April 2007.

[ZSPN09] A. G. Zajic, G. L. Stuber, T. G. Pratt, and S. T. Nguyen. Wideband MIMO Mobile-to-Mobile channels: Geometry-Based statistical modeling with experimental verification. *IEEE Transactions on Vehicular Technology*, 58(2):517–534, February 2009.